Born in Brighton and now living in Primrose Hill, London, Richard Hough served in the Royal Air Force 1941–1946, before becoming first a publisher and then an author. Among his outstanding works of history and biography are the bestselling *Mountbatten: Hero of Our Time*; *Captain Bligh and Mr Christian* (basis of the film *The Bounty*) and *Edwina, Countess Mountbatten of Burma*.

Also by Richard Hough

FICTION
(a trilogy)
Angels One-Five
The Fight of the Few
The Fight to the Finish

BIOGRAPHY
Mountbatten: Hero of Our Time
Captain Bligh and Mr Christian
First Sea Lord: Admiral Lord Fisher

HISTORY
The Great War at Sea 1914–1918
The Longest Battle: the War at Sea 1939–1945

RICHARD HOUGH

The Raging Sky

A Futura Book

Copyright © Richard Hough 1989

First published in Great Britain in 1989
by Macdonald & Co (Publishers) Ltd
London & Sydney

This edition published by Futura Publications in 1990

ISBN 0 7088 4554 1

Reproduced, printed and bound in Great Britain by
BPCC Hazell Books
Aylesbury, Bucks, England
Member of BPCC Ltd.

Futura Publications
A Division of
Macdonald & Co (Publishers) Ltd
Orbit House
1 New Fetter Lane
London EC4A 1AR
A member of Maxwell Macmillan Pergamon Publishing Corporation

For Allan Palmer
183 Squadron Typhoons
victim of German flak
1943

Chapter One

'WHAT'S YOUR NAME?'

She told him. 'Rachel Boland. And yours?'

'I'll tell you in a minute. I'm not sure I can remember right now.'

Rachel said, 'You poor thing. Can I help you out?'

He did not answer at first and she asked him again, placing her hand on his shoulder. He took off his gauntlets and then, slowly, his helmet and goggles, disconnecting the R/T socket and oxygen tube.

Then he said, 'No, I'm all right. Just got to reorientate myself.' There was oil on his face where it had been unprotected by mask and goggles. He wiped it with the ends of his silk scarf, but that made things worse.

Rachel said, 'If you can manage, come to the house for a wash. It isn't far.'

He pulled himself out of the cockpit as if he were an old man, gripping the top of the windshield. He seemed to realise for the first time that she was standing on the wing, and that the wing was on the ground: a most unnatural state of affairs. Then he remembered dizzily that he had just crash-landed, fast and bumpily, and that his Spitfire had a smashed but still hot engine; that it was half full of 100 octane fuel, and the magazines completely full with 20 mm cannon and .303 Browning machine-gun ammunition.

He jumped out hurriedly, clutching the girl's arm and hurrying her away from the wreck with its stench of mixed oil and petrol and glycol. When they were at a safe distance he apologised for this hasty treatment. 'Crashed aircraft are rather volatile,' he said.

'Oh, I know *that*,' she said, surprising him. 'But you might have needed rescuing.'

'Thank you very much ... My name's Raymond Cox, and as you've seen, I have just been shot down.' He pointed towards a large red-brick building with outhouses beside it and tall trees in the garden. 'Well, if that's your house I nearly crashed into it — not having much in the way of rudder control, as you can see.'

The tail of the fighter plane — now nestling on its belly like a downed grouse — was peppered with holes so that the slim fuselage looked like a colander. The young man suddenly realised that he had been extremely lucky.

First Raymond cautiously returned for his parachute, and then they walked side-by-side across the young spring wheat, looking as if they might be brother and sister. They were both dark — he with an exceptionally thick head of black hair, low across his forehead where it came to a slight point in the centre, above heavy black eyebrows. When he reached for the cigarette case inside his battledress, and shakingly lit one with a Ronson lighter, he revealed black hairs on the back of his hands, too. His dark brown eyes were fixed on the girl as he drew on his cigarette.

She held herself well and was pleasing to look at, a tidy oval face, he was thinking, and he liked her small nose and her olive-green eyes. Her cheeks were still pink from running, and she was breathing hard. Her dark brown hair was straight, and short except in the front where the fringe was inconveniently long and required a finger or a toss of her head to keep it out of her eyes. She seemed very young, perhaps sixteen or seventeen.

They found there was no need to telephone the police. A constable was already at the gate which led from the wheatfield into the road. He had leant his bicycle against a telegraph pole before taking off his trouser clips, and stepped out towards them with haste just within the bounds of dignity.

'I sees it was one of ours and telephoned the nearest aerodrome to report the matter, sir,' he greeted them with evident satisfaction. 'An' I sees you're not hurt, sir. I just hope you did for *them*, too.'

8

Raymond did not respond to this, but gave his name and service number. 'I'll just go and order some transport and a guard. You'll see that no one goes near the kite?'

The Reverend John Boland's study doubled as the vicarage drawing-room in these days of economising on light and heat, while the big kitchen, always warm from the Aga, served also as dining-room. The study was furnished with a number of worn leather armchairs which might have been bought from the surplus of a run-down London club, besides two sofas equally decrepit. The carpet was faded and looked as if it had been laid mainly for the comfort of the two old black labradors; while the rug in front of the fire was clearly the preserve of two black and white cats. To Raymond's surprise and interest most of the pictures on the walls were old brown photographs, and one or two paintings, of aircraft and aerial scenes.

A fire of mixed logs and coal burned welcomingly. John Boland — mid-fifties, bald, square-built yet not altogether stout — got up from behind his desk, seized his stick, and limped forward to greet Raymond. 'Come on in. Hear you've had a bit of a prang. You'll need a drink to settle you — I always did on these occasions.'

He poured out a stiff whisky for Raymond, and another, even larger one for himself. Rachel hurried into the kitchen to fetch some biscuits, and was at once replaced by a young man of about Raymond's age, in dressing-gown and slippers, who looked pale and drawn.

'This is my son Jack. He's something in flying, too, I'm afraid. He's got a squadron of Typhoons over at Horning — but as you see he's down with a spot of malaria.'

Of course, Raymond realised — Squadron-Leader Jack Boland, DSO, DFC. He had commanded a squadron of Hurricanes in Burma, and had taken over one of the first Tiffy squadrons on his return.

'How do you do, sir. I'm sorry about this sudden arrival on your doorstep,' Raymond said.

The young man nodded briefly.

9

When John Boland had refilled glasses, he sat down again and asked Raymond what exactly had happened. 'You obviously had a scrap?'

'No, Papa, he can't tell you,' interrupted his son. 'You know perfectly well it's against regulations. You'll have to wait for tomorrow's newpapers.'

'A fat lot they'll tell us. "Enemy planes attacked an East Coast town. Two were shot down and one of our fighters was damaged . . ." ' He sighed in disappointment and began filling his pipe from a tobacco pouch.

There was suddenly a ring at the front door, which Rachel went to answer. She returned to the study to announce that there was now transport for Raymond, and a party of RAF Regiment outside to guard his plane.

John Boland pulled himself to his feet, seizing his stick, and said cheerfully to Raymond, 'Come back and visit us again, won't you. Jack's a bit bored with life. I keep quoting Matthew chapter 20 to him — you know, "Why stand ye here all the day idle?" but it does no good.'

'Oh, really, Papa, that's not fair,' protested Rachel. 'You know how ill he is.' She began to escort Raymond out to the front door, carrying his helmet and gauntlets, but Jack intercepted her, taking the helmet. 'It's all right, Rachel. I'll see him out.'

When Jack had shut the inner glass door of the porch behind him, he turned to Raymond. 'Fancy you still flying Spit Vs,' he said. 'You need something faster to catch the Huns nowadays.'

'And to get away from Yanks,' Raymond added bitterly.

'How d'you mean? I assumed you had engine trouble?'

'No, it wasn't the Merlin's fault. Some sprog Yank shot me down.'

'Good God! Well, I'm afraid there's going to be more of that now that they're coming over from the States in hundreds. And maybe the other way round, too.' He opened the chipped front door. 'Come again soon — but by road next time.'

'Thanks, sir. And thanks for the hospitality.'

It had been his fourth shipping recce in two weeks. As Jack Boland was to say, 21 Squadron's Spitfires had proved too slow for catching the FW190s and Me109Fs which pestered the East Coast with tip-and-run raids from Holland, and to the pilots' disgust, they had been put on anti-shipping duties off the Dutch and Belgian coast, where convoys for Germany slipped along close inshore. First these had to be spotted and reported, then, as soon as the torpedo-carrying Beaufighters — the Torbeaus — could be briefed for an attack, 21 Squadron would be among the escorting fighters.

It was a long and tiring trip across the North Sea, flat on the deck — worse when escorting the Beaus, which were slow when carrying their tin fish. That morning, 29 April, there was slight mist forecast, then clear, with mixed cloud over the North Sea. Raymond had taken off as number one Yellow Section at 10.35 am. Today they were to run up the Dutch coast from Ijmuiden to Texel. There was always flak, sometimes heavy, and you had to keep an eye open for enemy fighters from Schipol and elsewhere. You sometimes received a few flak splinters, but it wasn't really hairy — unlike the escort work which could be very hairy indeed because the 109s and 190s never failed to attack the Beaus, and that meant a lot of mixing. 21 Squadron had lost five pilots in three weeks, and claimed seven 109s.

That morning they struck the enemy coast bang on target — a faint line of yellow-buff sandhills — and streaked along at full boost a mile offshore. Raymond spotted the twinkles of flak, from a flakship dead ahead, before he saw the ships themselves. Farmiloe, who was leading the flight that day, took them farther out, jinking hard against the flak, while they noted the nature of the convoy: flakship in the van and rear, a minesweeper which also had a lot of guns in the centre, and seven merchantmen — all quite small — but also a medium-size tanker.

No point in hanging around, so turn onto 245 degrees, and home again. With luck they would not be on the escort. They returned on the deck, too, which required concentration when you had to be looking back, up and to right and left all the way. Jack Farmiloe transmitted one codeword — 'Fishguard', meaning positive result — but otherwise there was silence for the next twenty minutes, the white-topped grey sea unfolding, mesmerising, just in front of them all the way.

Five miles off the English coast they would climb up to three thousand to cross in. And that's just what Raymond was expecting, when he noticed the water ahead and to the left being torn into a frenzy of white spray. Only an aircraft's gunfire could cause that, he knew from long experience. There was a second of puzzlement, of apprehension, of disbelief. 'Jumped' on your own doorstep — the humiliation!

But it was true. His mirror showed a snub-nosed fighter five o'clock above, its wings a blaze of muzzle flashes. 'Break!' shouted Farmiloe, and someone else irrelevantly called, 'Christ!'

Raymond felt the hits, more shuddering than flak splinter strikes, and saw oil splattering his screen. Then he thrust the throttle lever through the gate for emergency boost, and kicked right-left-right rudder as his Spitfire went into a climbing turn.

He felt no more strikes, and at five thousand turned again, seeing nothing because of oil film, over his canopy as well as screen now, ejected the canopy and still saw no more than clear sky above, and nothing below either — no Spits, no 190s, no ack-ack. Then, yes, a fast-moving grey-brown shape below, a great hunk of a machine with radial engine . . . and a single white star on its port wing.

Oh, Christ, one of those new bloody Thunderbolts — bloody American pilot, I'll bet, been here all of two days. 'Dear Mom, today I shot down my first German . . .' Doesn't anyone tell them *anything*?

And with that uncharitable thought his Merlin gave up. And who could bloody blame it? As Jimmy Brace had remarked over the R/T when his engine packed up five miles off Cromer, 'Silence is *not* golden . . .' And, with no canopy, the wind was fierce *and* cold as all hell at 150 mph.

The Spitfire's nose dropped like the head of a dying man, but at least the oil leak stopped, too, and by undoing his straps and reaching forward with a rag which he always kept along with his maps, Raymond was able to ease his hand round and wipe the screen. Then he switched off the fuel, pumped down the flaps — no hydraulics — and tightened his straps against the impact. And it was only then that he found he had no rudder control — none at all. There were also a great many holes in

12

his ailerons, and they weren't much use either.

So Raymond contented himself — not quite the right word he decided when he used it later — with setting the trim and praying that he would touch Mother Earth where it was soft and unobstructed.

Instead there was an old red-brick house almost dead ahead, flanked by two tall cedars and a spinney of lombardy poplars, standing on the edge of a village. Raymond banked the Spitfire very gingerly, straightened up, and spotted a suitable field, faint green with a newly sprouting crop, and just about long enough, beside the red-brick house.

The Spitfire scraped over the topmost branches of an unkempt hedge, touched the earth gently a hundred yards farther on, flattening the prop, tearing off the flaps without much noise, but skimming along on its belly for much longer than Raymond had anticipated. He knew he ought to get out immediately because of the fire risk, but he remained in the cockpit, stunned more by the shock of the attack than the crash landing, only half hearing the defiant song of a blackbird in the hedge.

Chapter Two

STIPLOWE USAAF BASE was on its best behaviour. Colonel Victor Schneider had been ordered to put on a show that would help cement relations between his newly arrived fighter forces and the RAF. The shooting down of Raymond Cox — not the first casualty of mis-identification — had been the determining factor. 'Get to know your enemy,' he had declared. 'But get to know your friends first.' So there was to be a party — a Saturday night party with the USAAF swing band and a bevy of WACs, a vanguard of the Women's Army Corps, and all the local girls who were fit to be present and who would decorate the occasion.

Stiplowe had been carved out of the East Anglian country-side by the 817th US Engineering Battalion in a fever of airfield building during 1942 for the arrival of the American Eighth Air Force. Farmers were informed that their land was being requisitioned for the war effort, compensation forms completed; and in came the construction gangs, laying down three concrete runways, a perimeter track with hard-standings off it, each hard-standing enclosed by blast bays against enemy bombing and strafing.

Behind the brick and concrete watchtower, a track was laid down leading to the domestic and administration buildings, the officers' and enlisted men's messes, the domestic blocks, the Military Police block beside the main gate, while two low, heavily camouflaged hangars provided cover for the maintenance staff working on the aircraft.

14

Stiplowe was like dozens of new American and British bases — lacking in decoration or embellishment of any kind, except only the flagstaff for the flying of the Stars and Stripes beside the parade-ground set into a close-cut lawn bordered by white-painted stones.

On 20 February 1943 the last construction gang had pulled out, and a skeleton party moved in to tend to boilers to prevent frozen pipes, to clean the floors, and supervise the GPO installation of communications equipment. But it was not until the last day of the month that any sort of life was fed into Stiplowe, with the arrival of the USAAF — truckload after truckload of maintenance equipment: from cooking ranges to lathes, bedding to toolkits, armchairs for the officers' mess to baseball equipment for the enlisted men's recreation.

Signs went up, tankers pumped thousands of gallons of high octane gas into the underground tanks, a final polish was given to the huge folding table in the parachute block, a train delivered five hundred bicycles and one hundred and fifty standard army-issue desks to Stiplowe Halt, and on the same day a Dakota became the first American plane to land on the south-east/north-west runway. Its passengers included General Ira Eaker's Chief of Staff, and a dozen more brass with clerks to inspect the base.

By the middle of March a small highly specialised town was operating, dedicated to the launching into the air, and the receiving back, and the maintenance of a group of three squadrons of Thunderbolt fighters. Twelve months earlier the farmer who owned this patch of East Anglia had been contemplating the prospects of his wheat harvest — and maybe on Saturdays going shooting over the fields and woodland. Now the guns were Bofors and Lewis, manned by RAF Regiment personnel, the 'birds' were somewhat bigger than pheasant, and the young wheat had long since been pulverised by earth-movers and suffocated by hardcore and concrete.

The spinney, which had been known as Brookeacre since Doomsday, now lay under a broad length of hardstanding between the watchtower and B hangar; while a short length of hedge, which was even older, had mysteriously survived

15

outside the WACs' sleeping block, and within twenty-four hours of the American girls' arrival was being used for hanging out army-issue underwear. It was just as swiftly named Pantyrow by the enlisted men, who were prevented from interfering with it by the high barbed-wire fence that enclosed the WACs' quarters.

By the time of the May dance, USAAFUK base Stiplowe was like some great living organism spawned arbitrarily onto the wide open landscape of Norfolk: a noisy, restless beast that might have been operating for as long as old RAF bases like Duxford or Wyton, but whose sounds and sights still alarmed the local villagers and wildlife.

Raymond Cox was saluted as he was driven through the main gate at 5.30 pm on the evening of the party. The USAAF staff car in which he sat in solitary splendour had been the object of a great deal of ribaldry back at Barton Heath, but Raymond was ordered into it by his CO, Sandy McWilliams, when it arrived for him at the officers' mess. 'Damn bad show not to accept the courtesy, Ray,' he was told. He had also been informed that he was to have a private meeting with the American pilot who had shot him up the other week — and Raymond had exclaimed that he would just as soon meet three 109s when he was out of ammunition and with a height disadvantage.

'Why in God's name do they have to make such a *thing* of it?' he protested. 'They just need to spend a bit more time getting clued up on aircraft identification ...'

'Anglo-American relations,' was the firm response.

So here he was, doing his bit for Anglo-American relations, in this Ford V8 staff car with a white star on the roof and sides, and PFC Hank Polensky at the wheel. A pair of Thunderbolts came in low overhead, massive beasts compared with the dainty Spitfire, wheels wide-splayed like some damn flying trolley.

The Colonel's office stank of cigar smoke like a bar at closing time. He answered Raymond's salute with his hands across his eyes as if shading them from bright light, and extended a hand of welcome.

'Lieutenant Cox, it's sure good to make your acquaintance.'

There was a slight figure in officer's formal uniform, silver wings on his chest, standing behind the desk. He had fair, thin hair, already receding, narrow-set blue eyes and a freckled complexion. He looked dusty but OK, Raymond considered, at the same time thinking that if this meeting was difficult for him it was certainly worse for this rooky lieutenant.

'This is Lieutenant Charlie Dee, Mr Cox. He has what you might say is an apology for you. You can say he was lucky not to kill you.'

'That goes for me, too.'

Charlie Dee stepped round the desk to shake Raymond's hand. 'I'm real sorry, sir', he said. 'I got no excuse and I'm just darn glad it was such lousy shooting.' He spoke with an accent like President Roosevelt's, while his Colonel sounded more like a Western cowboy — or that was Raymond's unknowledgeable interpretation.

'Not all that lousy! I counted thirty-seven .5-inch holes in my fuselage and tailplane, and a dozen more in the engine. *And* my armour-plate stopped three more.'

The Colonel had taken a bottle of Old Grandad bourbon from a drawer in his desk and was pouring out three stiff nips. He handed a glass to each of the two pilots. 'Here's to shooting down Krauts — and not each other.' Throwing back his drink, he then asked Raymond his score, as if it was his golf handicap.

'Not much recently,' Raymond told him. The strong whisky tore at his throat like a red-hot poker and his eyes pricked with the effort not to weep. 'The only time we see them is over the other side on shipping strikes, giving cover to the torpedo-bombers. Over here they are in and out too fast for us to catch them in our old Spits.'

'What about the Battle of Britain?' Charlie Dee asked. He was holding his empty glass so that it could be refilled if the Colonel felt so inclined.

'I only caught the tail end, when the worst was over,' Raymond told him. 'Well, yes, a couple of 109s and a Junkers 88. And I was lucky enough to catch up with a recce Dornier late last year.'

17

'Where's your medals then?' Charlie asked, glancing at the gap beneath Raymond's wings and top pocket. Charlie already had two colourful ribbons, though not for gallantry, and the Colonel had two whole rows. 'He'd have got a DSC if he was flying for us, eh, Colonel?'

'Sure thing.' And the bottle went round the party of three again.

Partly under the influence of the Old Grandad, Raymond began to warm towards the Colonel and his own opposite number who had so much to learn and appeared so openly keen to learn it.

'What about the 109?' Charlie continued. 'We heard it's quick in the dive.'

'That's its great trick. It can nearly always get away if it wants, and with its fuel-injected engine the pilot just throws his stick forward and it drops like a stone; while *we* have to go over onto our back or the engine cuts out with temporary fuel starvation.'

'Can you catch the bastards straight and level?'

Raymond shook his head. 'Not the F or G 109. We can out-turn them — but they can always get away. We're waiting for new Spits.'

As the two young pilots continued their professional talk, the Colonel listened, making occasional notes, until at last another young officer came in — evidently the Colonel's secretary — and said something to him in a low voice.

'OK, we're in business over at the hall in ten minutes, gentlemen.' Before leaving them, he grinned at Raymond. 'And don't forget you're the guest of honour and can have the pick of the girls.'

'Well, that's a generous invitation!' said Raymond, laughing.

'But only for tonight.'

When he had gone, Raymond turned back to Charlie. 'So, what do you make of it over here? It's a long way from home.'

'That doesn't bother me. The further the better.' Seeing Raymond's expression of surprise, he added lightly, 'It's easy for me because I haven't got one. Just a room in Pasadena stacked with a bed and some jazz records and my clothes.'

'What about your parents?'

'My mother left when I was just a kid, and then when I went to college my father lost whatever interest he had in me. So I lost interest· in him, and got on with my life by myself.'

The American showed no sign of concern at his abandonment, halting in Raymond's mind any urge to offer the comfort of shared misfortune by recounting his own circumstances.

'What did you do when you left college?'

'Joined the Army. I transferred to the Air Corps as soon as I could. All I think about is flying — well, maybe a bit about women.' His smile was just short of cheeky — a smile that would have turned flat with disappointment if it was not returned in kind. And Raymond decided he was not the sort of fellow you wanted to disappoint.

At this point the American stood up and suggested by a tilt of his head that they might leave. 'Which made it all the worse when I horsed things up,' he added.

'Oh, forget about it. You weren't the first and you won't be the last. There was one engagement in 1939 when a complete squadron of Spits took on a complete squadron of Hurricanes. It was called the Battle of Barking Creek. Both sides claimed victory and two planes were shot down before someone shouted "Hey!"'

Together they walked along the newly tar-macadamed paths that led them through the station buildings.

Far from feeling any residual antagonism towards this lively American who had done his best to kill him, Raymond felt a growing liking for him. It was already becoming an evening of contradictions. Everything about this airfield was similar to Barton Heath, and yet everything was so different. It was a fighter station like Barton — its function the same, the surroundings the same, the mechanics and routine of life the same — yet utterly different.

It was not that the parked machines were fatter here than the Spitfires parked in their bays a dozen miles away. But these Thunderbolts, these 'Jugs', had their extravagantly lettered names on the engine cowlings — '*Lie-Low Baby*' and

'*Virtuous Virgin*' were just two Raymond noticed — alongside paintings of naked, voluptuous girls with enormous breasts, as well as the more chaste but still prominent names of each one's pilot and his ground crew.

'There's my baby,' remarked Charlie, patting the fat fuselage of his 'Jug'. The bold letters **S** and **LM** were divided by the identifying American five-pointed white star, and on the engine cowling in sloping letters were the words '*Greta Garbo*' and a not-bad rendering in pink, yellow and black of the film star's face. 'The first woman ever to turn me on. Boy, do you remember that closing shot in *Queen Christina*? I wasn't going to have *her* stripped naked like some of these coarse bitches round here. Just take a look at that,' he added, pointing to a stretched-out blonde with legs twice the length of her body.

Then Raymond was thinking, just look at the way the men behave! All around him were enlisted men, ground crews, clerks and tradesmen of all kinds — and they bicycled along the paths or hung from overloaded jeeps (few walked), seemingly dressed as they pleased with headgear of their own devising, shouted wisecracks, or maybe threw a football around. Like the pilots, they were doing the same job as his own lot at Barton Heath, and no doubt just as well, but their manner and style were quite different. During the short walk over to the station hall, Raymond looked about him in wonder, enchanted by the casual yet professional air of an outfit that had arrived in Britain only weeks before and had not yet finished settling in to this raw airfield.

On the way the Colonel rejoined them. As he walked along flanked by Charlie Dee and Raymond, all the men who passed them saluted with that curious horizontal slap of the forehead which Raymond had never seen before.

'Evenin', Harry ... Hi'ya, Hank ... Saw your shootin' results, Bill, you ol' son-of-a-bitch ...' the Colonel greeted several of those he knew. Nearby, someone was running up a Thunderbolt engine, drowning all other sound. When it was cut, a more melodious sound emerged through the open doors of the station hall. They were playing 'Chatanooga

Choo-choo'. The 43rd's big band was hard at it, 'The Louiseville Loungers'.

A pair of startlingly good-looking WACs were on the door as hostesses, pinning daffodils to the lapels of the privileged guests and senior officers. 'Two for our guest of honour,' ordered the Colonel, and Raymond found himself being kissed on both cheeks as a bonus.

Am I dreaming? What is this? he wondered. Then he caught a glimpse of some blue uniforms — and there was Jack Farmiloe, grinning and winking like a demented monkey. He was standing drinking a pint of strangely yellow looking liquid — could that be *beer?*

Raymond's CO had elbowed his way through the crowds of airmen to greet Colonel Schneider. He watched them saluting and then shake hands. Sandy McWilliams was a stocky little man who used to play fly-half for the RAF before the war, the flattened nose bearing evidence of this, the deep scar on his forehead marking another form of injury — a crash in a Bulldog in the mid-Thirties. The CO had got through the Battle of Britain without a scratch, however, and with a DSO and DFC to acknowledge his twelve victories. He was one of those irrepressible Scots who flaunt their accent, and at interesting moments in the air, when they were being hard pressed, he became almost incomprehensible over the R/T. Raymond liked and admired him — they all did — but never felt entirely at ease in his company. Perhaps that was the reason he was such a good CO? As all his pilots knew, he was doing his best to get them new Spit IXs, which were 50 mph faster and nippier on the climb, too, but so far he had failed.

Now, after a few minutes chatting and laughing with Colonel Schneider, the CO turned to Raymond. 'The Colonel tells me this is entirely in your honour.' He looked wryly at Raymond, only half smiling. 'In which case it must be the only time an RAF pilot has been honoured for being shot down while half asleep.'

'Well, put like that, sir . . .'

'What other way can you put it?' But the CO added, 'Follow me for a wee dram.'

At the extreme right end of the bar there was special service for special guests — the special service being spirits, several of which McWilliams had already downed.

'My Baby and I, We see eye to eye ...' crooned the sub-Sinatra.

'You've got to give it to them, these Yankees,' said the CO. 'They get their pleasures set up without wasting too much time.'

There were fifty or more small tables packed into the hall, four or six airmen with their girls at each. The Louisville Loungers played on a raised platform, the big drum emblazoned with their name in slanting script decorated with stars; and on a cleared circular area in front of them the couples fox-trotted in tight embrace, cheek to cheek, though one couple was even attempting to jitterbug in the confined space.

The girls in uniform, about half the women in the hall, were mostly WACs, their smart, tight khaki uniform contrasting favourably with that of the British WAAFs, whose hair was shorter by regulation, and uniforms poorly fitting — except for those of a cluster of WAAF officers around the privileged end of the bar.

But there was also a scattering of civilian girls, and among them Rachel Boland, the girl who had helped Raymond from his cockpit after he had crash-landed. She was wearing a long red dress with long sleeves, quite plain, and a single string of pearls round her neck, her glossy dark hair reflecting the light from the overhead lamp — the only girl's hair that was not permed. She was smoking a cigarette, holding it as if for the first time, and talking to a WAC officer. She still looked no more than seventeen.

Charlie Dee came up to Raymond. He was smoking, too; almost everyone else was, and many of the American men had short pungent cigars. Raymond recognised the smell of a Camel, and when Charlie offered him one, flicking the base of the pack neatly with his thumb, Raymond took it with thanks.

'Who's that curvaceous cutie in red? Know her, Ray?'

'Just met her once. I nearly hit her house and she helped me out of my kite.'

'I think you ought to introduce me — and no cracks about my little error.'

22

Raymond laughed. 'So that's what it's become, just a little error — Charlie's clanger.'

Charlie put his arm across Raymond's shoulder. 'Come on, ol' buddy — lead me to her.'

Only five minutes later Charlie Dee was dancing with Rachel Boland on the crowded floor. They matched each other well, being the same height, and were laughing and talking as if they had known each other for years.

Raymond turned to the WAC officer he had been left with. 'I'd ask you to dance but I'm terrible.'

She took him by the hand and drew him towards the floor. 'I'll show you, Englishman.'

Her name was Louise Daintree, from New York, she told him, and it took Raymond a while to adjust to her accent. She was tall, fair, handsome, with unusually wide-set grey eyes and pale soft skin; like a couturier's wax model come alive. He was led firmly between the tables towards the packed dance-floor.

'I can see why you're an officer,' he remarked as she clasped him in her arms. 'Authoritative, decisive.' The whiskies he had downed with the Colonel and the two more he had been given at the bar were now going to his head, and he felt as if he had been transported to another world.

'Now just follow me,' said Louise Daintree from New York. 'Right foot forward — close like this you can anticipate my leg movements. I guess that's what the fox-trot's all about. I don't hold with this jitterbugging.'

From the corner of his eye he caught a glimpse of Charlie Evans and Bruce Cameron from B-Flight grinning widely over their pints of light American beer, and looking as anachronistic as Raymond himself felt in this environment.

'How do you like it over here?' Raymond asked. His voice had to carry only two inches, so he did not have to raise it. Louise's cheek was as soft as it looked.

'Oh, I like it fine. Just the cold — I do find it mighty cold and kind of draughty.'

'So ... we're so sleepy ...' The dancers now swayed to the slower, sentimental tune.

'I do love this one,' Louise whispered. 'And you're doing well. I do like dancing with you.'

She confirmed this by keeping him on the floor after the music stopped, tucking her hand through his arm as if they had been courting for months. Over her shoulder he saw that Charlie, too, was still on the floor with Rachel, and that gave him comfort, though mixed with a touch of concern. The pause between numbers was not long, and soon they were into an old Gershwin tune and the floor filled up again at once till the couples could only just move about.

'Now, I'm not going to do all the leading this time. You're doing fine, so you just lead me. I'll feel which way you're going, back like this, now round ...'

Raymond had a growing feeling that he was being pretty undeviously seduced, and he found the prospect both alarming and beguiling. He had never made love to a woman in his life, and held a half-defined belief that you did not do so until you were married, unless — as he understood it — you were prepared to risk a disease that could be fatal.

'I suppose you have a lot of girls at home, a boy as attractive as you,' Louise whispered. 'Have you got other brothers like you? And pretty sisters — I'll bet ...'

'No, no brothers or sisters.'

'Just your Mom and Pa at home?'

Raymond drew his head back and looked into the girl's wide-set, wide-open grey eyes, experiencing the old sensation of inadequacy touched with self-pity when he had to explain his background. 'No, I've got a father somewhere but I don't see him. My mother died soon after I was born. I was brought up by an aunt.' He smiled as if to reassure her. 'A nice aunt.'

The American girl clearly did not know how to cope with that news, so she put her cheek firmly against his. She smelt like the roses growing on the garden wall at 'Montrose.' 'Oh, never mind. We don't want to get sentimental, do we?'

After two more dances, Raymond appealed for a break. 'I'm not used to all this exercise,' he said.

'You *must* be mighty fit for what you do.'

'What I do is either sit in a cockpit or sit in the dispersal hut playing poker.'

But she followed willingly enough when he led her by the hand back to the table. Charlie and Rachel were already sitting there, drinking Coca-Cola and chatting easily.

24

'Hey, we were thinking you two were never going to stop — like those dancers who go on for days, doing it for money.'

Raymond held the chair for Louise. 'What would you like to drink?' he asked.

'I'll have a Scotch and soda,' she said promptly. 'It's no way to treat a party — drinking Coke.'

Raymond headed for the bar, threading his way between close-packed tables. The atmosphere was hot and heavy, and the smoke hung like a cloud beneath the low ceiling. The Louisville Loungers were now playing 'St Louis Blues', the trumpeter taking a slow, measured solo. Raymond realised he was feeling rather drunk and decidedly randy. But, after all, he told himself, it wasn't every day that an American Air Force Station put on a party just for *you*. 'Two scotches please.'

The Colonel was still there, talking to three pilots who were drinking beer. When he saw Raymond he asked if he was enjoying himself, then introduced him to the three other men. 'Ray here's got quite a score already, gentlemen. He fought in the Battle of Britain — could teach you fellers a trick or two.'

Raymond shook each hand in turn. 'That was when the Germans used to come over in hundreds,' he said modestly. 'They're not easy to find now — not on this side. Though they'll come up like wasps when you start going over with the bombers.'

'Right,' the Colonel confirmed. 'Hey, if I can get your Commanding Officer to agree, will you come over here and give us a talk? Maybe fly with us?'

'There're pilots better qualified for that than I am, sir.'

'I'll try it out all the same, if you don't mind.'

Raymond smiled his agreement, nodded to the three pilots, and slipped away with his drinks. Louise was all alone at the table, and he raised his glass to her, thinking how desirable she looked. 'That uniform is very smart,' he said.

She smiled, sipping her whisky and soda. 'Thank you,' she said, 'but I can't tell you how I long to slip out of this and into a pretty dress, something soft and light.'

'Yes, that would be nice, too,' Raymond agreed warmly.

'But we're not allowed to. Not on the station unless we're going on furlough. I can't wait for that. Maybe you could join me in London sometime? Show me your city?'

'That would be wizard.'

What was he saying? He had only just met this girl! A few dances and a few drinks. Anyway, he wasn't due for leave for three months. But when she extended her hand across the table and said, 'Another dancing lesson for you,' he got to his feet at once, if just a little unsteadily.

'My party night' was how Raymond later thought of that strange evening at Stiplowe — but only to himself. The mere fact of there being a party in his honour would be a shaming enough line-shoot, and any mention of it in the Squadron would be accompanied by guffaws. But, yes, it *was* his party, culminating in the oddest way — and, as much as he could remember of it, extremely pleasant.

He could recall quite clearly dancing with Louise again and again, many dances broken by several more drinks. Rachel and Charlie had disappeared for a while, Charlie later returning to explain that he was organising transport to get her back home. 'You two enjoying yourselves?' he added, with a wink at Raymond.

'Let's take a little air,' said Louise in mid-dance, and Raymond allowed himself to be guided off the floor. She led him through a thick blackout curtain, closing it carefully behind them, then opened a side door which led onto a path running beside the hall. It was quite dark — a starless, moonless night — but there were other couples outside, their presence marked by the glow of cigarettes and the murmur of voices. The steady beat of the band rose and fell as one or other of the doors was opened and closed behind people entering and leaving.

Raymond lit a cigarette and handed it to Louise. He felt her shiver, and she said, 'It's real nice to get some air, but, oh, it's cold! I don't want to go back in there, but I don't want you to leave. You're just too nice to let go.' She paused and then grasped his hand firmly. 'Come along with me.'

He was later in doubt about what happened from this moment. Some of it was clear, some of it was hazy. As she had been taking the lead from the moment she insisted on them dancing, this did not seem to be the time for Raymond to deny her wishes. She clearly wished him to come with her to the dimly-lit WAC officers' quarters, and he remembered her searching for a key in the shoulder-bag she carried, then opening a gate into the compound.

'This is my li'l ol' home in the west,' she said with a giggle, opening the door of one of the several small individual huts. She waited until they were both inside before turning on the light to reveal the simple furniture: a dressing-table-cum-chest-of-drawers, a wardrobe, a hand basin in the corner, a bed, neatly turned down by her servant, a small armchair and another chair — and that was about all. There was a rug in the middle of the wooden floor, an electric fire glowing red, and the window was heavily blacked out, with a decorative curtain over it.

Louise sat on the bed, unbuttoning her jacket, smiling up at Raymond and indicating that he should sit beside her. 'That's better,' she said, reaching her hands towards the fire and then placing them against his cheeks. 'Quite safe, quite alone, and quite warm — at last.'

Raymond felt dazed. It was difficult to relate these new circumstances with anything that had gone before on this curious evening. The only link was the distant beat of The Louisville Loungers and the presence of this young woman who had cut so remorselessly, yet pleasantly, into his life.

'Come along, sleepy boy. I hope you're not as slow as this when you're flying. And it *is* your party, Raymond.'

It was the first time she had used his name all evening, and he found it extraordinarily arousing but did not know how he should act next. Louise drew his face towards hers with her hands firmly holding his cheeks, and she kissed him with open lips for several seconds. He had kissed women before, usually at the end of an evening out — but not like this, with the certain knowledge that it was the beginning and not the end.

When she withdrew her lips she said, in half disbelief, 'This can't be your first time.'

He nodded and she laughed, kissing him again. 'Well, isn't that just sweet!' And in a businesslike way she turned off the light, leaving only the glow of the electric fire, and began rapidly to undress. 'Well,' she repeated, 'that is just sweet. First I have to teach you to dance, and then how to make love.'

Raymond had thought a great deal about the business of making love, had come near to taking the initiative several times, but had always flinched back at the last moment for fear of a rebuff.

But there was no turning back now, not with this soft-spoken, soft-skinned, devastatingly attractive American woman. The bed was too narrow to lie side-by-side, so she lay on her back, and he could just make out the curve of her shoulders leading to the softer curves of her full breasts, the lower part of her body concealed by the sheet that she had drawn over her thighs.

'That's right, my sweet ...' And she held him where no woman had ever touched him, brushing her hard nipples with his stiffness, repeatedly. 'Now you must talk to me, always talk.'

'I don't think I can,' he said achingly ... and at last she drew him down, throwing aside the sheet, and he felt the indescribably warm soft dampness holding him. So — this — is — what — it's — like. His whole mind and body in tumult. Many things might disappoint the first time, but never this. Never. Never! Oh, my God!

The final moment was secure in his memory for all time. But the remainder of that evening was like instrument-flying through heavy cumulus, rough and half-blind, but not without interest, and requiring concentration. He remembered that they made love a second time, dressing soon after, and even then she could not resist touching him again and again. He recalled returning to the hall, where the band played on as if nothing had happened and as if they had been on the dance floor all the time. So, the world really *could* stand still! Many of the same people sat at the same tables, and when Raymond glanced at his watch he saw with amazement that it was only just after ten o'clock. He was not even slightly drunk any more, as if that love-making had purged him and re-made him into a new being. *What do I look like*? he wondered; and then put the question aloud to Louise, who sat demurely at his side, her face newly made up, her hair in perfect order.

'Just fine, Baby,' she said with a worldly smile. 'How do you feel?'

'Different,' he said with emphasis; and she laughed long and loud.

The Colonel chose to stop by their table at that moment, Raymond later remembered, asking them what the joke was. They both stood up but were told to sit again, Louise saying, 'Just a silly private joke, sir.'

'You two seem to have got acquainted real fast,' he said. 'Perhaps we can tempt him back here again. Now, Ray, I promised your Commanding Officer we'd have you back at base by eleven o'clock. Seems you've got an early show.'

'Oh, sir, we reckoned on dancing some more,' Louise appealed.

But Raymond was on his feet, quite steady now though still in a half-trance of disbelief. 'Good night, Louise. Thank you for everything. Let's meet again.'

'You bet,' she said warmly, then turned to the Colonel. 'With your permission, sir.'

Chapter Three

LATE JUNE 1940: almost three years previously. He had just got his wings up. Looking back, he saw himself as a boy then, inexperienced as a pilot, inexperienced in life. He *must* have been young, and foolish, to have ventured on the enterprise at all. Curiously enough, and quite unsuitably, the events of that final morning of his search came back to him now as he lay utterly exhausted after that first love-making with the American girl.

Raymond had known at the time it was a damn-fool thing to do. But the need to know had burned so deep for so long that he also knew that the pain could only be relieved by the answer to it. Was *he* still alive? What did *he* look like? Where and how did *he* live?

He had spotted the advertisement in an old copy of an American magazine, but the address was England: 'Trace Your Ancestry' — it was irresistible. But the reply which came was cautious, suspicious even. They were not accustomed to receiving enquiries about ancestors a mere generation back, they wrote. They were not a missing persons bureau, nor (heaven forbid!) a private detective agency.

Raymond decided to go to see them. Their office was above a shop in Bromsgrove, of all places. The Battle of Britain had just begun, so anyone in RAF uniform was respected, a pilot was automatically a heroic figure. He was received sympathetically by an elderly man in a dusty, book-lined office. This genealogist did not appear to have even a secretary, but judging by the pile of letters on his desk, many of them unopened and with foreign stamps, he had plenty of work on his hands.

Raymond told him the position briefly and without embellishment. 'I just want to know. I've no feeling of hostility, only curiosity. I don't want to interfere in any way with his life — if he is alive.'

The man listened until he had finished, then was silent for perhaps half a minute, pinched his lips with his first fingers, smiled and said he would do what he could. 'Mark you, Cox is quite a common name, and he may have changed it to another anyway.'

He had brushed aside any offer of payment. 'You're doing your bit for your country; I'll do my bit for you.' Then he got up and accompanied Raymond to the door.

Two months had passed without a word. Raymond completed his abbreviated course at his Operational Training Unit on Spitfires, and joined 21 Squadron in 10 Group on 26 September. He arrived at Langley Down just as eight aircraft were landing, one or two in a bad way. They had lost two, and a third had landed at Middle Wallop out of fuel. Feeling very much the new boy and an outsider, Raymond waited in the mess for the officer pilots and the CO to come to the bar for a pre-dinner drink.

But it was all right. Up until now, and throughout his training, Raymond had been made conscious (you could not avoid it) of a rather futile hierarchical scale based on length of service. 'Get some in!' ... 'There goes a new sprog!' ... and all that. Under the pressure of combat over the past weeks, at 21 Squadron everyone seemed to have fully grown up.

The CO confined himself to a faint raising of the eyebrows when Raymond told him he had done only twenty hours on Spits. 'I'll take you up in the morning,' the senior man decided.

And that morning flight was to be his only squadron preparation for the desperate fight for control of the skies over southern England. To lose it must lead to invasion and probably to the subjugation of the nation, like France and three-quarters of Europe.

31

On that same day of Raymond's arrival, when 21 Squadron had suffered so badly, the Luftwaffe had struck the Spitfire factory at Southampton, halting all production and killing many people. On the next afternoon, the plots building up on the Sector plotting board showed clearly a big raid heading for Bristol and its aircraft factories, confirming a change in tactics.

The day's fighting was already over before it occurred to Raymond that in his first ever action he had been defending his home city. They had been ordered up to rendezvous over Wincanton, and had picked up the enemy stream five minutes later. It had been a rough introduction to battle, but the defenders had been far more successful than on the previous day. The enemy fighters were operating at the very limit of their range; and their protection of the bombers, all of which were turned back or shot down, was only sketchy.

Raymond failed to make a kill on his first op, but he was elated at the squadron's success in defending Bristol, scoring four without loss. So there was a party afterwards, with much broken furniture. The next morning there was a notice on the board from the Prime Minister himself: 'Pray congratulate the Fighter Command on the results of yesterday ...'

It was a good start to Raymond's operational career.

By the middle of October 1940 the daylight raids from across the Channel began to fizzle out as the Luftwaffe was forced to concede defeat. Fighter Command was as strong as at the start of the battle, and by the end of the month could relax its vigilance slightly. Leave was granted, and Raymond's coincided with a letter from Bromsgrove. It was from the genealogist, who apologised for the long delay. It had proved a difficult nut to crack, 'but now, cracked it was'.

Raymond spent three days in Bristol with his Aunt May, who had taken a war job in the canteen of a nearby factory. 'Oh, darling, I can't take time off. I'm terribly sorry,' she had answered Raymond's plea. But she did take one afternoon off and they went for an enormous walk over the Downs with Bonz, her manically lively Jack Russell. It was a beautiful late autumn day, but at that time it was impossible to escape from the sounds and sights of the war: fighters from Colerne and Kemble, test aircraft from Filton, training aircraft, Wellington and Hampden bombers, and on the roads military vehicles and anti-invasion gunposts and anti-tank obstructions.

The next day Raymond had to announce that he was leaving for a couple of days, and he did not deny too vehemently May's assumption that he was visiting a girl. She left the house before daybreak on her bicycle, and the last Raymond saw of her was her faint outline pedalling down the drive, the dim little red tail-light fading into the distance. Then he gave Bonz and himself breakfast, patted the little terrier goodbye, and drove off in Delilah, his Alvis sportscar, along almost empty roads to Worcester, wearing his civilian suit and a cap.

Number 27, Marchmount Street, north Worcester, did not sound very promising. Nor did the reality amount to anything very interesting. It was a short street between two main roads, and featured haphazardly scattered semidetached houses built sometime between the wars. The ground floors of one or two of them had been converted into shops, and one of them into a Food Office for dealing with ration cards. This was something of a blessing because it meant there was a steady procession of people walking to or from it, which made Raymond less conspicuous — or so he hoped.

There was also a queue outside this Food Office, mostly of women, many with prams, all chattering away contentedly in the mid-November sunshine. In the office window there were Government posters about recruiting offices and air-raid precautions and what to do if you lost your identity card. Number 27 was six houses away. Like the others, it had a dormer window in the roof, and a little balcony on the first floor above the ground-floor bow window. It was clearly not the property of a man of substance, but was distinctive in one respect; its small front garden was exceptionally well kept, weedless and immaculately tidy — a birdbath in the centre of a lawn without a flaw, its edges trimmed like an army haircut, lobelia still blooming in dead straight lines, healthy looking mixed dahlias in the right bed, roses in the left bed beside the steps leading to the porch and front door.

It was the garden of someone who cared and fussed, but lacked imagination. If a couple lived here, judging by the shining whiteness of the net curtains, the bright brass on

33

the front door and the spotless tiled porch, she was just as particular as her husband.

Raymond walked on, studying the face of every middle-aged and elderly man he passed. How old would he be? Somewhere between forty and sixty. May had never given a clue; in fact she had hardly ever spoken of her one-time brother-in-law. At the corner were a couple of boys playing conkers. Raymond stopped and spoke conspiratorially to them: 'Do you want to make a couple of bob — a bob each?'

They stared at him, in their eyes a trace of caution struggling with avarice.

'What's the trick, guv?'

'No trick. All you've got to do is knock on the door of number 27 along there, and if a woman answers ask her when Mr Cox is due home. And say "please" and smile. OK?'

The taller boy asked, 'What if she wants to know why?'

'Tell her a friend of her husband's sent you and he's got a surprise for him.'

'OK. You going to pay us now?'

Raymond gave him a shilling. 'The other bob when I meet you back here in ten minutes.'

The two boys ran off, the conkers dangling on their strings. Raymond walked for a while up the main road, then turned round. They were waiting on the corner, the tall one again attacking his friend's conker. They saw him approach and ran to meet him.

'About twenty to five. "Always on time, tell your friend" — that's what she said.'

Raymond walked back to the car, drove down the main road and turned off back into Marchmount Street. It was 4.35 according to the Smith's clock on the dashboard. The queue at the Food Office had diminished to three or four people. The sun was low over the Welsh hills to the west. He pulled his cap well down before driving off, and then realised the absurdity of hiding his face.

As a man on a bicycle turned into the street at the far end, Raymond let in the clutch. He was travelling at little more than walking pace when he passed No. 27, where the man had dismounted and was pushing open the gate. Raymond saw him glance up at the unusual sight of an open sports

34

Alvis driving slowly down his street, which saw few enough cars anyway. Raymond saw a tall but rather bowed figure, hatless, with a full head of grey hair and a grey-black moustache, hornrim spectacles. He wore cord trousers and the cycle clips revealed black boots that were earth-encrusted. He wore a cravat instead of a tie and an old tweed jacket with bulging pockets.

In a fleeting second all this was etched into Raymond's memory so that he knew he would now recognise the man anywhere, at any time. Looking in the rearview mirror of his car, he saw the man carrying his bicycle up the steps, pausing at the top to look back again at the disappearing vehicle. Raymond found this faintly unnerving, even though he knew that it must be the Alvis rather than the driver which had retained the man's curiosity.

Later, Raymond rented a bicycle and checked in to stay at a pub which conveniently stood round the corner from Marchmount Street. After a high tea and a couple of pints of bitter he began to feel overcome with the urge to tell someone else that he had now seen his father for the first time in his life. But who was there to tell? Like most people, his friends from school had already been scattered by the war. If he rang up the officers' mess at Langley Down to tell them, they would think he was either drunk or mad. Only Aunt May would know how he felt. But even she — tolerant, loving and kind as she was — would be hurt that he had not confided in her first. 'But, Raymond,' she would have protested, 'why didn't you *tell* me? Why didn't you tell me on our long walk — or last night at supper, or . . .?'

'Because, my darling May,' he would have had to reply, 'You would have warned me of the risk I was taking, of being hurt, of being disappointed and of regretting it. But whatever the outcome, I *have* to know.'

To escape from his racing thoughts and speculations, Raymond took himself off to the cinema and saw an old Fred Astaire-Ginger Rogers film. Then he had a couple of whiskies as a nightcap, asked to be called at half-past six, and went to bed.

He had calculated that his father finished work at 4.30. A 4.30 pm finish suggested a 7.30 am start, and therefore leaving home at 7.20. Raymond wheeled his bicycle out at quarter past and pedalled along to Marchmount Street. The weather had broken and it was drizzling. The street was empty of people and traffic — except for one man on a bicycle, wearing a yellow cape, and already at the far end.

Raymond stepped on the pedals and raced down the street after him. He saw the man turn left, but by the time Raymond reached the end of the street there were several bicyclists now in sight. None was wearing a yellow cape. Furious with himself, he overtook several of them, and then decided to take a chance and ask one of them if he had seen a friend of his wearing a yellow cape.

'You mean old George Cox? Yes, he went his usual way down Spiggot's Lane.'

'Where's that?'

A pause for surprise. 'Well, back there, on the left of course.'

Spiggot's Lane was a footpath running between allotments. It was muddy, with puddles from the drizzle. At the far end there was another major road, and on the other side of that extended iron railings enclosing lawns and flowerbeds, a Gothic tea-room, a statue of Queen Victoria, tennis courts closed for the winter. A sign read: *The Municipal Gardens. Open 7.45 am. Closed at dusk. Regulations* ... and then much small print. The board stood next to the double iron gates, which at 7.45 precisely were opened by a man who was wearing a yellow cape, and who had parked his bicycle against the railings.

A bus passed by, followed by an army convoy of one-ton trucks, which allowed Raymond only intermittent glimpses of the man remounting his bicycle and pedalling it through the gates and along the asphalt path. Raymond still had no means of properly identifying the figure, but all the evidence — the muddy gardener's boots, the immaculate garden of number 27, the timing — seemed to confirm that this was his father's place of work. Head gardener at North Worcester Municipal Gardens.

By the time Raymond managed to cross the busy road, the man had vanished, but he followed the asphalt path round a shrubbery and found that it led to a low, wooden building that was clearly some kind of an office and gardening headquarters. The drizzle had turned to a steady misty rain but Raymond could see through a window the outline of a figure moving about.

He could go now. He had found and identified his quarry. No one would think the worse of him for ducking away. No one would ever know, even. It was not as if he had been vectored on to a *Schwarm* of 109s and didn't fancy the odds. He had accomplished what he had set out to do. Go on, then, get on to the saddle of this old hired bike and return the way he had come — all the way back to Clifton, Bristol, and the ven of 'Montrose'.

Instead, Raymond dropped the bicycle into some rhododendrons and walked up to the wooden building, where there was a face watching him through the windows. It disappeared as he approached, but almost at once the door opened and his father stood there. He had taken off his yellow cape and was dressed in the same working clothes he had been wearing the previous evening. He eyed Raymond suspiciously: a tall young man, black-haired, without even a hat to protect him from the rain which poured down his face, wearing a posh flannel suit but with his trouser turn-ups tucked into his socks.

'What do you want?' The voice was harsh with a Midlands accent, a trace of fear in it, anxiety showing in his dark eyes. He was taller and more muscular than Raymond had judged from the glimpse he had caught of him last night.

How many times had Raymond imagined and rehearsed this moment? Now that it had come he was so frightened that for a moment he could not speak. Then at last he said, 'You're my father, George Cox. I'm your son Raymond.'

The man responded so swiftly it was as if he, too, had rehearsed this moment, this confrontation with the adult metamorphosis of the infant he had abandoned almost twenty-one years ago. 'I don't want to see you, do you hear? I don't want you here. Get out of my gardens. Go on, GET OUT!' His voice rose to a shout and he waved both arms threateningly, as if shooing hens.

Raymond looked into his angry dark eyes knowing that he would never do so again, and would never understand, never learn the secret of this man's hatred of his own son. Then

37

he just shook his head, saying nothing, and turned away. But the voice had not quite finished. It had more to say, more to half-shout in the ugly Midlands accent: 'And do your duty and get into uniform, you coward! There's a war on.'

As Raymond entered the officers' mess bar, Jack Farmiloe looked up in surprise.

'Good God, Ray, what're you doing back before your time? You must be a glutton for punishment.'

He bought Raymond a drink before inquiring how he had got on at home.

'Got a bit bored really. My mother was out all day and everyone else has gone off somewhere.'

'Your father at work, too, I suppose.'

'That's right.'

Next morning at the dispersal Raymond asked 'Chiefy', the Flight-Sergeant in charge, if there were any kites needing an engine test. 'Yes, R-Roger. Ready in five minutes.'

All Raymond wanted to do now was to get off the ground, into the pure air, to dart among the cumulus, indulge in a few aerobatics. And that is just what he did — until a voice came over the R/T with his callsign:

'Daisy Red One, are you receiving me, over?'

'Loud and clear.'

'Daisy Red One, there's a possible bandit north. Angels twenty-six. Steer zero-one-zero, and buster. Out.'

It could only be a photo-recce plane checking on the damage to some poor northern city which had been bombed last night. Raymond's height was a mere fifteen thousand. But the adrenalin was already flowing fast. So he went through the gate as instructed, and R-Roger responded nobly, the rate-of-climb needle moving rapidly from 1 to 2 and then higher. But it was forty minutes before the controller had brought him near enough to identify the twin-engine plane heading south-east flat-out back to its base.

This was a very experienced pilot with a couple of very accurate gunners, one with twin machine-guns in the rear of the ventral gondola, all of them now following him around with short, sharp bursts of tracer as he made a series of rear attacks, the jinking of the 88 making accurate deflection firing difficult. Raymond's Spit was hit many times before, guided by a barely controlled fury, he pressed home to less than one hundred yards and got in a long burst on the port engine. A lick of flame suddenly blasted into an inferno and the 88 flicked into a spin, at the same time shedding the entire wing.

Raymond watched the fireball drop into cloud. Far below, a single parachute hovered above it, the swinging figure scarcely visible. For a second Raymond wondered about this only survivor's feelings ... which set him to wondering about his own, after burning to death three young men twenty five thousand feet above the earth. But he found there was less pity and compassion than fuel in his near-empty tanks. Remorse might come later. Or it might not.

'Daisy Red One, bandit destroyed,' Raymond transmitted.

Then he had gone home. That was 13 November 1940, and the following night German bombers left over five hundred civilians dead in the ruins of Coventry.

Those German aircrew like those people of Coventry, had been dead for two-and-a-half years now. And still the killing went on. There would be more today, of that there was little doubt. Ten minutes to six o'clock; 21 Squadron dispersal on immediate readiness. The NAAFI van was outside, serving hunks of bread and marge and mugs of hot sweet tea. Nick Moeran and Archy Duke (both Australian sergeant-pilots) were playing shove ha'penny. The CO, a fanatic even at this early hour, had got up a four of bridge. Two pilots were reading old creased newspapers in which the crossword puzzles had long ago been completed. Raymond was half reading a crime paperback with a green cover, but making little progress, his mind slipping back time and again to the events of the night before. Louise Daintree — well! He kept repeating her name and thought about rhapsodising to someone else on the wonders of making love — containing himself with the notion that this was unlikely to be news to any of his fellow pilots, who would mock him for his naiveté. '*Oh, stale gen, Ray,*' he could imagine the thick Australian accent of Archy Duke from Adelaide. '*Never met one that wasn't fuckable.*'

39

So Raymond was happy to nurse the memory to himself, soon even giving up his attempt to fill in the memory gaps and forgotten details of that most odd Anglo-American evening. And, anyway, the telephone was ringing.

Jack Farmiloe, Flight Commander, took the call, jotting down notes. 'Yeah ... yes, OK, got that ... yeah, yeah. We'll be there, sir.'

It was as if everyone in the hut had been frozen, tea mug halfway to lips, hand halfway to the ha'penny board, and Chiefy with his hand on the doorlatch, ready to go out.

Farmiloe replaced the receiver, turning to his audience. 'Well, it's on, and it's ten-tenths at two thou.'

The Intelligence Officer — known as the IO or the 'Spy' — who like most of his kind was inclined to fuss, tried to draw everyone's attention to the board for a last check, but they all knew what was on it and what they had to do. 'Chuck it, Spy, we've got to get airborne.' The lines on the board showed a rendezvous with the Torbeaus twelve miles off the Dutch coast, then a run north until they hit the convoy a few miles south-east of Den Helder. If cloud height was really going to be no more than two thousand feet, it was going to be a dodgy do in Spit Vs when the Schipol fighter boys interrupted proceedings.

That was *not* how the CO had put it, but that is how it would be. They would almost certainly be outnumbered, there — whereas by contrast it was always more comforting fighting on this side of the water, where the Air-Sea Rescue Services were all poised to fish you out, and anyway you could sometimes glide back to dear old Blighty.

Rendezvous had now been fixed at 6.50 am. The ground crews had the engines running, all twelve of them, blue exhaust smoke rising into the cold dawn. Raymond's kite was two bays to the left, next-door to the CO's, to whom he was flying number three, with Archy Duke in R-Roger as his number two. Raymond ran towards his Spitfire, Bonz as usual at his side, helmet clutched in his small jaws. Barney Hart, Raymond's rigger, was standing on the wing, ready to take the helmet from the dog, and give Raymond a hand up before helping him with his helmet and straps. Raymond wouldn't even have to remind him to feed Bonz and keep an eye on him until he returned. In the cockpit everything was neatly laid out, as always, parachute straps laid back ready to clip into the box.

The slipstream tugged at Raymond's black hair as he climbed up and slipped into the cockpit. Barney leant over like a nurse preparing the patient for an operation. He was a cockney from Bow (house bombed, wife killed) who unselfconsciously hero-worshipped Raymond, his fingers itching to add to the swastikas painted beside the cockpit. 'Give 'em merry hell, sir.'

It was always the same, 'merry hell', a curiously contradictory term. Raymond looked up and smiled, then adjusted the rheostat on the reflector sight. This had been an unfailing part of his cockpit check since the time he had switched it on in a sudden crisis, when a Junkers 88 broke cloud right ahead of him, and he had been blinded by the sight's brightness and failed to blow it up, depriving Barney of a celebratory bit of painting.

Squadron-Leader McWilliams was the last to be settled. Above the sound of his Merlin, he was talking into the ear of his fitter and gesticulating, but then as he checked his ailerons and rudder controls, looking left and right and behind, and when he checked that everyone's engine was running, and when he raised his hand, signalled chocks away and began to taxi forward onto the perimeter track, he reflected the aura of a leader. The routine that they all followed assumed in his hands a special authority.

Barton Heath had a single, rather narrow tarmac runway for visitors' use, or for their own use in exceptionally damp conditions. But they all preferred the grass, and thought runways were strictly for sprogs. Besides, on grass you could take off four abreast, or the whole squadron abreast if you were shooting a line for the C-in-C's benefit. Now Raymond formed up on the CO's starboard wing, and — when the CO raised his arm momentarily — he moved his throttle steadily forward through its quadrant.

The Spit always needed careful nursing at take-off partly because of prop torque, which had to be compensated by strong opposite rudder, but chiefly because the close-set wheels made it skittish, especially on any sort of uneven

41

surface. But the four machines of the CO's section kept reasonably close formation as they accelerated across the grass, bumping a little until first the tails lifted, then after a few more bumps the aircraft themselves cleared and they were airborne.

Undercarriage up. Radiator closed, ease prop pitch back, check instruments, boost four easing to three-and-a-half. Follow the CO into a gently climbing turn. Met was right: cloud base at exactly two thousand feet. Archy Duke's starboard wingtip was brushing it as they completed the turn downwind. Below, the last section was just airborne and over the hedge at Barton's perimeter.

By 6.12 am, 21 Squadron had been wordlessly formed up in three sections of four, the CO in the centre section, the twelve Spitfires bobbing slightly in the turbulance, course 084 degrees, the grey spread of Great Yarmouth to the left. Once over the coast, the CO took them down to near zero feet, and Raymond, like the others, reconciled himself to the silent wave-hopping across the North Sea.

6.37 am they had to circle twice, slowly and almost brushing the wave-tops, before they caught sight of the twin-engine Torbeaus coming in from the west, flying as low as they were. There was no question of misidentification with a Beau, with its stubby nose, stubby radial engines, and the torpedo — the 'pickle' — hanging awkwardly from the belly.

The Torbeau leader fired a green Very, tapped out the letter of the day on his lamp, and turned his squadron north-east to close the coast. The cloud had lifted slightly, but the base was uncomfortably low, giving the Spits little manoeuvring room. The CO formed them up protectively behind the Torbeaus so that they had to throttle right back to avoid overshooting their heavily loaded charges.

The Spy had told them that it was believed the Germans had installed some short-range, very low-seeing radar along this critical bit of coastline, and this seemed to be confirmed when a pair of 190s, followed by two more, sprang out of the murk from the east.

'Bogeys three o'clock.' The CO's voice was matter-of-fact, and he took them up to cloud base at around three thousand. 'There'll be more, har-r-r-k my words.'

'Dingbat leader to Strawberry leader,' said the Torbeau leader. 'Target dead ahead and we're going straight in.'

Raymond could just make out the dark blur of ships ahead, already sparkling with flak; then he turned his attention back to the four enemy fighters flying parallel to them, range around two miles, their threatening stubby silhouettes testing their nerves. Fifty miles an hour faster, more heavily armed than they were, every sane fighter pilot respected these vicious Focke-Wulfs which were as manoeuvrable as they were low down, and could be caught only in the tightest of turns.

The enemy reinforcements came unexpectedly — but not unseen — from the west: twenty or thirty 109s flat on the sea, looking like a swarm of grey trout swimming with the current, and heading very fast for the Torbeaus, which were already being crisscrossed with tracer flak from the ships. These torpedo-carrying planes had broken formation and had scattered across the grey sky like pigeons hearing a shotgun. Their aircrew might be scared too — must be scared — but showed no signs of it as they headed for the strongly defended ships from all heights and directions in order to divide the fire.

'All Strawberry aircraft, get in among those 109s and watch your tails.'

Raymond felt the breathtaking rush of adrenalin mixed with naked terror that always seized him before tight combat. He had every confidence in his skill, all the pride in his record, and all the awareness that the final arbiter was often the devil luck — the luck that could as suddenly put an enemy plane smack into your sights at killing range as it could leave you with your blind spot uncovered for the fraction of a second needed to bring high explosive tearing into your cockpit. Then it would smash human tissue just as decisively as the complex of steel and fuel, alloy and unused ammunition, and propel you, dead or in flames, into the sea.

Raymond was fully aware of all this, of the crazy unpredictability of odds, of the unjust vagaries of combat chance, which — even as he glanced to starboard — revealed the sudden scarlet and yellow glow of another Torbeau taking a direct hit. Archy Duke must be feeling as he did, but without his experience.

43

Then, a split second later, mind and body were concentrated on the fighting to the exclusion of all else — concentrated, like a surgeon making his incision, on the centre dot of his reflector sight. Suddenly, there was his darting target of mottled camouflage, blatant black cross and the heart of it all, the enclosed cockpit, and the head and shoulders of the German pilot. But this time, Raymond wasn't quick enough.

'They're bloody hard customers at Schipol, make no mistake,' the CO had once warned. 'Take no liberties and give them everything.' Johnny Warner, on seeing one of his mates go down, had taken the last exhortation too literally; he had slipped inland and raked from end to end one of the most heavily defended airfields on the Continent. He came back slowly, with 22 cannon hits in his wings and fuselage, but an air recce photo showed ten wrecked 109s spilt all over Schipol.

That was last November and Johnny had long since gone; and for a moment here, six months later, Raymond thought he might be joining him in his watery grave. The 190s had joined the fray, and one with a yellow spinner was tapping out 20 mm cannon shells in his direction at very short range. Someone was shouting, 'Break Ray!' and he did, but only after feeling the thud of hits somewhere behind him.

Raymond hauled back into a left climbing turn so tight that he partially blacked out. The 190 had no difficulty in following him, and he could see the intermittent flashes from the wing cannon proving that his adversary still had him at full deflection. Tighter, tighter, back, back, back. He could feel the first flutter of a stall, and at this height no one could pull out of a spin. Round and round. The corkscrew pursuit lasted only seconds but felt like minutes.

Then Raymond saw the Focke-Wulf suddenly fall away — not in a spin but in an effort to escape from his tighter turn. He immediately kicked left rudder, pushed down his nose and, amidst a mêlée of plunging, climbing, turning fighters and Torbeaus, he pursued the 190 down to a few feet above the sea. He fired a one-second burst at maximum range and the 190 pulled away like a sprinter from a long distance runner. Curse the Spit. Curse it — too slow, hopelessly too slow!

But, as suddenly, the needle of luck swung his way again with the appearance of a long-nosed machine a few hundred feet above, a scarlet-nosed 109 in a shallow turn as if disorientated. Raymond pulled back on his stick, pushed the throttle through the gate for emergency boost, and tucked in behind him, range 600, reducing through 500. Resist the urge to open fire at maximum effective range, closer, closer.

He *must* be spotted. But, no, the 109, grey-camouflaged, the numeral 4 on its fuselage, straightened out and headed back to the coast. Raymond was right underneath, and at about 150 yards he pulled out, steadied on a 10-degree deflection. At this range, under these conditions, he could pick his spot. A once-in-a-lifetime true sitting duck. His cannon and machine-guns poured in their jet of destruction, into the wing-root, the cockpit and rear of the engine, taking the machine to pieces before his eyes.

He pulled up hard to the right, aileroned left again, and watched the fragments fall — but did not wait for them to hit the sea. There were other things to concern him. For example, where was everyone else? Neither friend nor enemy was in sight, only two burning ships like small volcanoes emitting volumes of smoke and flame, and the faint streak of the Dutch coast.

Raymond remembered that he was still at emergency boost, pulled back the throttle, searched the sky again and headed west. He was not altogether surprised at being alone. The hurly-burly of close combat often ended, seconds later, in empty skies; which made it all the more surprising to see, far to the north, a fighter emerging from the cloud in a shallow glide. He turned to intercept it, again opening throttle, and recognising the familiar silhouette of a Spitfire. So the fighting had climbed to above cloud level, that was the only conclusion. And now he would not be returning alone.

In a few more seconds he made out the squadron letters, and then — my God, what a coincidence! It was R-Roger, Archy himself, reunited with his number one.

But not for long. As Raymond pulled in beside him, he saw that the cockpit canopy had been released, and that the cockpit was empty. So Archy had baled out. But why? On this side of the Spit there was no sign of damage. It remained on a steady course, the glide neither steepening nor shallowing.

Had Archy baled out in a panic? No, Raymond saw, as he pulled up a few feet above the Spitfire. No, he had not baled out at all. He was still in the cockpit, slumped right forward, his head to the left of the stick. Now Raymond understood. Archy had been shot, and in his dying moments had released the hood and his straps, then died before he could get out.

Raymond flicked over his switch to transmit, recognised the futility of talking to a dead man, and watched with sickening resignation R-Roger, prop spinning, Merlin in good heart, airframe little damaged, close the sea and strike it in a tall plume of white foam, and at once disappear.

There was no debris, nothing but bubbles. Perhaps one day poor old Archy's body would float free and be picked up by a Dutch inshore fisherman. Meanwhile, as a mark of respect Raymond circled low over the spot before heading once more for home.

He knew the sad routine:

> *Dear Mrs Duke,*
> *It is with deep sorrow that I am writing to you with the*
> *sad news that your gallant son . . .*

'Quite a donny, sir, so they say. The CO got a 109, and Sergeant Milford got one and damaged another. How about you, sir?'

Raymond pulled himself stiffly from the cockpit, pulled off his helmet and threw it angrily back on to his seat, ignoring the proffered hand and jumping from wing to the ground. The sight of the three long, angled holes in the fuselage and the raw turned-in edges made by the 190's cannon switched his state of mind as if the shots had just been fired instead of thirty-five minutes ago. Bloody tactful of Barney to say nothing, especially as they meant much unrewarding work for him. And bloodyminded of himself to ignore his rigger.

He lit a cigarette, drawing deeply on the smoke. They always tasted special after an op. Then he looked up at Barney, who was hauling out his parachute and helmet.

'Yes, you can paint on another swastika.'

Barney grinned broadly. 'Well done, sir. Oh, I'll enjoy that — and we'll soon have those scratches dealt with.' His expression changed as he added anxiously, 'And Sergeant Duke, sir? He's even later than you are.'

'He won't be coming back at all, Barney.'

'I'm sorry about that, sir. I likes the Aussies.'

Raymond said nothing. He bent down and gave Bonz the warm helmet to carry.

Chapter Four

'ALL RIGHT,' the CO agreed, 'So long as you can get to the dispersal in thirty minutes and you leave your number.'

'Ten minutes, sir, that's all I'll need. You know Delilah.'

'I *do*, Ray — and don't you get killed in that machine. To go for a burton in a car — well ... Just you remember Robbie Burns:

> "Know prudent cautious self control
> Is wisdom's root"'

'Obviously your Robbie Burns would never have commanded 21 Squadron, sir.'

The invitation had come, correctly addressed *Flying Officer Raymond Cox, Officers' Mess, RAF Barton Heath*, and written in a round schoolgirl's hand. Mums and Papa would so like you to come to family lunch on Saturday if you can get the time off. Then directions, not really necessary, to the Vicarage, West Aitcham.

Raymond had bought the Alvis Speed 20 in 1940 as much for its line as for its speed — which was close to 100 mph if you could hold it on the road. From its huge P100 chrome headlamps and long vented bonnet and the fold-flat windscreen in front of the driving seat to the finely tapering tail, the Alvis was aesthetic perfection. The B-Flight chief fitter had tuned and balanced the triple SU carburettors to fullest efficiency, and Barney Hart had exercised his painting talent with 'Delilah' in sloping lettering along the bonnet. (He had also wanted to duplicate Raymond's swastikas along the cutaway driver's door, but the offer was firmly declined.)

There was, strictly speaking, no petrol ration for Delilah but somehow there was always fuel in the tank, and if the gauge fell low, the next day it magically showed full again. In return for this unstated privilege, Raymond was always happy for Flight-Sergeant 'Chiefy' and the groundcrew generally to pile — a dozen at a time — into the four seats and on the running-boards to be brought to and from dispersal to living quarters, and often down to the local pub in the evening.

There were other private cars on the squadron, and there were other dogs, too; but just as Delilah was top car, so Bonz was top dog, the first to pick up the sound of distant Merlin engines when the squadron returned from an op, first to reflect elation at a pilot's success, first to reflect the gloom when a pilot failed to return. (Archy Duke's death had caused Bonz to mope for a whole day.) Raymond had taken Bonz up in a Spitfire once or twice on engine tests, but the terrier liked best the Squadron Tiger Moth, in which he sat, well secured on a couple of parachutes, head in the slipstream and watching the world below go by, in a state of blissful contentment.

Raymond stopped his car beside the hedge over which he had dead-engined ten days earlier, and saw that the farmer had harrowed the long slash the Spitfire had cut across the field and had already drilled in more seed. In a few weeks time there would be no evidence of his crash landing, and he reflected philosophically on the ironical consequences of being shot down by a nice young American, escaping death more closely than with the Focke-Wulf just the other day — but also leading to a welcome bed on one evening, and now a welcome back to the Boland vicarage.

The village of West Aitcham — a manor house, two or three larger houses, a few shops, twenty or thirty smaller houses, and the solid Norman church with its gravestones and yews — lay beyond the entrance to the vicarage. Raymond drove slowly up the gravel drive, in much need of raking and weeding, and beneath overgrown rhododendrons and laurels, to the small sweep in front of the door.

Rachel, carrying a basket of muddy eggs, saw the car and came alongside the driving seat as Raymond brought it to a halt. 'Goodness, what a dashing machine! I suppose you have to drive fast if you're flying Spitfires. And why Delilah?' She was taller than Raymond remembered her, and almost absurdly young and pretty as she pushed back the over-long black fringe from her eyes.

'I just thought it sounded nice. But then someone said she was a treacherous woman.'

Rachel laughed. 'But beautiful, too. If you were an American you would paint her on the bonnet without many clothes on.'

'Or none at all. Did you see those Thunderbolts that evening at Stiplowe?'

'I certainly did,' she said, laughing again and stroking Bonz. 'I was taken on a tour of them.'

Raymond climbed out of the driving seat, tying Bonz's lead to the steering wheel. 'Oh, let him come in. The boys will love to play with him — you know, our dogs.'

'He'll tear the place to pieces,' Raymond warned.

'There's nothing left to tear.'

They walked over to the dark brown front door, which was in need of some paint. 'I ought to have brought you some flowers, or something. But there's nothing this side of Norwich. Anyway, it was very kind of you to ask me.'

Rachel led the way in, putting down her basket in the porch. 'I'm afraid it'll be a busman's holiday for you. Jack's coming over from Horning, and Papa will want to know exactly what you're up to.'

'And your mother?'

'Oh yes, you didn't meet her last time. She was away at one of her London charities.'

As before, Rachel led Raymond into John Boland's study. He was cleaning his pipe by the fire and looked up welcomingly. 'Good to see you again. So glad you could come.'

'Very good of you, sir. I'm on "30 minutes" so you'll forgive me if I have to sprint off if the 'phone rings.'

50

Bonz was proving uncharacteristically shy with the two aged labradors, who thudded their tails hospitably but did not rise from the faded carpet.

'Jack'll be here in a minute.'

'How is he?' Raymond asked.

'Oh, he's all right. He gets these tertian malaria bouts every so often and has to rest afterwards. They make him depressed and rather cross, with bad headaches. He caught it out in Burma during the Arakhan fighting. He had a squadron of Hurricanes out there. At the end he and a sergeant-pilot were the only two left. We were lucky to get him back.'

The Vicar picked up his stick, which had been hanging by its crook from the mantelpiece, and limped over to the sideboard. 'He managed to lay his hands on a bottle of whisky from the mess last week. Like some?'

Dorothy Boland then came in, square in shape like her husband, white hair that did not seem important in her life, a healthy, pleasing appearance though, and bright blue eyes: a real matriarchal figure. She greeted Raymond warmly and excused shaking hands — 'covered in flour and goodness knows what' — and told him to sit down. 'No cook on Saturdays, which is most inconvenient as it's John's day of rest. So you'll have to put up with me. Steak and kidney pie, but lucky for you, all I'm making is the pastry.'

Rachel was playing with the dogs, trying to arouse some interest from the labradors in their lively guest Bonz, but without much success.

Noting a photograph of an old biplane on his host's desk, Raymond asked him about it.

'That's a Pup. Father of the Camel. I liked the Pup better. It handled more predictably.'

'What else did you fly, sir?'

The vicar topped up Raymond's glass. 'Call me John, please. I never got higher than your rank.' He smiled as he added some soda from a syphon.

'Oh, the old FE. I flew those quite a bit. There's one,' he added, pointing to a brown photograph on the wall of a machine with the engine and prop behind the pilot, who sat out in front in a sort of basket with a single Lewis machine-gun, more exposed than the driver of an Alvis Speed

20, and with nothing between him and the tail-plane except for naked struts.

'How fast?'

'About 90.'

'Same as my car.'

Rachel, now lying on her back on the floor as she played with Bonz, interjected, 'And the same as what we have in the garage.'

Puzzled, Raymond asked what she meant.

'It's our secret. I'll show you after lunch.'

From the drive they heard the sound of a car approaching and a minute later Jack Boland joined them, complaining of the cold, which was not surprising after three years in the Far East. He was in uniform and Raymond noted the ribbons of the DSO and DFC beneath his wings. He gestured for Raymond to sit down again and served himself a generous draught of whisky, holding the bottle up to the light and mock-complaining to his father: 'Looks as though I'll have to bribe the barman again. "Lay not up for yourselves treasures upon earth where drink doth corrupt," eh, Father? Matthew 6:19.'

'Well, nearly, but not quite.'

Unlike the other two men in the room, Jack Boland had a fair complexion and blond hair, grown rather long — by carelessness rather than intention, Raymond guessed. He obviously took after his mother, who, as Raymond noted later, clearly doted on her first-born. His eyes were bright Scandinavian blue, his hands long-fingered unlike his father's stubbiness, with nicotine stains on the first and second fingers of his right hand. He had about him the same air of authority as Sandy McWilliams. Raymond was quite sure that he himself did not possess this, yet while wondering where the new leaders would be found, he had to admit that he had seen suddenly promoted officers assume the mantle of office with speed and efficiency, especially during the last phases of the Battle of Britain.

But while Raymond's CO gave every appearance of equability and nervelessness, Jack Boland was clearly highly-strung. The words spilt from him rapidly, as if anxious to be away, so anxious indeed that the last words came up almost as a stutter.

52

He also laughed a great deal, a rather high-pitched bray, as often at what he himself had said as at what others had said. It was completely in character that Jack Boland was a heavy cigarette smoker, taking short, hard puffs so that sometimes the tip of his cigarette was long and glowing and the ash had no time to form. Twice Raymond watched him light up again when a half-smoked cigarette lay burning in the ashtray.

But none of this led to the slightest doubt in Raymond's mind that Squadron-Leader Boland was a fine leader. Just as, say, the role of Macbeth can be played in different and highly contrasting styles, so fighting leaders, Raymond knew, can be equally effectual playing their part in quite different manners. At the top, for instance, look at the difference between Air Marshals Park and Leigh-Mallory, C-in-Cs 12 and 11 Groups in that great battle of three summers ago: the first a cool, calculating New Zealander, and Leigh-Mallory the emotional showman.

All this passed through Raymond's mind as he listened to Jack Boland telling his father and his equally interested sister about the week's events at Horning — the improving reliability of the Typhoon, and the wear and tear of keeping up standing patrols during daylight hours against tip-and-run raiders, but the necessity of doing so if they were ever to catch them.

Then Dorothy Boland called them into lunch, the vicar knocked out his pipe into the fire, Jack also threw his newly-lit cigarette into it, the labradors hauled themselves off the floor in the hope of scraps, and the cats appeared from somewhere though pretending they were above being interested in food, while Rachel carried Bonz in as special guest. There was a jug of beer on the table, and cabbage and baked potatoes alongside the big pie.

Addressing Raymond, Dorothy Boland asked briskly, 'Your family? Tell us about them, where you live and all that.'

Raymond felt the grey tide of inevitability wash over him. It was always the same, and always wretched. Why? It didn't seem to bother that American. I'm a big boy now, he would shriek at himself silently. But it was no good. It was like an incurable speech impediment, to be suffered.

So when he answered he hoped that none of the distress was revealed in his voice. 'I don't have much of a family ...' And he told them about his mother dying and his father just disappearing. (Nobody would ever, *ever*, know about his father.) Ending up, 'So you see, all rather negative.'

Her eyes were regarding him sympathetically, and he felt the eyes of the others on him, too. Jack poured out the beer, and some cider for Rachel.

'Mark you,' said Dorothy Boland cheerfully, 'you can sometimes have too much of a good thing. I quite like this lot,' she said, waving her hand about the table, 'and there's another one you haven't met; so that's three altogether, or four if you count John as needing attention — as he sometimes does. To say nothing of this house, which is like a fifth member of the family and a very difficult child — greedy, expensive, overgrown, awkward, untidy, dirty, demanding and requiring constant attention, the wretched spoilt thing.'

'But you love it,' said Rachel, pointing her fork. 'You can't have too much — house, family, everything, really. Omnivorous, that's how someone described you. You know you love it.'

'Well, I suppose so,' Dorothy admitted with a hearty laugh. 'But why the Church lumbers its slaves with cold, gaunt castles I fail to understand.' She turned back to Raymond. 'But tell me about your aunt, and where you live,' she asked him.

'Well, she was something of a saint, I suppose. She was my mother's elder sister, so when my mother died, Aunt May adopted me. She was only twenty-two, and had very little money, but my father never offered her any. So she brought me up, somehow sent me to a decent boarding school, and she never married. She *was* my family. So it was a bit of a blow when she died.'

They had pulled her out of the rubble soon after four in the morning, Raymond was told. 'She's a tough old nut,' one of the heavy rescue team said. '*I've* never seen anyone so knocked about and still alive — and I've seen a few.'

Raymond was directed to N Ward in the south wing of the hospital, the only wing relatively undamaged, though they were still sweeping up the glass and it was bitterly cold — for not only was there no heating but there were no windows either, or very few. There was a screen round May's bed, more to keep off the draft than to provide privacy. The doctor, who looked younger than Raymond and was grey with fatigue, told him straight out, 'I'm afraid she's not going to live. It's a miracle she got here alive. Though of course we'll do our best.'

Raymond did not enquire about her injuries, and never learned later. He preferred not to think about May's robust frame being broken and twisted. She had beaten him at tennis until he was seventeen and could walk the wolds and the Mendips at Raymond's own fast pace. Mercy be to God, her face was only slightly cut, so she might have been asleep rather than unconscious. But the arm with the drip was bandaged above the elbow, and the rubble dust remaining in her hair was pathetic evidence of the condition in which they had found her as well as of the pressure on the hospital emergency staff.

Raymond held the other hand, which was cold and limp. It was a fine hand that could play Chopin preludes with tenderness and precision, as well as paint in oils and smash a lob at the net, but Raymond was thinking more personally about it holding his own hand while crossing the road, putting him on the seat of the swing, nailing a safety bar across his bedroom window, and also smacking him when that was called for.

She opened her eyes without recognition and without any change of expression, peering straight into his. Raymond found this disquieting and spoke her name. 'It's Raymond.'

Her eyes were closed again when the beginning of a smile awoke on her lips and she said clearly, 'Dear Raymond, it's nice to see you. You are kind. Have you brought Bonz?'

'No, but I'll find him. Are you in any pain, May?'

She did not reply. Raymond continued to hold her hand for a long time, against the sound of tinkling glass and trolley wheels, voices of distress and decisiveness, and — outside — the sounds of ambulance bells, of shouting, of falling masonry and straining vehicle engines — of a great city bringing itself back to life.

It must have been at least a 500 kg HE. The crater was ten feet deep, and it had utterly destroyed the detached house on one side and almost levelled the house on the other side where the Clutterbucks lived — lived *and* died, as it turned out.

The bomb had fallen in the front garden and only a part of the rear wall remained, with May's painting of Burford high-street still clinging to the inside at an acute angle. There were fragments of furniture to be seen in the rubble, but the only other thing to remain intact was the front gate-pillar with the name 'Montrose' etched in Gothic lettering within a stone panel. May had wanted that removed when she had bought the house five years ago. 'We've never even *been* to Scotland,' she had said, laughing at the inappropriateness of it here in Clifton, Bristol. 'We must just have a number.'

But Raymond had argued for keeping it. 'It's like changing a person's name. And think of the pride of the first occupant — a fine proud fellow in sidewhiskers, certainly in shipping, who took his family to Scotland every year, and ordered the name from the builder and had it engraved in Gothic script on his stationery, too.'

'You're a silly old sentimentalist,' May said, but she gave way. And now there it was, quite unharmed, although its duplicate pillar had joined the rubble.

There were an air-raid warden and a policeman talking to each other by the 'incident', and several others behind the rope which had been strung round the scene of demolition. Another bomb had fallen plumb in the middle of the road, leaving white-scarred trees and scattered branches.

The policeman saluted Raymond and the warden stood respectfully at attention. He had Great War ribbons on his chest, and the policeman — Raymond remembered later — had a fine walrus moustache.

'This was my house,' Raymond said. 'I've just come to see if anything is left.'

'Well, you can see for yourself, sir ... I'm very sorry. And I'm afraid there's bad news about the occupant.'

'Yes, thank you, I know. She's my aunt, and I've seen her. Is there any sign of her dog? She was asking for it.'

The policeman looked at the warden. 'You were here last night, Charlie. Did you see one?'

'We were pretty busy, sir, as you can imagine. But there was one tied up down at the station when I got away for a cuppa soon after the all-clear. Little fellow.'

Raymond asked for directions, said he would be back to see if there was anything to salvage, and was reassured by the policeman that someone would be keeping an eye on things.

It was Bonz all right, tied up with string and shaking as if shell-shocked. Someone had put some milk in a saucer for him but he had not touched it. When Raymond called his name he leapt forward, spilling his milk, to the string's full stretch.

Bristol survived that ferocious bombing, but May did not. When Raymond returned to the hospital the sheet had simply been pulled over her face.

He always minded much more that May never saw Bonz safe once more than that he himself never saw her alive again. On the long grinding train journey back to his squadron in Yorkshire, he reflected with dismay and astonishment that this small and engaging dog was now the most important living link with his past. The loneliness, grief, and then self-pity this realisation brought about was forever fixed in his memory, along with the squealing starts and stops of the train through the night, the huddled figures with kitbags on blacked-out station platforms, the rise and fall of siren notes in the Midland cities, and the intermittent flashing of gunfire and bomb bursts.

When Raymond arrived back with his squadron, the CO grunted his sympathy, ordered a pale ale for Bonz and a double whisky for Raymond. 'It'll bloody well improve your gunnery,' he said. 'Controlled anger always does.' And that was true: it had been getting better ever since.

Raymond rapidly filled the vacuum of shocked distress around the vicarage table by reverting the conversation to Jack's squadron and his Typhoons. 'You've got the tail trouble taped now, have you?'

'You've heard about that?'

'They kept falling off in a dive, didn't they?'

'Not *always*,' Jack said with a little nervous laugh. 'Just sometimes. But all right, now. And catching a 190 is like your car overtaking an Austin 7.'

Baked apple and custard followed, with a pot of tea. John Boland excused himself for what he called his Saturday afternoon chore — 'Not really a day of rest. Sermon's got to be written.'

'What's your theme this week, Papa?' asked Rachel.

'In view of your little contretemps the other day,' he replied, smiling at Raymond, 'which we're so pleased has brought you back to us, I thought of "suffering the strain of good intentions".'

Jack said, 'You mean Raymond being shot down by that crazy Yank, Papa?'

'He's not crazy,' Rachel protested. 'He's very, very nice' and extremely kind, and anyone can make mistakes.'

'Not in war, one can't,' her father said firmly, 'speaking as an old pilot myself. But speaking as the voice of the church, there's more to it than that.' He stomped out of the kitchen, laughing. 'As you will no doubt learn from me tomorrow, young lady.'

Raymond insisted on helping Jack and Rachel with the washing-up. 'You said in your letter it was family lunch,' he said. 'And it's been a wizard family lunch, so now it's going to be a family clear-up.'

And that was exactly how he felt as Rachel threw him a drying-up cloth: part of the family, thanks to this welcome. He had, long ago, stayed with some distant cousins in Yorkshire, like this a big family, full of animals as well as children of all ages, and when the week was over and he came home he was filled with melancholy and loneliness. Nor had it helped that he was never invited there again.

'What's this secret you're going to reveal, Rachel?' he asked as he dried the last glass.

'I was going to show him Tiger, Jack. Is that all right?'

'Of course. Give him a pat for me, as I've got to get back to Horning. There's a new sprog pilot who needs knocking into shape.'

The sun had now broken through, after a morning of low cloud, and they went out through the kitchen door into a cobbled yard which sprouted many docks and nettles. There were neglected loose boxes and a tack-room with windows obscured by spiders' webs and dust. At one end there was an old greenhouse, its roof bent like an old man's back and with little glass left. He hoped the tiger was more securely installed.

'We used to have a groom and coachman when I was little,' Rachel explained. 'And two gardeners. But they all went off to the war ages ago, and anyway we couldn't afford them any more.' With Bonz at her side and looking up at them every few steps, she led Raymond to a large wooden building beyond the stable yard, standing alone. By contrast this was well maintained, the wood recently creosoted, even the windows clean. Rachel took out a key and opened a side door.

'This is Tiger's lair,' she said, switching on a light.

Raymond stood just inside the door, staring in wonder at the machine filling the entire building with only feet to spare. It was an aeroplane, its fuselage covered with a tarpaulin, its wheels off the ground on protective blocks, its tail held up by a wire so that it assumed a flying stance. Even before Rachel triumphantly ripped off the cover, Raymond had recognised the configuration: it was an old Tiger Moth, identical to 21 Squadron's, with the name '*Tiger*' — and a painted head of that animal beside it — beneath the cockpit.

'What do you think?'

'I don't know what to think. Are you storing it for someone?'

'Of course not, silly. It's the Boland family runabout. Before the war we used it all the time. Jack used to go to school in Tiger. Papa landed on the playing fields at Eton, and I used to fly Tiger, too. Not strictly within the law. But I went solo when I was fifteen.'

Raymond looked at her incredulously. 'So you really are all flying mad?'

'Yes, Papa infected us with the flying bug when we were in the cradle. Although he ended up with a smashed leg, the Great War gave him the disease.'

Bonz had recognised the machine as quickly as his master and was hopping up and down by the rear cockpit trying to get in.

'There's another sufferer from the disease,' Raymond told her.

'You mean Bonz flies?' It was Rachel's turn to express amazement.

'Can't keep him away. He likes my Spit too, but prefers our Tiger Moth. So do I, really. He's going solo next week.'

Rachel picked up the dog and, standing close to Raymond, said, 'Oh, Ray, what a shame about this beastly war. We could all go flying together *now*. Hedge-hop down to Eton and take Arnold out to tea ...'

Raymond laughed. 'Perhaps I could take the Squadron Tiger instead. Would you come with me?'

She looked into his face, her eyes flashing. 'You bet!' she exclaimed.

'Rachel! Rachel!' Dorothy Boland ran through the door, caught sight of Raymond and, panting as if finishing the hundred yards sprint, cried out, 'Call from your squadron. You're on immediate readiness.'

Raymond called out, 'Bonz, come on, it's flying time ... Good-bye, Rachel. Thank you for a lovely lunch, Mrs Boland.'

'Dorothy,' she corrected him emphatically — something which he remembered warmly later. 'Good luck!'

Delilah started at the first touch, just like his Spit, and Bonz leaped into the front passenger seat. Driving might be second to flying but it was still good fun.

A mile from Barton Heath, he saw a section of four of his Squadron Spits low and climbing, L-Leather, the CO's kite leading, then turning east for the coast. He was doing 80 mph along the short stretch of straight road before the main gates, changing down twice and double-declutching (not showing off, the synchromesh was worn). The guard could recognise Delilah's exhaust note — just as Bonz knew a Merlin's — and had the gates already open for him. A perfunctory salute — more a wave and a grin — and seconds later Raymond was on the perimeter track, past the watchtower — another wave — picking up a couple of erks, who had thrown their bikes onto the grass and raised their thumbs.

'Thanks, sir. There's a hell of a flap on.'

'I know. It rudely interrupted a conversation with a pretty girl.'

'Conversation, sir?' one of them asked darkly.

Bonz was out first, his adrenalin reacting to the crisis as rapidly as anyone's. 'What's on, Jack?' Raymond called out to Farmiloe, who had a sidcot on under his leather jacket, indicating an imminent high-altitude trip.

'Some Yanks are in trouble and we've got to do something about it.'

Raymond dug into the back of his locker for his silk inner and wool gloves to augment his leather gauntlets, hating the prospect of high flying because of the cold, the need for oxygen, and because (most important) the clip-wing Spit Vb wasn't much good above fifteen thousand. The Spy had fixed a map of the North Sea onto the board and all eight of them listened to him while they kitted up.

Spy was at his best when there was a flap on. His measured phrasing and 'pulpit voice' (as the CO called it) were irritatingly pedantic when there was time to spare, but soothing and mind-concentrating when it was panic-stations.

'Eighty Forts left for Emden, here, in waves late this morning, to bomb the U-boat yards. They knew they'd meet trouble but thought they could manage on their own. But by here (and he indicated a point thirty miles west of the Schleswig-Holstein coast) the first lot were taking a beating and called up for help for the rest on the return trip.'

Jack Farmiloe broke in, 'What are all those fuckin' Thunderbolts for? Just for shooting us down?'

The Spy's expression did not change. Coolly, he said, 'They're not fully operational yet, and we've said we'll do what we can. If you take off in five minutes, they'll be about here when you intercept them. Look out for stragglers — they're the ones they go for. The 8th Forts pack a sting and they'll be extra trigger-happy so never fly towards them. And there'll be more Spits and Typhoons around.'

Raymond stuffed the maps into his flying boot, and with Farmiloe led the others out into the warm, clear afternoon at a trot. He was leading Blue section, Farmiloe Red section and in command.

'Take Bonz, will you,' Raymond said to Barney. The dog was, as usual, keen on acting as co-pilot. The Spit, with its sixth swastika shiny black below the cockpit, was ticking over and chocks were away without asking, and his section of four moving forward before they had done up their straps.

Blue section beat Red by a hundred yards, taking off down-wind without asking permission. For number two, Raymond

61

had Sam Chapman, a twenty-year-old ex-public schoolboy straight from OTU, who had only been up once with him and had not seemed all that promising. For an op like this Raymond would have preferred someone with more time in. He had seen too many go for a burton on their first trip, and he knew he would be over-anxious about him, especially after the loss of Archy Duke.

Farmiloe took them over the coast at five thousand, climbing steadily with the sun behind them at $4\frac{1}{2}$ boost. As they were looking for a scrap, there was no point in keeping under the German radar and they wanted all the height they could get with their inferior performance. The visibility was unlimited, and to the south-east they could see the Dutch coast etched as if on a map, with all the islands and indentations they usually saw laterally at low altitude, and the Danish coastline more than one hundred and fifty miles distant to the north-east.

Some desultory heavy flak was thrown at them from the island of Terschelling, the only sign of hostility so far. Raymond turned every ten or fifteen seconds to squint into the sun — 'beware of the Hun in the sun' was the first tactical lesson they learned at OTU — and ruddered right, left to cover ahead and below.

Farmiloe — 'old razor eyes' — was the first to spot the trouble. He had Red section a little ahead and above, and called out, 'Strawberry, Red One, big friends below, ten o'clock.'

Raymond told himself he should have spotted them earlier. There were at least thirty B-17s flying in combat formation of stacked vic-threes, though ragged after all the flak and fighters they had been through. They were about five thousand feet below them, ten miles distant, and they were being kept busy by swarming single and twin engine fighters, looking at this distance like mobbing starlings. They were making head-on attacks, closing the formations at a combined speed of over 500 mph, many of them inverted and dropping away like stones after their pass.

'Strawberry aircraft, go in in pairs, try to get them as they attack. Don't follow them down. Out.'

Faintly a voice chimed in, the CO: 'Strawberry, Red and Blue, Strawberry leader here. We're on our way home. Pick the 110s if you can. We saw no 190s. Watch your fuel. Out.'

They were right over the stream now, some of the bombers showing evidence of damage or with feathered props. There were 109s all over the sky, above, below and level with the bombers. Bees round a honeypot, and angry ones at that. The odds against the bombers were ludicrous. Their only advantage was that most of the German pilots must have used some or perhaps most of their ammunition.

Anyway, they had not come all this way just to weigh up the odds and go home again. Raymond spotted a 110, and glancing at Chapman to make sure he was with him, turned and went after it with his throttle wide open. Check reflector sight intensity, slip off button safety shield, settle in your seat. Check turn and bank. And get him. The twin engine plane was lined up for a full deflection attack on the B-17 and was taking a lot of tracer cross-fire from the guns of two more bombers. It did not seem to worry him in the least. But the second he spotted the two Spits closing in, the pilot pulled away.

They went after it, Chapman's machine proving marginally faster and pulling ahead. But neither was fast enough to overhaul the 110, which turned towards the German coast, dipped into a shallow dive and was gone. Raymond swore to himself. 'Oh, God, how much longer are we going to have to fly these bloody old crates? Can't even catch a 110 . . .'

He turned back towards the bomber stream. There were one or two orders on the R/T. 'Red Three, break off. It's no good following them down.' And, 'Cannon jammed, fuck it!' But the Germans seemed to have melted away like frightened wolves about a corpse, certain in their knowledge that they could outpace their enemy, and ready to return once the escort had left.

But, five miles to the east, Raymond spotted a straggler and at once called Chapman, 'Blue Two, follow me.' He headed straight for the damaged B-17 with an engine smoking and at least half a dozen 109s torturing it with simultaneous attacks from different directions.

'Watch my tail, Blue Two.' Although they were coming in on the 109s out of the sun they couldn't hope to surprise them. German control would be listening in and must have warned their pilots. Already they were turning in to face the two Spits. But one 109 was slower and was still climbing away. Raymond kicked his rudder, checked again gun sight intensity, and went after him.

Chapman was above to the right and a little behind. Quite right. Good boy. And how he would be sweating! Raymond could just see out of the corner of his eye the looming shape of the beleaguered bomber but was giving all his attention to the 109. It was an old 'E' with clipped wingtips — just like his Spit. He hadn't seen one for months. But as he knew from his own first encounters back in October 1940, a tough adversary all the same.

The 109 was turning steeply, Raymond followed it, pulling hard on the stick, getting in a short burst at full deflection. He saw no strikes, and was not surprised.

'Blue Two, climb above me — fast!'

'Roger, Blue One.'

Suddenly the 109 flicked with breathtaking speed onto its back. The pilot evidently intended to fall away and outdive him — as he certainly could have done. But he left himself exposed, dead ahead of Raymond's guns, nil deflection for another fraction of a second. And Lady Luck was with him. But it needed needle-sharp reactions and a practised eye, as well, to get in a burst, cannon and .303 Brownings. A thousand pieces of Messerschmitt came screaming towards him, a hailstorm of metal.

It was a good early lesson for young Chapman, and a good too-late lesson for the Luftwaffe pilot who should never have done anything so silly. For the dive which should have taken him clear of danger became a dive to death — if he was still alive after suffering that ferocious hail of high-explosive and steel.

The other attackers, who may or may not have seen Raymond's sharp piece of shooting, had disappeared, all except one, neatly spotted by Chapman — the kid was doing well — some five thousand feet above. Another 110. Raymond sent Chapman up after it, and almost at once it showed the black cross on its fuselage as it banked and headed for home in a steep dive. Like the rest, he was after bombers, not Spitfires.

'Blue Two, let it go. Form up to port of big friend.'

It was the first time Raymond had been able to take a good look at the B-17, and a terrible sight it was, too. Its port outer engine was still streaming smoke, the prop dead. Cannon holes punctured almost the whole starboard side of the fuselage, inevitably killing the waist gunner and probably most of the cockpit crew. The ball gunner and his ball had disappeared, leaving a gap in the belly of the bomber, and there was an enormous hole in the starboard wing outside the second engine which had ripped the aileron to fragments.

The crew member at the controls in the shattered cockpit — the only man who appeared to have survived — was so occupied with keeping the B-17 flying that he did not for a while see his escort. Raymond closed in almost to the plane's wingtip, the pilot glanced in his direction, raised a hand briefly from the wheel, thumb extended, and returned to his task. Raymond, wondering how long he could stick it, tried to imagine what it must be like inside the bomber, the stench of blood, the bodies of his mates lying where they fell, the gunners amongst the piled spent shell cases, perhaps one or two still alive and bleeding to death, the physical strain of compensating for that hole in the wing and loss of an engine, while ahead of him the survivors in his group faded farther and farther into the distance.

There was no sign of any fighting ahead and the B-17's escort appeared to have been reinforced by several more squadrons of Spitfires and half a dozen Typhoons. They would be all right now. But almost half the width of the North Sea remained to be crossed, and their B-17 was steadily losing height and speed.

The sun was low in the west, but visibility remained unlimited and it was possible to make out the bulging coastline of East Anglia, right down to the Thames estuary. The remainder of the bombers had almost disappeared, leaving behind two more stragglers who could not keep up, both of them with escorting fighters to give them support and encouragement.

Raymond was having difficulty holding his Spit down to the bomber's speed, and they were using more fuel at this uneconomic speed than at 180 mph. One minute too slow, the next too fast. 'Blue Two,' Raymond called up, 'go ahead and return to base. But watch your tail — there may be the odd bandit around.'

'Roger, Blue One.' Like an unleashed dog, Chapman's Spitfire surged ahead to catch up with the others. Raymond reckoned there were still thirty miles to go and they were down to five thousand feet. The bomber's dead engine had stopped smoking, but when Raymond took his plane tight in again he could clearly see the strain on the pilot's face as he struggled to keep the big bomber straight and level.

They were below one thousand feet as the bomber staggered over Great Yarmouth. Looking down, Raymond could see people in the streets and the anti-aircraft gun crews staring up at the crippled machine, waiting for the inevitable crash. Raymond would not be able to keep flying much longer either. He had been onto reserve tank for almost half an hour and the needle showed zero. But he decided to stick with the B-17, guiding it towards the nearest airfield, Ludham, which was less than five minutes away, and calling up Sector to warn of the imminent arrival. 'You'll need the blood wagon, too.'

Rocking his wings, he took station ahead of the bomber. They were not much above tree-top height now, but he could see the Ludham R/T mast. 'Come on,' he called uselessly. 'You can make it.'

The American had evidently spotted the runway ahead, and laboriously the bomber banked, almost brushing the tops of some trees, straightened up, and throttled right back. Watching from above, Raymond didn't think the pilot was going to make it, and reflected on the irony of his crashing and killing himself now, after such a long struggle. The bomber did touch a hedge, the props carving through the fresh greenery, but it staggered on, the pilot — thank heavens — choosing to land beside the runway rather than on it, with the risk of sparks and fire which that would entail.

It touched, bounced high, touched again, almost burying its nose, then ploughed deeply into the soft grass amidst a cloud of soil and debris. It slewed from side to side, casting off its damaged starboard wing and coming to rest at last and at right-angles to the runway, at once assuming the grotesque appearance of a dead giant sloth.

Raymond wasted no time. His engine must already be running on air and hope. He lowered undercarriage and flaps, and came straight in down the runway, touching alongside the crash-landed bomber and almost crashing himself into one of two ambulances that were racing across the airfield. As his Spitfire slowed, the engine died, and he came to a halt in silence after more than two hours of flying. That was well timed, he told himself. Very well timed. He tried to laugh but gave up. He was just too exhausted.

'Are you OK?' A jeep had stopped beside him and a squadron-leader had jumped out and climbed onto the wing.

'Yes, I'm fine. Unlike that lot.' And Raymond indicated the crashed B-17. There were a dozen vehicles round it. He decided he would prefer to avoid seeing the removal of the bodies. But he wanted to see the pilot and congratulate him, and he had an opportunity of doing so an hour later in the sick bay. He was lying in bed, grey-faced, smoking and sipping a hot drink.

'Thanks, buddy. I wouldn't have made it without you.'

'That was a great landing,' said Raymond, sitting on a chair beside him.

'Not bad for first time.'

'How's that?'

'I'm the rear gunner. The only one not hit. Someone had to bring the ship home and get my buddies properly buried.'

'All dead except you?'

'No, Hank and Bo Peterson are alive, but not too good.' Raymond glanced sympathetically at the small weasel-faced American. He had noticed it before: you couldn't tell about guts. Who would have picked him out from a crowd on the sidewalk of his home town and said, 'That man's got exceptional guts.' And, after flying a crippled bomber, without any experience, back from Germany with all his mates dead or wounded, and landing it wheels up, more or less in one piece — well, this air gunner would live the rest of his life buoyed up with the knowledge that, when tested to the limit, he had showed what he could do.

Raymond patted his arm. 'Got to go now. Let's give up this stupid flying game — get ourselves nice desk jobs.'

The air gunner winked. 'You betcha.'

Chapter Five

THREE WEEKS PASSED before Raymond saw Lieutenant Louise Daintree again. The memory of that evening of dancing, drinking and seduction glowed as a warm memory through the tumult of flying and fighting, sometimes on patrol at 5 am as the light lifted from the east across the North Sea, sometimes landing in darkness, guided back to the bays by the ground crews' torches. 21 Squadron seemed to be regarded by 12 Group as maids-of-all-work, ordered to take on anything in spite of their obsolete aircraft, hard-bitten veterans who never complained.

Then one evening, after a long day during which they had flown down to Manston in Kent, refuelled and joined a Spitfire Wing on an escort operation, the CO took Raymond aside and said, 'That Colonel over at Stiplowe keeps telephoning. He's reminding me of a promise I made that I would let you go over and talk to some of their pilots.'

'Are you asking me if I want to go, sir?' Raymond was dead tired but the suggestion at once sharpened the memory of that earlier visit.

'Well, do you?'

'Yes, sir, but will you come, too? I'm not going solo on this op.'

'OK, I'll tell him we'll both come.'

Saturday dawned dirty and wet. 'Harry clampers, sir,' announced Raymond's batman as he brought in early morning tea. 'The Squadron's stood down.'

And later, when Sandy McWilliams came into the mess for breakfast, he said to Raymond, 'Right, today we invade the Americans.'

They left in Delilah, with Bonz sitting in the back and the hood up against the rain. 'She'll impress the Yanks more than my old staff car,' the CO said.

And so she did, the US Colonel insisting on looking over the shining six-cylinder engine and driving round the perimeter track. Then they gathered in the lecture hall with cups of coffee and, with Sandy McWilliams and Raymond beside him, Colonel Schneider addressed the fifty or more pilots of 382 Group.

'Next week we're going operational at last, men. None of you has seen any combat yet.' He paused to stare at Charlie Dee in the second row. 'Except on the wrong side. But I have with me here this morning two pilots who have seen more combat than the Red Baron in the last war, and they know a few tricks of the trade. These may save your undeserving asses when we come to mix it with the Krauts ...'

McWilliams spoke first, and Raymond wondered what these Americans — none less than three thousand miles from their homes, and so recently arrived in this green damp land of rain and mist — would make of his CO, or whether they would even understand his strong Scottish accent. However, there was no arguing the fact that Sandy McWilliams looked the part of the veteran fighter, the tough guy, a James Cagney figure who could fight his way out of any trouble. He talked incisively, with the help of blackboard and chalk, indicating the best method of attacking a *Staffel* of German fighters forming up to attack a bomber group which the Thunderbolts were escorting. The Americans smoked, sprawled, legs on desks, sipping coffee, throwing cigar stubs into the spitoons. A casual, seemingly undisciplined lot but, as Raymond noted, they really were fascinated. Their attention never strayed, and they filled page after page of their note-books.

Raymond followed, at once feeling comfortable with this keen audience, as he recounted the lessons he had learned, some of them the hard way. 'There was a notice on the back of the ready-room door on my first squadron with "do's" and "don'ts",' he told them. 'The most important one, I learned from experience, was "Get in quickly — punch hard — get

70

out". Sounds obvious but it's tempting to hang around if you miss with your first pass . . .

'Now here's a trick you may not believe, but it saved my neck once. I had three 190s on my tail, the pilots tossing a coin to see who would cut me to pieces. No use tight-turning, no use climbing, less use diving. But I suddenly remembered once being right behind a four-cannon Hurricane when it opened fire during ground attack practice, and being amazed at the amount of muzzle smoke that came straight back at me. It was just as if that Hurricane had a rear gunner.

'So I turned my kite upside-down — just to add to their astonishment — and fired off my cannon and machine-gun ammunition. The lot. Next time I looked they had all gone!'

This was greeted with a round of laughter. 'No shit!' 'Can you beat that!' 'Che-r-r-ist!'

Questions rattled out afterwards. Colonel Schneider thanked McWilliams and Raymond, and led them off to the officers' mess for a drink. Lunch was served cafeteria-style, hot and plenty of it — beef hash, french fries, ice-cream, more coffee. By chance Raymond found himself sitting opposite Lieutenant Louise Daintree at the table reserved for WACs and senior officers. It was like returning to a dream from which you had reluctantly awoken. She looked up from her coffee and smiled. 'Welcome back to Stiplowe. I hear you've been teaching the boys. How did they behave?'

'They behaved very well. I hope they learned something. It was a sort of exchange for my dancing lesson.' He looked into her grey eyes, and the memory of that evening returned as clearly as if it was last night and not two dozen ops ago, with all that tumult and danger of attack and defence, killing or being killed, which had happened since, up there in the raging sky. He looked across the table at her long fingers holding the cup of coffee, and he remembered how they had held him and moved with such ecstatic pleasure as they lay on her bed. His glance took in the khaki tie she had unknotted so swiftly, the brass buttons of her jacket she had undone so deftly, and the lapel insignia of the head of Pallas Athene, with its ironic hint of virginity.

She turned to the Colonel on Raymond's right and said, 'Don't you think, sir, that we should invite these Englishmen

71

regularly. It would be swell. And it would be good for Anglo-American relations.'

'Smart idea, Lieutenant,' he said, raising an eyebrow at Raymond. 'I guess we'll work on that.'

Colonel Schneider excused himself. 'I have a message that the weather is lifting and I want to get the boys into the air.' He indicated that Raymond should not get up. 'Just you keep right on talking to Lieutenant Daintree. Her specialty is intelligence.' He grinned, clamped a cigar in his mouth and marched from the dining hall.

There was no one else left. Around them the kitchen staff were clearing the tables. Louise said, 'This *is* a real nice surprise. How long are you staying?'

'I have to take my CO back in a few minutes. Would you like to see my car — and my dog?'

'Sure. Both.'

Bonz jumped up and down at the full stretch of his lead. Louise picked him up and held him to her face. 'What a sweet little boy!'

'One of Caesar's dogs of war — aren't you Bonz?'

Louise clearly got the allusion all right, Raymond noticed; and said, 'He's a war dog because he flies Spitfires and he was bombed.'

'How's that?'

Raymond told her about his dog's escape from the rubble of his house, but he said nothing about May. Somehow his memory of his aunt did not conform to the occasion or the lust he now felt for this American girl. Instead he asked, 'Can you get an evening pass? I'd like to see you again.'

'Not necessarily on this base, you mean?' Louise said with a smile.

Raymond nodded. 'I thought maybe we could have an evening in Norwich. I know its jam-full of service people, but it's all there is, and we could go to the pictures.'

'Pictures?' she seemed puzzled. 'You mean we could take in a movie?'

'I've got a twenty-four hour pass from Monday morning,' he said, hoping he could fix it.

'OK. I'll manage something — the Colonel's very obliging.'

He arranged to pick her up.

And then Sandy McWilliams appeared and asked to be driven back. 'I've just heard we've got to do an evening recce.'

The clouds had lifted and broken to expose scraps of blue sky. Raymond put the hood down. Other WACs had gathered round to admire dog and car. In a sudden gesture of informality the CO blew them kisses as they drove off, and they approved of that.

On the short run back to Barton Heath the CO told Raymond that they were earmarked for Mark IXs. 'First deliveries in a couple of weeks.'

Raymond blew the horn in celebration. 'That's wizard, sir. They're faster than 190s, I've heard, and leave 109s standing.'

The next day Raymond lost Sam Chapman. The boy had done just enough ops to get over-confident. They were doing another run with Ventura medium bombers to Abbeville from Manston. The Ventura was obsolete before it first went on ops, a flying coffin. 'If there's anything worse than facing a *Staffel* of 190s in old Mark V Spits,' Farmiloe had remarked before take-off, 'its facing a *Staffel* of 190s in a Ventura.'

Fortunately they had a Wing of Spit IXs and a Squadron of Typhoons to support them, too. For once, the reaction was rather slow and the Venturas finished their bombing run without loss before 109s and 190s came charging in — from above, as usual; one quick pass then out.

In the mêlée that followed, Raymond lost his number two and tacked onto a pair of Typhoons that were beating off a *Rotte* (or pair) of Focke-Wulfs that were making passes at a straggler Ventura. But almost at once he spotted far below, three long-nose 109s closing in on a clip-wing Spitfire — that could only mean 21 Squadron.

'Badger aircraft — break!' he transmitted. 'Three bandits up your arse!'

Raymond was diving flat out with 480 mph on the clock and his Spit shaking like an old man with the palsy. Before he was close enough to identify the plane he knew that it was his lost number two. Oh God, nothing could save him now! But he shouted, 'Sam, break for Christ sake!'

Either his or Sam's R/T was not working, but the dark grey smoke pouring from the Spit's exhausts suggested that he was aware of what was behind him and had already pulled the plug for maximum boost. Even with the advantage of height, Raymond could not close the gap in time. The nearest 109, closing without effort — or so it seemed — shot Sam Chapman to pieces ten miles north of Cap Gris Nez. The Spit was on fire and he did not get out.

Like smash-and-grab raiders, the 109s turned and flashed for home, leaving Raymond, low on fuel, with nothing to do but fly on, nursing his remorse and anger.

Off Ramsgate a British destroyer threw up a few shells at him, more out of boredom than with serious hostility. Raymond flashed the letter of the day but could not be bothered to take evasive action. He did not even feel particularly angry. Dejection and a sense of futility had crept over him as he thought about the unnecessary loss of Sam Chapman's life. Why were they always fighting with one arm tied behind their backs? In 1940, when they were supposed to be heroes, no one outside Fighter Command realised that they were fighting against cannon with peashooters and that most of their fighters were actually outpaced by some of the German bombers.

And three years later, it was just the same. *Plus ça bloody change plus ce qu'est la même chose.* Those poor bloody Ventura crews — only the other day they had lost eleven out of twelve attacking a power station near Amsterdam.

Raymond called up Manston and was told to divert to Hawkinge. He cursed, glanced at his fuel-gauge needle which was nudging zero, and replied crisply, 'OK, but you'll have to pick me up out of a field.'

In fact, he made it to Hawkinge, going straight in without asking permission. Taxi-ing too fast across the grass to the caravan which served as a control-tower in this much-bombed field, he reflected that perhaps he had been in the game too long, was battle-weary and short-tempered. Since September 1940, apart from odd spots of leave, he had had only three months away from an operational squadron. And those three months were spent instructing at an OTU which was almost as stressful as patrols and shipping strikes.

For once, he showed scant courtesy to the ground crew that received him. 'Get a bowser and fill her up, and make it snappy,' he ordered.

Half an hour later, Raymond was flying alone back to Barton Heath, keeping well clear of the London and Chatham balloons, trying to work himself into a better frame of mind but still haunted by the sight of Sam Chapman, one of the nicest of the recent replacements, going down in flames. For him the sudden awareness that the worst fate a pilot could endure was unavoidable as the heat rose and the agony became overwhelming while he struggled to release the hood and undo his straps, and the last scream of the engine was like a chorus of torment with his own scream, and the impact with the fire-extinguishing sea: the merciful sea, not the sea of Conrad that 'has never been friendly to man'.

Raymond always relished flying alone and found it a liberation from the discipline of formating with the others, worse still on a Wing show when you felt like a poor bloody infantryman keeping in step with a thousand more. So he felt better, but, oh God, so tired, as he flew close to Stiplowe (he'd be there tomorrow to pick up Louise, he remembered with a flash of mixed excitement and apprehension), and steered for the Barton Heath circuit.

'Strawberry green one: permission to pancake.'

'Roger, Strawberry green one.' The voice was the only sign of life. There were a dozen Spits in their bays, a dozey looking Dakota by the control-tower and not a human to be seen anywhere.

It was almost dark and they switched on the runway landing lights for him. Still feeling bloody-minded he landed on the grass anyway and taxied at reckless speed for the dispersal.

Barney Hart — bless him — came running out of the dispersal almost as fast as Bonz, and guided him in, installing chocks and climbing onto the wing to help him out. 'Thought we were never going to see you, sir, until the dog began barking. Any trouble?'

'No, Barney, no trouble at all,' he lied.

It was not until he was on his way to Stiplowe that he began to face the reality of the task that lay ahead. It was, he realised, quite one thing to dance with a woman after a few drinks, and then gladly allow himself to be seduced before returning to his own bed. And quite another proposition to accompany and entertain an American woman he scarcely knew for lunch and dinner. What were they going to *talk* about? The long hours between the two meals stretched ahead like a North Sea crossing in poor visibility. He had at least taken the precaution of booking a room in the best Norwich hotel and he had looked up the programmes at the various cinemas.

Raymond was saluted by the guard who opened the white barrier, and he saw Louise standing in the sun outside the WAC quarters. He had forgotten that she had said she would be in civilian clothes, and for a moment the transformation made him speechless. She was dressed in a short pleated skirt with a white blouse and a short, camelhair jacket, with a very saucy little hat on the side of her head. Silk stockings were rarely seen in England, and hers contrasted with the ugly lisle stockings of the women in the British services and with the civilians who usually had nothing to wear on their legs. A large leather bag with a brass clasp was slung over her right shoulder.

'What a transformation!' Raymond exclaimed, at the same time turning to another WAC dressed as smartly at her side.

'I guess I'm not sure how to take that,' Louise said with a laugh. 'Do we look that bad in our khaki?'

Raymond shook his head in embarrassment. A fourth figure now joined them. It was the ubiquitous Charlie Dee carrying a small suitcase under one arm and an enormous book by John Steinbeck under the other arm. He put his luggage down on Delilah's running-board and introduced Joan, a happy, round-faced brunette from Philadelphia, who turned out to be superior in rank to Louise, and, technically, to Raymond himself.

'We wondered,' said Charlie, taking Joan's arm, 'Whether we could sit in the back of your sport car for the ride into Norwich. That is, if you've forgiven me now.'

Raymond laughed. 'It's not good policy to refuse favours to superior officers,' he said, opening the vestigial back door and helping Joan in. 'No dog to keep you company, but plenty of wind.' He erected the rear Auster screen, adjusting the wings' angle to their comfort. 'I'll keep the speed down below one hundred.'

With four, all Raymond's anxieties about conversing with his American girl were resolved, and they made a noisy and compatible party, even breaking into song as they drove through the eastern suburbs of the city. Then as they passed the first shattered remains of buildings, the burnt-out shell of a church, a terrace of demolished houses, the two girls, who had never been to the city before, fell into a shocked silence.

'How do people still *live* here?' Louise asked in an awestruck voice.

'You get used to it — and it's much worse in the East End of London. There they were bombed every night for three months, and they're not free of it yet.'

They drove into the centre of Norwich past the noble cathedral — amazingly still intact — down King Street and past the castle and the maze of streets around it. There had been some more relatively light bombing a few nights ago and several streets were blocked off: '*Keep Clear. Unexploded Bomb.*'

Louise and Joan exclaimed at the casual way people strolled past the destruction. 'My, let's not have our lunch near here!' Louise said, turning in her seat to address the two in the back. It was market day in Norwich, and being a Saturday there was also a great influx of American and Allied servicemen, all seeking distraction from their dangerous or tedious war work. Pedestrians in the narrower streets spilt off the pavements and many glanced in wonder at the slow-moving open Alvis with its two pretty women and two airmen.

Raymond got them a table at a fish restaurant he knew up a little lane off Exchange Street. Joan turned out to be lively, bright company. Charlie Dee, with his strongly contrasting eastern, educated accent, and Louise with her standard New Yorker's voice, both loved all this. As the big pieces of grilled plaice with white parsley sauce were put in front of them, Raymond remarked on the wide spread of their homes. 'Pasadena, Philadelphia, New York and Bristol, England — which is about six thousand miles from California.'

'And here we all are eating fish in a bombed British city, and getting along pretty well,' Charlie commented.

'Maybe it's the only good thing the war's done, but that's all the more reason to enjoy it.'

Charlie and Joan wanted to go sightseeing afterwards. 'You've got all this swell history and I'm going to gobble it up,' said Joan, adjusting her pillbox hat and applying dark lipstick. She turned her head to Raymond as he helped her on with her coat. 'And are you going to be a sweet boy and drive us back in your sport car tomorrow?'

So they were spending the night in Norwich, too, and assumed that Louise and he were, also. Same hotel? he wondered. Perhaps they would meet at the reception desk. 'Of course. It'll be an 8 am start, though. Is that too early?'

'Any time is too early when I'm with this sweet boy,' said Joan. And the pair walked off down the street arm in arm, steering a course through the crowds.

An Astaire-Rogers movie was playing at the Royal, and Louise and Raymond headed in that direction, Louise taking his arm in a warmly proprietorial manner. It was an old picture and the audience hummed along to some of the familiar tunes. Louise held his hand. 'You can't sit in a movie-house not holding hands,' she said loudly so that the couple behind laughed.

In the middle of Norwich, in the middle of countless airfields, in the middle of a war, even the most respectable hotel only questioned couples who were ostentatiously unmarried. Raymond signed the book as Flying-Officer and Mrs Raymond Cox without, to his surprise, experiencing a qualm of conscience. The earlier presence of Charlie and Joan had stilled his anxieties and broken down his shyness. The obvious fact that they too were sharing a bed for the night made the whole proceedings seem natural and not particularly daring.

They followed the old maid, who insisted on carrying his case and Louise's bag along the heavy panelled corridor and up a wide staircase decorated with paintings of rural East Anglian life, and, at the top, the standard wartime dual portrait of King George VI and Queen Elizabeth. '*God save the King.*'

Louise kicked off her high-heel shoes and threw herself on the bed. 'My, I'm tired,' she exclaimed. 'Oh, but it's real swell to get away to civilisation after all these weeks. Aren't you a clever boy finding this place?'

Raymond took off his jacket and opened the window, letting in the late afternoon sounds of the city. The May sun was still high in the sky. Sometimes he had brooded on the improbability of his seeing this next summer. In 1940 he never expected to see the fresh leaves of 1941, and after some savage losses on sweeps over France that summer, it had seemed rather unlikely that he would live to see 1942. Yet now it was May 1943. It hardly seemed fair on the other fellows who had not made it ... especially Sam Chapman, whose mother must still be suffering day and night after the news of his death.

'Hey, Englishman, too much thinking and not enough action!' Louise lay back with her hands behind her head, and she was laughing. 'Thinking's no good in your line of business, Ray. Come and kiss me instead.'

He bent over her, succumbing to the softness of her lips, breathing in her scent of roses. Beneath the blouse of fine silk he felt her breasts, cupping each in his hand in turn. Her tongue ran gently inside his mouth, and then she pushed him away quite firmly, so that he wondered if something different was expected of him.

'Too many clothes,' she said, heaving herself up. 'And I'm hot and tacky.'

She undressed with remarkable speed and complete unself-consciousness and strode naked to the bathroom without a further word. He had never before seen a naked woman walking, let alone like this, with the proud grace of a Nubian. Why it should seem so different from the numerous women he had eyed on the beach in their sketchy two-piece swimsuits he could not understand, and he mocked himself for finding this experience faintly shocking.

At the door she turned provocatively revealing her full shapeliness and the splash of hair as fair as on her head, and the full breasts that required no support from the bra she had thrown on the bed. She smiled and said, 'Well, that's all. There's no more to see. Now I'm taking a tub.'

Raymond lay on the bed in his shirt and trousers, thinking of the unfamiliarity of the situation and wondering what May would have made of it. He liked to think the sensible May, while never giving him any sex instruction or advice except to keep clear of prostitutes, would have approved of this innocent initiation at the hands of an experienced woman.

For a while he could hear Louise splashing about in the bath, singing one of the songs from the film they had just seen. Then she called out cheerfully, 'Come on in.'

When he went into the steam-filled bathroom, Louise was standing on the mat, soaking wet and with no sign of a towel. 'Come along, Englishman, it's nice like this. Get those damn clothes off.' She helped unbutton his shirt and trousers, breathing heavily, and still smelling of the scented water.

With difficulty, Raymond protested, 'But you're all clean, and I haven't even washed.'

'It's better like that. I like it.'

Without her shoes on, she was still almost as tall as he was, he noticed, as he held her in his arms in the hot bathroom, feeling her wet breasts and thighs against him, holding his hands tight against her smooth wet back.

'I guess we won't do it like this after all — it's kind of awkward,' she said, nudging him towards the door and grabbing a towel from the rail.

They lay side by side on the towel, touching and feeling one another, at first gently and then more fiercely.

'I told you last time, you have to talk,' she said firmly.

'It's not easy,' he said, grinning.

'Try.'

They were holding one another between the legs, moving their hands.

'Well, that's nice for me.'

'And for me. But you can do better than that.'

He moved so that he was astride her, looking into her grey welcoming eyes. Her whole body was still glistening wet from the bath, and he told her she was right — it was nice like this. Perhaps even better if he had taken a bath, too.

'No, no.' She put her arms round his back and tried to pull him down. 'Come on, Ray, it's time. My God, it's time.'

'No, no. It's my time to say no.' Though he craved to come into her and have it over, he decided he ought to resist. For a few moments he kneeled over her body, just looking at her face, not touching her anywhere.

Louise was not prepared for this delay. 'What are you *doing* to me?' she cried out, her face creased in agony. 'Come *on!*'

'Oh no.' He laughed, but lightly touched her breasts.

She manged to get a hand up behind his head, grabbed a hank of his hair and pulled down hard. This hurt, and he allowed his face to fall against hers. She had him now — held him strongly and held him tightly against the dampness between her legs. He ceased resisting, and fell with his whole weight onto her body, and into her.

It was no use pretending that either of them could talk now, and it seemed as if an age passed before he murmured into her ear, 'Well, my goodness!'

Her cheek was wet, and when he put his lips there he tasted salt. 'What are you crying for?'

'The agony,' she answered, speaking slowly.

'I thought you liked it.'

'For a second I thought I'd die. And then . . . oh God, it was wonderful. And, baby, *you* took command.'

He liked 'Baby', and the sharp 'a' in the way she pronounced 'command'. He kissed her again, moving his whole body firmly against hers. 'Don't cry any more. I'll take a bath now and then we'll eat.'

She rolled herself up in the big bath towel, like a chrysalis, and watched him as he got off the bed and crossed the room.

The dining-room was like a morgue suffering a visit from the unwelcome living. The permanent residents sat at their permanent tables, each with their private supplies of their favourite sauces and packets, and their personal table-napkin rings which were placed beside them by a waitress as they sat down. Their elderly murmured conversation was like the drone of monks muttering the Magnificat, and the waitresses' voices the muttering of responses.

Scattered amidst these venerable bodies were the totally contrasting tables occupied by officers of many ranks and nationalities — Polish airmen of ferocious good looks and immaculately uniformed, with their wings insignia high on their right shoulders; Canadian naval officers from mine-sweepers and MTBs; Free French airmen; Bomber Command flying officers with DFC ribbons and haunted eyes; ack-ack gunners, and a number of Americans not yet comfortable in this unfamiliar environment. All had their women beside them, some in uniform, some in long dresses and a few, like Louise (who had packed only a nightie and some necessities), in short dresses.

Subdued by the aura of solemnity and austerity in this large pillared room, the conversation of the young people was soft and decorous — for a while at least. But as the evening wore on, and the beer and spirits and occasional bottle of champagne flowed (only the Americans could afford *that*), the talk became louder and less restrained. As this roughly coincided with the departure of the permanent residents for the lounge to hear the voice of John Snagge on the 9 o'clock news, this new boisterousness gave offence only to any waiters above military age.

'Come and join us, you two?' A couple of Australian Flying-Officers and their girls squeezed up and welcomed Raymond and Louise. 'Shop talk forbidden, mate,' added one of the men.

'That's one rule we don't need to worry about,' Raymond retorted, and introduced Louise, who created considerable interest with her New Yorker's voice and exquisite good looks. The two Norwich girls did not look best pleased at first, but the circulation of drinks soothed any jealousy and indignation (silk stockings indeed!), and after a while they agreed to all go on a pub crawl.

It was still full daylight at 9.30, something Louise found hard to understand, and the pub customers had spilt out into the streets. The Australians seemed to have a special aptitude for reaching the crowded bar and coming back quickly with full glasses. 'No wonder we're winning the war,' exclaimed one of the local girls, called Mavis, as she sipped her fourth port and lemon. The Australians talked sentimentally of home and the bush and the desert and the beaches, and they listened enraptured to Louise on the jazz spots of Harlem.

Just before ten o'clock the air-raid sirens sounded, moaning across this much-damaged city. A few people headed rather shamefacedly for a shelter down the road, but most of them struggled to get a last round in before closing time.

The Australians wandered off towards the nearby park, calling out cheerfully, 'Good on you, mate,' when Raymond told them he and Louise were heading back to their hotel. He felt drowsy but not in the least drunk, and completely at ease with Louise now. For the first time in his life, he would be sharing a bed with a woman. All night. Waking up to find her there in the morning!

'Every day a new experience,' he said half to himself.

'What do you mean, honey?'

Raymond laughed, and tried to turn the question aside by speculating, 'I wonder what those Aussies are doing right now?'

'Same as most men with pretty girls late in the evening.'

'I suppose you think I'm ridiculously innocent.'

'Not ridiculously. Touchingly.'

Raymond asked the hotel staff for a morning call at 6.30, and they went to bed at once. He felt more confident about making love now, as they seemed so completely compatible.

'I'm getting rather fond of you, honey,' Louise said. 'We mustn't get too serious.'

'Why not.'

'Because we won't be able to do this very often, and we don't want to get hurt, do we?'

Raymond ran his hand from her breast to her cheek and back — to and fro. Suddenly he asked, 'Why were you really crying earlier?'

'I told you. It hurt so, you holding me back like that.'

'Is that really true? I don't understand.'

She did not answer that, and he lay quiet and still beside her.

Louise was the first to speak. 'No, it's not true. I was crying for you.'

'For me?'

'Sure,' she said almost fiercely. 'The Colonel told me you've lost twelve buddies since March, and you lost your number two the other day and that made you real sad.'

'It's no good being sad.' He paused and then said pensively, 'I wonder who told him that. Sandy, I suppose. Now why would he do that?'

'I don't know, Ray.'

My God, she was crying again.

She went on softly, 'I just don't want you killed, Ray. Don't get killed like that other boy.'

Raymond reached out and touched her wet cheek. 'No, I won't get killed. I'm a great survivor. But people *do* get killed in a war, and this one's going to last a long time yet.'

He fell silent and moved close against her. She was breathing deeply and regularly now. My God, he thought, she's *sleeping* with me! So this was what married life was like. But what a surprise she was, this sweet soft girl from New York! Not just what the Americans would call a 'lay'. She was bright, and she cared. What's more, she cared about *him* and did not want him to be killed. No more did he, of course — but since his aunt May had died there had been no one else outside his squadron, only scattered childhood friends he had not seen for years, who would do no more than merely note his being killed as just one more name in those long RAF casualty lists.

Then he went to sleep, strangely comforted, with an unformed feeling that his mind and body had just undergone some kind of metamorphosis.

Chapter Six

SQUADRON-LEADER JACK Boland said, 'You're not getting Spit IXs, not for a while anyway. Sandy doesn't know it yet, but he will tomorrow. Production's running late and 11 Group are getting them for dealing with the tip-and-runners.'

'We're supposed to deal with tip-and-runners, too,' Raymond said indignantly. 'And a good deal more. I tell you, sir, it's getting to be like Bloody April '17 when the Fokker DVIIs were cutting the RFC to pieces — your father will remember.'

'I'm sorry, but you may as well know the worst.'

'Twelve of our chaps have bought it since March. I lost my number two ten days ago, and when I look at his replacement green from OTU it's like looking at a ghost.'

Jack Boland lit a new cigarette from the one he had half smoked. 'Look, Ray, I know how you're going to reply to this, but I'm going to ask the question all the same. Will you transfer to 69 Squadron? I'd like that, and can fix it.'

They were sitting on the grass at the end of the lawn in the early June sunshine, jackets off, waiting to be called in for lunch. Rachel was on her way over to them with a tray of drinks. Dressed in a green light cotton dress, with no stockings and sandals, she was looking about fourteen. Raymond had ten seconds to give an answer, but he only needed one.

'You know I couldn't do that, sir.'

'Just call me Jack while we're here.'

'First it would be disloyal to my CO and my squadron. Second it would be yellow — switching from an obsolete kite to the fastest and newest in the RAF when the rest of them are still lumped with Spit Vs.'

Rachel arrived and set down the drinks tray, before sitting cross-legged beside them.

'What are you two arguing about? Too nice a day for argument.'

To Raymond's surprise, Jack told her of his transfer offer, but as if she already knew about it. 'I'm a flight-commander short, but Ray's not interested.'

'You never said anything about promotion,' Raymond said. 'Flight-commander?'

'Does that make a difference?' Jack said, winking at his sister.

Raymond did not reply at once. Commanding a flight was growing up. It had been a desirable aspiration, something he supposed *might* happen one day — like going to bed with a woman — but not something he had seriously contemplated. In a curious way there was a parallel between the two, both marking a stage in the process of maturity.

'Well, does it?' Jack repeated.

'Come on, say "yes",' Rachel said. 'And take this drink to celebrate. Think of it — Tiffies!'

'But how can I face the others? Farmiloe and the CO and the rest of them, or my new number two?'

'Pilots are being shuffled about all over the place all the time. There'll be a signal from Bentley Priory and that'll be that. Come on, you've done three years on Spits — more than your whack. And you're becoming a rare bird — ex-Battle of Britain and still going strong.'

Raymond suddenly saw the offer in a new light. Not only was it an opportunity for promotion in rank and responsibility, it was a generous and flattering offer, and it was about time he showed his manners.

'It's very good of you, Jack, and I appreciate it.'

'And you'll do it,' Rachel said eagerly.

'OK — and thank you.' Raymond raised the glass and looked into the bright blue eyes of his new commanding officer, and added, 'I just hope I won't disappoint you.'

'You won't do that.' Fingers always busy, Jack was pulling at the grass and arranging it in little piles.

John and Dorothy Boland, each clutching a glass, then joined them from the house almost as if the gathering had a prearranged scenario. Raymond stood up and offered to fetch them chairs.

'No, we'll sit on the grass like you,' said Dorothy. She sat down cross-legged, like her daughter and looking for a moment not much older than her, while her husband arranged himself more awkwardly, his false leg stuck out straight in front of him.

'Well, is it good news?' asked the vicar, looking from his son to Raymond. So it *was* a family plot; and Raymond was struck again by the closeness as well as the generosity of this all-flying family upon whom he had descended, engineless, out of the sky.

'It is for me,' said Raymond. 'But I'm still worried about my squadron – my old mates.'

'Of course, of course, dear boy. But remember Paul to the Philippians: "Forgetting those things which are behind, and reaching forth unto those things which are before."'

'Oh really, Papa!' Rachel exclaimed, 'you'll make him shy. What he wants is practical stuff on the Typhoon — a flying manual not Bible quotes.'

The invitation for this lunch visit to West Aitcham had come from Jack Boland himself, telephoning from Horning, and he had given no hint then that it would be anything more than a social occasion, as before. This time Raymond had not come empty-handed, having succeeded in winkling a bottle of whisky out of the officers' mess barman, and a rare large tin of tongue from the catering officer. It was a happy outing for Bonz, too, who had even stirred some activity into the two black labradors, who were humouring him with a few playful rolls on the lawn.

The enormity of Jack's offer and of Raymond's decision summoned up images of new fighting, new machines, new responsibilities very remote from this peaceful setting in which it had been taken, and he consciously attempted to dispel from his mind both the past and the future and yield instead to the delights of the present. The bees were humming busily among the June flowers bordering the stream which lapped past this end of the garden, and white cabbage butterflies fussed around a patch of nettles, nearby. A light breeze was setting the poplars whispering, and stirred the leaves of the pollarded willows bordering the stream. Raymond was reminded of the reproduction of Renoir's 'The Luncheon at The Boating

Party' which had hung in the hall in 'Montrose'.

And then, at first faintly and distantly but slowly becoming louder, there came the deep throb of many aero engines. High above appeared the tiny gleaming silver crosses of massed B-17 Flying Fortresses forming up for the North Sea crossing to their target in Germany.

They all stared silently at the sky, watching the first contrails forming as the bombers hit a cold layer, the white lines pointing towards their destination.

'They're off to Wilhelmshaven,' said Jack Boland matter-of-factly. 'And for the first time 382 Group are providing escort.'

'Charlie Dee will be in action,' Raymond said, imagining the excitement at Stiplowe as they prepared to scramble and join up with the 'big friends'.

'Let's hope he doesn't shoot down his Colonel,' Jack remarked sharply.

'You're not to talk like that,' Rachel said defensively. 'It's time to forgive and forget. And if you're not careful, Papa'll start quoting Ecclesiastes. Besides, if it hadn't been for Charlie we wouldn't have Ray here now.'

Raymond noticed Jack Boland's strange expression as he glanced at his young sister, and he puzzled why he could not decipher its meaning. Was it proprietorial, or suspicious, or just concerned?

The sound of the booming bomber formations was now fading, and they could again hear the lapping water and the rustling leaves. Would it be like this for ever and ever, Raymond wondered? Every gentle sound of peace and quiet broken by the jagged cacophony of war? He was just a schoolboy when the golden silence of the country — round his boarding school, round Bristol and the Cotswolds at home — had last been reliable and sacred.

'Come and have lunch,' said Dorothy Boland, rising suddenly. 'It's a cold meal. Raymond's kind gift of tongue, and some chicken. We could bring our plates out here.' She offered a hand to help Raymond to his feet, and tucked her arm through his as far as the back door.

Raymond was not on standby until 5.00 pm, but Jack had to leave after lunch. 'Your posting will come through later this week — can't give you the day. But I want you to familiarise yourself with the Tiffy, but not at Horning, and it obviously can't be at your place.' He was sounding no-nonsense professional now in the moments before he left, and Raymond felt this was a preview of what it would be like to serve under him as a flight-commander. Not a comfortable man.

'I want you to get over to Coltishall the day after tomorrow, 0900 hours. If you make a fool of yourself, no one'll notice in that great menagerie.' Jack smiled briefly and bleakly. 'The beast won't give you any trouble.'

His car was ready, the driver standing with the door open. Raymond stood momentarily to attention. 'Right, sir, I'll be there.'

He then took a walk along the bank of the stream with Rachel, feeling completely at ease with this girl he had encountered only briefly before, including that strange evening at Stiplowe which she had spent with the American, Charlie Dee. By contrast with Louise, he found his feelings towards her were protective and brotherly, and when he helped her cross a muddy patch on the path, he experienced none of the electrical response he would have felt through physical contact with the American girl.

Rachel, he decided, was strictly family, and he had no wish to disturb the merciful protective skin he felt growing over his old isolation and vulnerability by taking advantage of the kindness and privileges these Bolands had offered him. Besides, there was her age. He assumed she was still at school, but had never asked.

It was all the more surprising, therefore, as they stood on the footbridge watching the water flow past, when she suddenly announced that she was going to London the following day to join up.

'Join what?' Raymond asked in astonishment. 'You're much too young.'

'No, I'm eighteen. Nineteen next month. And that means I can join the ATA.'

'You're joking!' The Air Transport Auxiliary! The idea that this schoolgirl (or such she seemed) might be delivering

89

RAF aircraft around the country seemed too ludicrous to be considered seriously.

Rachel dropped a stick over the rail and turned to watch it reappear on the other side. Poohsticks for a little girl. But, oh, not a bit of it! 'I am *not* joking,' she said firmly, close to outrage. 'I soloed when I was fifteen, and I bet that was before you did. Not quite legal, but I did. Jack checked me out and Mummy and Daddy watched. What's more, I've done 150 hours on Tiger and have flown a Puss Moth, a Gipsy Moth and a twin engine Dragon. And lots more.'

'You're pulling my leg.'

Her smile was half mischief, half satisfaction, and he knew she must be telling the truth.

'Well I'm damned. You mean we might see you delivering new Typhoons to us over at Horning?' He was not being serious but she did not rise to the bait.

'You just wait and see.'

If she was accepted, she continued as they strolled home, she would be in uniform and on a training course before the end of the summer. 'And I bet I *will* be accepted. Daddy has spoken to Amy Johnson and he knows the Commandant. Anyway, I'm a very good pilot.'

'I believe you,' he said. 'And I'm sorry I misjudged your age — and your abilities. You've probably flown more different types than I have.'

'I expect so,' she said laughing, blowing her fringe out of her eyes. 'Now tell me how to fly a Spitfire. I'll have to know that, too.'

Two days later it was Raymond who had to learn to fly a new aircraft. He parked Delilah outside the officers' mess and there found Jack finishing breakfast. Coltishall was like a city compared to Horning or Barton Heath, with big hangars and many types of aircraft, including Walrus amphibians used for air-sea rescue, two-seat black painted Defiant turret fighters which had proved such a disaster but were now on some unidentifiable hush-hush work, and several squadrons of Spits, all of them Mark IXs.

At Barton Heath every face was familiar to him, but Raymond recognised no one in the Coltishall mess except his future CO, who took him off at once to his Typhoon, A-Apple, which was parked in an obscure corner on the far side of the airfield. Raymond had never before seen one of these brutish machines close to, on the ground. It had none of the grace and style of the Spitfire, but stood on its wide-splayed undercarriage like a boxer, heavy chin extended, eager to get into the ring.

They walked round the big machine together, Raymond noting the heavily canted thick wings sprouting four 20 mm cannon, and the massive air-intake beneath the nose. Jack said, 'Some critics say the Tiffy's a flying steamroller, and he's a heavy brute all right. You've got nearly twice the Merlin's horsepower in that Sabre engine, too, which is why he shows well over 400 mph on the ASI without any trouble. And for take-off you set the rudder tab control full right to offset torque, and you'll have to use a lot of right rudder, too.'

Jack patted the big tailplane. 'But once he's up — and you can't call the Tiffy a "she" — he's more manoeuvrable than you might think. Given the strength, you can throw him around the sky and he's quite forgiving.'

Raymond had brought his own helmet and gauntlets, while Jack lent him a parachute. 'Climb in and I'll show you the drill.'

The cockpit was spacious compared with the Spitfire's, and there were winding windows like a motor-car's and other unfamiliar items like an explosive cartridge starter to turn the massive 24-cylinder engine. Jack showed him all the switches and sequences, concluding, 'If you remember everything's twice what it is in the Spit: weight of controls, response time, height needed for a slow roll or loop, landing speed, acceleration, diving speed — remember all that and you won't go far wrong. Give yourself an hour and take it easy.'

Jack closed the door and Raymond pulled down the unfamiliar canopy over his head. The Sabre engine burst into explosive life after the third cartridge, blowing back an immense amount of exhaust smoke, and he taxied onto the perimeter track, using the brake to swing the nose in order to obtain some forward vision, and checking magnetos where he stopped.

Given permission to take off, Raymond opened the throttle steadily, waiting for the expected swing and the promised acceleration. Very little happened, and he was thinking: *Piece of cake — nothing but a piece of cake!* Then the big prop seemed suddenly to get a grip, and as it did so, thrusting the machine into fast motion, the torque started to do its work, too, threatening to throw him off the runway as the tail lifted, and then — thankfully — the whole great brute was airborne and climbing at a speed Raymond had never before experienced.

'Well, what do you think?' Jack asked him later.

'Tough but exhilarating.' He pulled himself out of the cockpit seat and climbed onto the starboard wing. 'He goes all right,' he added, putting his foot into the step and lowering himself to the ground. He laughed at Jack's amused face. 'I did a loop at six thousand thinking that would be comfortable, and had to pull like hell to keep him from diving in. And he threw a lot of oil on my screen.'

'The Sabre's inclined to do that. I always carry a rag with me. You can open your window and ease your hand round to the screen and give it a wipe. If it's very bad you have to land looking out of the side, or standing up — I've seen that.'

Raymond took off his helmet. 'Anything else, sir?' he asked with an audible element of irony.

'Never fly without oxygen. The fumes get into the cockpit. We've lost a lot of chaps that way.' He led Raymond to the tailplane and pointed to a double line of rivets round the fuselage. 'I think you know about the tail falling off. But we've fixed that with a bit of reinforcement.'

'Are you sure I ought to make this move?' he asked. 'It seems a high price to pay for promotion.'

Jack Boland uttered one of his high-pitched brays. 'You get used to anything in this life,' he remarked philosophically. 'See you at the end of the week.'

There is a pub called the Nelson Arms at Mappin Broad, one of dozens so named in Norfolk, the Admiral's county of birth. It is all that an American imagines an English country pub to be, with low oak beams and inglenooks, a dartboard and skittles, sawdust on the floor and ale drawn from the wood.

Somehow they had not correlated that with having to drink warm ale in warm weather but they put up with it, and it was a good deal stronger than American canned beer.

Soon after their arrival the Nelson had been adopted by 382 Group aircrew for off-duty evenings when there was no dance or film show at Stiplowe. Because the Thunderbolts' rôle was that of bomber escort in the summer of 1943, they had clearer off-duty hours than the British 12 Group fighters, which might be placed on thirty minutes' readiness, or even immediate readiness at short notice. For this reason RAF fighter pilots from Horning, Ludham, Coltishall, Barton Heath and other nearby airfields only got to the Nelson on evenings when they had been stood down.

Luckily for 21 Squadron they were stood down by Sector on Raymond's last night. He had been on the Squadron longer than anyone else, had seen three COs come and go (luckily only one killed), and had flown under half a dozen flight-commanders. Even allowing for his brief 'rest' as an instructor, someone had worked out that he had served one hundred and thirty weeks of the squadron's total life of two hundred and fifty four weeks. When the news of his transfer was made known, the 'Spy' had produced an exclusive 21 Squadron Long Service Ribbon with three bars, each representing a year of service, and this he was forced to wear on his last-night party at the Nelson.

Raymond drove five of his flight comrades in Delilah, and the rest of 21, together with the Spy and the Adjutant, arrived in the CO's car and a Commer 15 cwt van.

After a few drinks, with Bonz asleep on the bar, for once taking no part in the proceedings, Raymond confessed to Farmiloe, 'I'm feeling pretty sentimental about all this, Jack.'

'So you should,' his Flight-Commander said, topping up Raymond's glass with beer from his own. 'And *we're* having to drown our sorrows. Losing you and *not* losing our old Spits in one week is a bad show.'

'Perhaps we ought to have a song. What about that old favourite, *The Dying Airman*? That'll chase away the Tiffy gremlins.' So he began, and after a line or so everyone there joined in:

'Oh, the bold aviator was dying,
And as 'neath the wreck-age he lay (he lay),
To the sobbing me-chanics about him
These last parting words he did say:

'Two valve springs you'll find in my stomach
Three spark plugs are safe in my lung (my lung),
The prop is in splinters inside me,
To my fingers the joy-stick has clung.

'Oh, had I the wings of a little dove,
Far a-way would I fly (I fly),
Straight to the arms of my true love,
And there would I lay me and die.

'Take the propeller boss out of my liver,
Take the aileron out of my thigh (my thigh),
From the seat of my pants take the piston,
Then see if the old crate will fly.

'Then get you two little white tombstones,
Put them one at my head and my toe (my toe),
And get you a pen-knife and scratch there,
'Here lies a poor pilot below'.

'Take the cylinders out of my kidneys,
The connecting rod out of my brain (my brain),
From the small of my back get the crankshaft,
And assemble the en-gyne again.

'And get you six brandies and sodas,
And lay them all out in a row,
And get you six other good airmen,
To drink to this pilot below. Oh —

'Take the cylinders out of my kidneys,
The connecting rod out of my brain (my brain),
From the small of my back take the crankshaft,
And assemble the en-gyne again.

'And when at the Court of Enquiry
They ask for the reasons I died (I died),

Please say I forgot twice iota
Was the minimum angle of glide. Oh —

    'Take the cylinders out of my kidneys
    The connecting rod out of my brain (my brain),
    From the small of my back take the crankshaft,
    And assemble the en-gyne again.

'And when I join the Air Force
 Way, way up in the sky (the sky),
Let's hope that they know twice iota
Is the minimum angle to fly. Oh —

    'Take the cylinders out of my kidneys
    The connecting rods out of my brain (my brain),
    From the small of my back take the crankshaft,
    And assemble the en-gyne again.'

Like a good Scot, Sandy McWilliams the CO was drinking
neat whisky, so was well on by the time everyone else was
into their third pint of beer. He had taken very badly the
news that their new Spits were to be delayed, seeing this as
some reflection on his own weight and influence at Fighter
Command, and because of his gloom everyone had avoided
him over the past couple of days. Tonight he was slightly
more cheerful, and a great deal more aggressive. For several
minutes he had been reflecting quietly, leaning on the bar
and scratching Bonz under the chin. Then Sandy suddenly
burst out, 'I've got it, fellows. Listen to this:

    Spit Fives are fine
    For shooting a line
    And gunnin' the Hun from the sky-aye
    The Spit Five is fine —
    Sod the Mark Nine
    For pranging a 109 — out of the sky-aye

'How's that, ma wee bairns?'
There were some alcoholic cheers and a cry from someone
at the back, 'Och aye, a proper Robbie Bur-r-rns!'
'Who said that?' yelled the CO.
And at that moment the first few pilots of 99 Squadron
entered the bar with a party of WACs, smiling curiously at

the noise and hilarity. On spotting them, Farmiloe said, 'Right, we'll repeat it for the Yanks.'

'No, it's too rude for the ladies.'

But they sang it all the same and it was received with cheers and offers of drinks all round.

Everyone knew about the widespread bad feeling between the American enlisted men and the relatively underpaid British and Allied servicemen, who had neither the money nor the silk stockings for getting the best girls. *Over-paid, over-sexed, and over here.* But amongst the officers, and especially the aircrew who shared the same risks and also suffered such heavy casualties, there was a lot of mutual understanding. Which is why Charlie Dee had got off so lightly after shooting down Raymond, and why he should be mixing now with the 21 Squadron pilots, at their invitation, for Raymond's leaving party.

Raymond pushed a beer towards him and said cheerfully, 'Don't forget the Typhoon looks much more like a Focke Wulf 190 than a Spit looks like a 109, Charlie.'

'Yeah — *and* we're going to be seeing rather more of you guys, too?'

'How's that?'

Charlie pushed his freckled nose close and lowered his voice. 'Guess you haven't heard — and it's top secret. Even the Colonel doesn't know. But the Typhoon boys are joining us in looking after the big friends.'

Raymond focused his eyes with care and told himself to sober up. 'Say that again, Charlie. You mean we're going to be on American bomber escort ops?'

Charlie nodded. 'Sure thing.'

'But, for Christ's sake, we've not got the range. We can get to the Dutch coast and back, but not much more.'

Charlie put his mouth to Raymond's ear, and uttered the single word 'Tanks'.

Raymond frowned, and Charlie said, 'Yeah, tanks. Drop tanks. We're getting them, too. Increases our range to 325 miles.'

Raymond let this news sink in and decided he liked the feel of it. So now, instead of shipping strikes and occasional rhubarbs and anti-tip-and-run patrols, and escorting medium bombers into France, they were going to get the real thing, and with the Americans — escorting the big friends into Germany and bringing up the enemy fighters in droves. He wondered if even Jack Boland knew about this yet . . .

Raymond was suddenly aware that a lot more Americans — pilots and WACs — had now arrived and a very considerable party had developed, spilling out into the gardens which ran alongside Mappin Broad.

Charlie nodded towards the door, where khaki figures of both sexes were still pouring in. 'There's your date, Ray.'

'Who do you mean?'

'Who do I mean? Don't be dumb. The beautiful Louise, of course.'

And he was right on both counts: she *was* there, and she *was* beautiful. Raymond picked Bonz off the bar, and struggled to the door with a whisky in his other hand. She had caught sight of him just as she managed to get inside, and was smiling and calling soundlessly above the hub-bub.

Louise gathered up Bonz in one arm, and Raymond took her other arm to lead her to a far corner. 'This is my escape route.' He unlatched the side door and ushered her out into the garden. She set down Bonz, who jumped about their legs with pleasure, and they walked over to a weeping willow at the water's edge.

'It was nice of you to come to my farewell party.'

'How's that? What's going on?'

'I'm leaving 21 Squadron tomorrow.'

He was flattered and happy to see that she looked startled and dashed. 'Oh no, Ray, you mean . . .'

'No, its all right. I'll be at Horning — and that's a bit nearer.'

'Oh, Ray. Oh Jesus! I couldn't bear you to go away.'

They were standing close together, faces only inches apart, and he stared into her appealing grey eyes. 'I can hardly bear not to kiss you here and now.'

Louise turned to look at all the airmen and WACs thronging the lawn, several of the nearest facing towards them as they stood together under the willow. 'Gee, Ray, why are your evenings so goddam light? Back home it'd be dark by now and we could just kiss and kiss. But WAC officers can't behave like that in public.'

Raymond touched her hand as he passed her the glass of whisky. 'We'll just have to make love with words,' he said. 'Do you remember Norwich? Only a few days ago. And you were all wet from your bath and I had all my clothes on?'

'But not for long.' She smiled.

Raymond laughed. 'I don't think I can bear this. When can we meet again and lie naked together?'

She sipped the drink and passed it to Raymond. 'Call me up from Horning as soon as you can ...'

Eventually Charlie Dee spotted them and came over with another WAC officer. So did Jack Farmiloe with a pretty girl in a blue dress, and then Sandy McWilliams, very drunk but quiet, and the Spy, who was also fairly drunk. Then the party started all over again, but outside now ... and just before closing time half a dozen of B Flight suddenly seized Raymond two to each leg and one to each arm, and hurled him into the river.

As Raymond followed Jack Boland into the dispersal hut, he found a scene familiar anywhere throughout the operational airfields of Fighter Command. There were a dozen or so pilots — sergeants, flight-sergeants, a warrant officer or two, and junior commissioned officers. They lounged about reading, smoking, playing cards, shove-ha'penny or darts, sipping mugs of NAAFI tea (ready mixed with sugar and tinned milk), some wearing flying boots and yellow Mae Wests. All around were photographs and posters pinned to the walls, reflecting the enduring interests of the men who used this hut: colour drawings from *Esquire* of impossibly-proportioned, scantily-clad women; German aircraft recognition drawings, and clips from cine-camera film showing enemy targets being raked by 69 Squadron's cannon fire. Alongside the bulletin board and beneath the ancient propeller was the Squadron Information blackboard showing the state of readiness of the two flights, the names of the pilots, and the serviceability state of the Squadron's aircraft.

All this was so familiar that in order to feel completely at home all Raymond was left to do was to relate the faces to names and ranks. He might still be at Barton Heath except that the CO, who set Squadron style in all things, was quite different, *and* he himself was arriving as a flight commander responsible for half the pilots.

Everyone got to their feet when they saw Jack had entered, looking curiously at Raymond with that scarcely visible downward flick of the eye to check if he had any ribbons under his wings.

Jack Boland was quick and businesslike in his introductions. 'Chaps, I want you to meet Raymond Cox, new B-Flight Commander. New to you but not new to ops. There are not many of us left now who go back to the summer of 1940. Ray, this is Tubby Eccles, A-Flight Commander — you'll be having a lot to do with him. And Robbie Simpson, "Wicks" Wileski from guess where, Barney MacQueen — and don't confuse his Canadian accent with an American one, he's very sensitive about that, "Cobber" James from down under . . .'

One face after another flashed before Raymond, narrow faces, round faces, scarred faces, near-baby faces, about one in three with moustaches, nearly all dark-haired, which made the CO's fair hair and skin that much more distinctive. As usual, a very international crowd.

Introductions had just been completed when four more pilots walked in together, two of them still wearing helmets, the other two with the outline of the tight rubber oxygen mask etched on their cheeks, and each with his 'chute over one shoulder.

The first pilot began, 'Are we interrupting a public meeting or something?' Then he saw Jack Boland and apologised.

'We have a new Flight-Commander,' Jack explained. 'You can meet him after the Spy's finished with you. Well, how did it go?'

'OK, sir. Sammy picked up half a tree in his air intake, but he doesn't seem much the worse for it.'

After the four pilots had disappeared into the Intelligence Officer's room, Raymond said, 'Can I have my lot together for a few minutes, sir?'

Jack was lighting one cigarette from another, as usual, but that didn't delay him. 'Sure, Ray. B-Flight pilots gather round.'

There were eight of them, including the Pole and the Canadian. Raymond knew that they were looking him over critically. He was the key man who could lead them into fatal folly, or guide them steadily with the mix of dash and judgement that made a good leader in the air. They knew he couldn't be a real dud to have got this appointment. But why so long being promoted? That second stripe on his battledress shoulder was so clean it must have just recently been sewn on. And wasn't it unusual to have done three years and the Battle of Britain without a gong? What was his score, if any?

Raymond knew these questions must be going through the minds of these eight men. And they would find out in due course. Meanwhile, he did his best to put on a show of informal authority while letting them do most of the talking. Listening to them each describe what they had been doing, he began to discern the first inklings of their character and qualities. He liked particularly a very young-looking pilot officer with uncombed hair and a straight prominent nose. He had dark brown intelligent eyes and a purposeful air about him, and he sensed that Jamie Miller was never going to let anyone down in a tight spot.

Nor would Wicks Wileski. Raymond had seen many times the ferocity and dedication of the Poles, the first to have their country raped by the Wehrmacht and their undefended cities razed to the ground by the Luftwaffe. You could sense their anger and burning desire to kill whenever they set off on ops, so that sometimes they had to be restrained — and even then they might pretend not to understand orders.

There were a couple of other men who stood out, and no one, so far, disappointed him. 'If there's no panic on this afternoon we'll meet in my office later for more chat. And bring your logbooks. Thank you.'

Had he done all right? He thought not too badly. Now let's see you perform in the air, he thought.

The opportunity to do that occurred sooner than he had expected, cancelling the proposed meeting. Soon after lunch the call came through from Sector. Dusk rhubarb. Two sections of B-Flight, behind Pas de Calais. Scramble 2100 hours. Targets of opportunity. Jack said, 'You'd better go,

Ray. It's throwing you in at the deep end, but it'll do the troops good.'

'Of course, sir. I wouldn't think of anything else.'

Raymond had inherited his predecessor's plane, H-Harry, and had tried it out after lunch. 'Yes, OK,' he had reported to Chiefy. 'It's rather like going to bed with a gorilla, but she'll do.'

'Any special — er — insignia you want painted on, sir? A name or anything? I can have a word with the rigger.'

What the Flight-Sergeant was circuitously asking was whether any swastikas should be painted on the nose of H-Harry.

'No, no name. My dog doesn't approve. But seven swastikas if you like.'

'Right, Sir. That'll be done,' Chiefy said with satisfaction.

When Raymond led off Blue and Green sections, with the sun low in the west, his three pilots were aware, and suitably impressed by, his score, which was one more than the Pole's, 69 Squadron's highest scorer after the CO. He had Wicks as Black Section leader and a pair of sergeant brothers — almost identical twins, Roly and Harry Hobbs — as number twos.

They landed at Manston to top up their tanks, and when Raymond led them off again, the sun was just tipping the rich rolling fields of Kent. He had led sections of four many times with 21 Squadron, but this was something new — as Flight-Commander with this tough brute of a machine with four cannon and a speed low down almost 100 mph faster than the Spit. He gloried once again in the Sabre engine's power as he led them in open finger-four formation right down on the deck, scattering livestock in the fields for the short distance to the coast.

Dip down over the cliffs to the sea, brushing the wave-tops. Ahead the white cliffs of Gris Nez already visible through the light evening haze. The flak was always ready — always, day or night — but it gave them a few seconds advantage if the warning radar did not pick them up until they were almost on them.

A mile from the coast, when they would certainly have been picked up visually, Raymond pulled back on the stick, at the same time giving full fine prop pitch for maximum climbing speed. Light flak from three directions sprayed them as they went up almost vertically back into the sun, the tracer lines following them, at first deceptively slowly, then at breakneck speed, whipping between them.

'Green One and Two, break off now. See you later. Out.'

They were at ten thousand feet and free of the light stuff in just half the time a Spit V took. Roly Hobbs did not need to be told to weave. The black spots of the 88 mm flak peppered the sky, the red-yellow heat of each puff proof of its deadliness. One exploding right in front of Raymond caused him to duck — as if that would help! — and rocked him about as if he had suddenly dived into a cumulus thundercloud. The heavy flak lasted less than half a minute, and then they were out of range — and at once Raymond led his number two down to the deck.

There was something uniquely exhilarating about flashing over the French countryside low down like this, lifting up over the woods and down again to hedge height, ever watchful for the power cables, especially since, many months ago now, he had seen his number two tear his Spitfire to pieces in cables with an almighty yellow flash. The Germans had built a number of flak towers in the Pas de Calais as an answer to low-level attack; and Raymond, who knew this part of France as well as he knew Norfolk, kept well clear of their known locations.

'Target at 3 o'clock, Red One,' Roly Hobbs suddenly called.

Raymond turned to the right, banking steeply, and at once picked up the long line of olive-drab vehicles driving away from them, a dim red light on the tail of each. It was a small army convoy, moving at dusk for safety, heading for Lille which, according to Raymond's map reckoning, was about five miles distant.

'Follow me in — not too close, Green Two.'

Raymond had already set the light intensity of his reflector sight low, and had slid back the safety shield of the gun button when he had crossed the coast. All he had to do now, in the three seconds before he was on top of the rearmost lorry, was to check his turn-and-bank instrument for any drift and line up the centre dot of his sight. The road was dead straight, dusty white and lined with tall poplars. His cannon began

102

hammering as he squeezed, and the first shells tore into the road, hitting short. Raymond eased the angle of dive a fraction, and the shells ripped into the last vehicle, tearing it apart. He could not run the full length of the convoy as the shallow dive was bringing him too close to the treetops, but at least half a dozen were already blazing and running off the road and into the trees before he pulled up and turned sharply left to make room for his number two.

Raymond caught a glimpse of figures leaping from the leading vehicles, several of which had smashed into one another, and racing for the ditch. Sergeant Hobbs was starting his run, his cannon muzzles flickering in the half-light, adding to the murderous mayhem and the intensity of the blaze. How many men were screaming, dying, in that inferno? One minute perhaps they had been chatting, playing cards, grumbling that they were late for supper, speculating about their quarters in Lille; the next moment they had been shot or burned to death in a tangle of twisted, jagged metal and glass.

'Tough tit!' as his first CO used to say. Raymond had long since trained himself to resist speculation or guilt: all that sort of thing was left to his dreams now, for, like his shooting, there was only one target for his thoughts and that was flying and surviving.

Alerted by the blazing inferno which lit up the countryside flanking the road, the outer flak defences of Lille had spotted them and were blasting off 88 mm in a low trajectory.

'Follow me, Green Two,' Raymond called and he set off on an easterly heading. 'Go in quickly. Punch hard. Get out!' With the failing light he kept higher, at around one thousand feet, which gave them a wider arc of vision. He knew there was a canal near Courtrai which was often gratifyingly rich in barge traffic and little defended. Roly Hobbs was correctly weaving, watching their tails. All over Belgium and north-east France the fighters would be scrambling, listening for news of their course and whereabouts. It was almost dark now, but the moon would rise in another ten minutes, when it would be time to turn back.

It must have been a new and so far unidentified airfield. Raymond knew their position near enough to be confident it appeared on no RAF map of this area. It was a small grass strip, easy to overlook — and the more dangerous for that. They were about ten miles short of Courtrai and they were almost on top of it, the first flak slamming at them before they realised their mistake. A blue searchlight caught Raymond like a moth in its beam, and the multiple 20 mm tracer criss-crossed him seemingly from every direction.

Half blinded by the glare, he kicked each rudder pedal in turn and concentrated on his instruments in order to lose altitude quickly. He could feel that he was being hit, and the gunners could hardly miss with such a sitting target. For one ghastly moment his instruments showed he was almost upside-down. The next moment he was straight and level again, and a few seconds later, mercifully, he was out of the searchlight's beam and the firing ceased as suddenly as it had started. One wing was heavy but the engine sounded OK and the oil pressure and temperature were normal. My God, he was lucky!

'Green One to Green Two — are you OK?'

There was no answer.

Raymond transmitted again, 'Are you OK, Green Two?'

Silence. Perhaps it was not surprising that he had gone in but, oh God, what a start as Flight-Commander — losing your number two on the first op! Raymond felt sick with a sense of failure and defeat. It might not, strictly speaking, be his fault that they flew into that hornets' nest, but that's not what the records would show. And what would Jack Boland have to say?

Raymond angrily pushed from his mind his grief and anger, and concentrated on flying his damaged machine home. Steering 285 degrees and with the moon behind him, he flew out at Nieuport, the flak evidently judging that he had had enough for one night — at least until he was well out to sea and climbing, when an unidentifiable ship off to the left gave him a few rounds to think about.

'Strawberry, Green One,' Raymond transmitted on Channel B. 'Strawberry, Green One to Dogdays, transmitting for a fix — ten, nine, eight . . .'

'Steer 293, Green One. Dogdays out,' replied the female voice crisply.

Ten minutes later Raymond was in the Manston circuit, asking for permission to land. His arm was aching from the strain of holding his Tiffy straight and level, and to add to the gloom and depression, he realised he would have to spend the night here. He would not be allowed to take off again in his damaged kite, and someone would have to fetch him in the Tiger Moth tomorrow.

There were two figures to guide him in to his bay, but only one had a torch. Raymond switched off and opened the canopy and door, glad of the fresh night air after ninety minutes of breathing oxygen. His hair was sodden with sweat and his shirt was sticking to his skin.

'Well, you've been a long time, sir,' a cheerful voice called up to him.

'My God, Sergeant Hobbs, is that you?'

'Yes, sir. I'm sorry I came back alone. I lost you in the flak and lost my bloody radio at the same time.'

Raymond sat for a moment, feeling the breeze cooling his head. 'I really thought you'd bought it.'

Roly Hobbs pulled down Raymond's retractible step and helped him to the tarmac. 'The buggers don't get me as easily as that,' he said with a laugh. 'But I see they've knocked you about a bit.'

Raymond saw that most of his port aileron had gone, and there were big cannon holes in the fuselage. The rigger picked them out with his torch beam, counting, 'One, two, three . . .'

H-Harry had been hit at least a dozen times by 20 mm shells and for a moment Raymond was almost overcome with double relief.

'Let's see if the bar in your mess is open, Sergeant Hobbs.'

'I'll open it if it isn't, sir.'

Chapter Seven

SQUADRON-LEADER JACK Boland stood on the steps of the officers' mess, sipping a last cup of breakfast tea and smoking a third cigarette. Raymond observed that he was tapping a foot as well as dealing with his tea and cigarette, so that, as usual, there was plenty going on. Jack looked up at the sky for the fifth time in the last minute and muttered, 'Bloody clampers! Of all days, bloody clampers!'

'Why "Of all days", sir?'

'The drops are due at noon and I wanted to try them out.'

Raymond had been waiting to hear this ever since Charlie Dee had revealed the gen, but he knew he had to go through the business of asking.

'Drop tanks,' added the CO. 'They'll give us another hour's endurance. Hang 'em under the wing — drop 'em when they're empty. I've had my kite fitted up to take them, so was going to try them out. The Yanks are getting them too.'

'Why, are we flying with the Americans, sir?'

'How d'you know?' It was more an accusation than a question.

'Only asking. I presume these tanks will mean some sort of change for us.'

Several more pilots had joined them outside the mess, including Raymond's opposite number and A-Flight commander, Tubby Eccles. He had a calmness and serenity about him which nicely set off Jack Boland's high-tension temperament.

Jack offered him a cigarette. 'Now Ray knows, you may as well know, too, and you can tell the rest of the chaps. But these long-range drop tanks are still on the secret list so absolutely no gassing about them outside the Squadron.'

Tubby said, 'It sounds a good wheeze, sir. A pity we can't try them out today. I've just been talking to Met and they say there's no chance of a clearance until late this evening.'

The CO gave instructions that everyone — 'especially you, Tubby' — should get in a couple of running circuits of the perimeter before being stood down. Jack Boland was going through a keep-fit phase — for everyone except himself. He just went on steadily and heavily drinking and smoking. As he turned and walked away to his office, he indicated that Ray should accompany him. Bonz followed at heel, a subdued dog when there was no flying, and his own canine Met forecast told him there would be none today.

'I'd like you to come with me over to my place for the day, Ray? Is that OK?'

'Of course, sir. I'd be delighted.'

'I think we all regard you as one of the family now. And there are one or two things I'd like to talk over.'

Reaching his desk, he raised the non-scramble black phone and asked for an outside line.

'Operator, Aitcham 39.' He slipped another cigarette between his lips and Raymond gave him a light. 'Mums, good morning. Harry clampers here, so you'll have two extra for lunch.' He laughed at her response. 'Good old Mums. Be with you in about half an hour — if we can manage to navigate over to you. Yes, I managed to get some for Papa.'

'Some,' Raymond realised, meant only one thing: some whisky.

'Do you mind us driving in your car, Ray? So much more interesting — and you can see better in fog, with the screen flat.'

Car was second best to cockpit, and Bonz leapt into the Alvis like a new dog.

The Speed 20 started at first touch of the button, and Raymond halted only at the guardroom on the gate.

'Tell the Adjutant I'll be at home if wanted.' Jack returned the smart salute and they drove off into the murk, P100 headlamps reflecting brightly and giving them ten yards of visibility.

'I want you to know, Ray, that I regard you as my number two — successor if I go for a burton.'

107

'That's nice of you, but what about Tubby? He's far senior to me.'

'Tubby's fine. We're lucky to have him. I've complete faith in him and he runs a good Flight: he wouldn't be here if he didn't. But he's not got your flair and imagination. Nor your experience, for that matter. That's why I want to talk over the Squadron's future. Things are changing quite a bit — so's the future of the Tiffy. We'll talk about it when we get there. Easier away from the station.'

Raymond had never felt completely at ease with Jack Boland — he was not quite sure why. He admired him and his quality of leadership, and it was flattering, if somewhat embarrassing, to hear him talk like this. It was impossible to feel wholly relaxed with the sort of vibrancy the man emanated, and his unpredictability could make all his pilots jumpy from time to time.

But from a professional (and survival) point of view, it would be hard to find Jack's equal. His briefings were crisp and uncompromising and he was brilliant in the air, as both pilot and leader. He seemed to have eyes in the back of his head, and several pilots owed their life to his quick reactions and thinking.

Raymond turned off the road and into the vicarage drive.

'You are the most hospitable family I've ever known,' he told Jack, as he pulled on the big handbrake lever and switched off. 'Even the fog's better here.'

'I think Mums and Papa feel they've sort of adopted you.' Jack let himself out of the car, clutching the bag he had carried from his office.

Raymond released Bonz from his lead. 'That's what Bonz feels, too.'

'And then, of course, there's beloved Rachel.'

Raymond turned, ready to smile in agreement, but saw Jack's face for a fleeting second frozen into an expression more quizzical than friendly. Then, all in one co-ordinated movement — or so it seemed — he took a last deep pull on his cigarette, ground it out on the gravel, winked at Raymond, and said, 'Come on in — you and your ridiculous dog.'

Raymond had never before visited West Aitcham at this time of the day. It was like catching a woman without make-up. Breakfast had not yet been cleared, and Dorothy came downstairs in a dressing-gown. 'I'm sorry for the mess, Ray,' she said, putting her arms round his neck and kissing him on the cheek. 'We're not very good in the mornings. John stays in bed until about 11 o'clock: he always says his leg doesn't like the dawn. And Rachel's gone shopping. But I'll get you some tea.'

Jack went upstairs to see his father, carrying the bag with him, after telling Raymond to make himself at home in the study. The room was in its usual shambles, books and papers and empty glasses all over the place. He sat down to read the newspaper, noting that the island of Pantelleria in the Mediterranean had been captured and that the Americans were still doing well in the Pacific.

Jack and Dorothy Boland came in together a few minutes later, Dorothy with a tray of tea and biscuits. 'You two can get on with winning the air war now,' she said, and turned to go. The labradors, followed by the hero-worshipping Bonz, padded out after her.

Jack sat down at his father's desk, telling Raymond to pull up a chair. Then, with an ashtray and pencil and paper at hand, he began talking fast and fluently about their flying future. 'There are two broad strategical concepts that affect us,' he said. 'And of course they're related — everything's related when it comes to winning the war in Europe. First is the invasion across the Channel. That won't be this year; it'll be next year, probably in about twelve months time. Then there're the preparations for this invasion, which include the strategic bombing of Germany — her industry and oil and communications. That's already started, as we all know.'

Unable to keep his hands still, Jack was drawing a side-on view of a B-17 bomber, complete with gun positions.

'First the bombing. We've already seen that the American daylight bombers suffer heavy casualties when they rely on their own defences. That's why Colonel Schneider and his lot and many more are over here — but there're not enough of them. Not yet.'

Out of the corner of his eye Raymond noticed a figure silently enter the room. He turned his head and saw Rachel tiptoeing across the faded carpet, with a finger to her mouth.

Jack looked up, too, and smiled a welcome. To Raymond's surprise he made no objection when she sat down to listen.

It was a long and highly technical conversation, to which Rachel listened in silence and with evident concentration and comprehension, not even turning her head when the dogs returned to the room. The job of 61 Squadron, and two other Typhoon squadrons, was to provide close escort for the B-17s and B-24s on the first and last stages of their operations over enemy territory, the longer-ranging Thunderbolts taking over at stage two.

'And stage three?' Raymond asked.

'That's when we're most needed, but can't help. Up to the target, over the target, and withdrawal. There's no fighter that can reach that far into Germany. Not yet.'

'You mean there will be?' Raymond felt Rachel's dark brown eyes watching him, then turning to her brother for the answer.

'Yes, but not for a while.'

'You mean a single-seat fighter to Berlin and back?' Raymond found the idea inconceivable. Six, eight hours in the air, *and* the flak, *and* 109s and 190s all over the place!

'Yes. Enough said.'

Jack Boland turned his attention to the other new rôle of the Tiffy. 'Bombs and rockets. We're going to be the Stukas of the return to Europe. Close co-operation with the ground forces.' They would be called up at short notice to deal with artillery, tank concentrations, operating from forward air-strips on liberated soil.

'The boys are not going to like that.' Raymond was thinking of the jealously-guarded exclusivity of the fighter pilots, enhanced by the Battle of Britain: top button undone, silk scarf, easy-going discipline — except in the air of course.

'They'll have to put up with it.' Jack swiftly drew a picture of a Typhoon with four rails suspended from each wing, each carrying a rocket with a heavy, lethal head. He pointed his pencil at the completed drawing. 'They'll pack the same punch as a broadside from a naval cruiser. But for the moment we're remaining fighters and we'll be seeing a lot more of our American friends.'

Jack Boland now began a long debate about how best to protect the bomber formations, partly based on American experience. 'There's one thing the Yanks got wrong when designing the gunnery defence of their heavies,' he said, sliding the earlier drawing of a B-17 in between them. 'They allowed for every angle of attack except head-on, which requires a lot of skill and nerve, as we know — so the forward armament is the weakest. And our job therefore, will be to catch the Hun as he comes in, flat out — and sometimes upside-down so he can slip away quicker . . .'

At 12 o'clock John Boland limped into the room, looking cheerful, rubicund and ready for a party. Jack and Raymond had risen to their feet but the vicar told them to sit down again. 'Shan't need the desk, not today. War today, sermons tomorrow. "They shall beat their swords into ploughshares . . ." But not yet awhile.' He turned to Rachel. 'My darling, I think our gallant boys in blue may be ready for a pre-prandial. Will you do the honours?'

It was not easy to resist the Bolands' hospitality, and Raymond noticed that, as usual, the smell of whisky was already heavy on the vicar's breath. Some time ago Raymond had concluded that his drinking was a consequence of the pain in his leg, which also caused him to sweat at only moderate exertion. There was some sort of justice in this ex-pilot from World War I having his meagre ration of whisky supplemented by the RAF, however unofficially, during World War II.

With whisky bottle and syphon and glasses placed beside him, John Boland poured out heroic drinks for the three of them. As they talked about the war in general and flying operations in particular, Raymond felt the effect of the whisky spreading over him like a soft blanket, comforting, encouraging and warming.

At the same time Raymond felt even more that he was slipping into a kind of membership of this family — these people who filled his need to be recognised, to belong, after those years in the wilderness ever since May's death . . . years occupied only with violence and killing, ever close to personal mutilation or death.

Except for the vicar, they all mucked in with the preparations for lunch. Outside it remained heavy with fog, and with that peculiar chill of East Anglia near the sea, even in late June. At one point, as they were washing new potatoes at the sink, Dorothy stopped and put an arm round Raymond, nestling close to him and whispering in his ear, 'It is lovely having you here, especially unexpectedly like this. You *must* come more often.'

Raymond looked up into her clear blue eyes, so like her son's that it was almost uncanny, and said, 'That's up to the boss, Dorothy. As often as you like, as far as I'm concerned.'

She kissed his cheek and put a kettle on the stove. 'Jack, you're to bring Ray here more often,' she called to her son. And from the study across the corridor, her husband John answered, 'Hear, hear!' Then, 'Another little life-saver for the kitchen slaves?'

After lunch, Dorothy rounded up Rachel and Raymond. 'Come on you two youngsters, it's time the dogs had a walk. John, you'll be having your usual nap. So what about you, Jack?'

'I think I'm going to bed, too. Damn it, I think I've got an attack coming on.'

Raymond had already noticed that he was sweating, but had put it down to the whisky and the pints of beer for lunch. Jack was dabbing his forehead with a handkerchief, and Dorothy studied his face anxiously. 'Poor dear, yes you go to bed and I'll call Dr. Sproat.'

'No need, Mums. I've got my pills. But, oh God, what a curse!'

For once, the dogs did not seem too enthusiastic about a walk, and even Bonz was subdued and content to come to heel. Rolling swathes of mist — like a bad Hollywood interpretation of an English fog — added to Raymond's growing sense of unreality. Was it all that drink at lunch, to which he was unaccustomed? He looked at Rachel by his side, dressed in a sweater and slacks and gumboots — a real country girl.

'Any news of your ATA interview?' he asked her, to bring back a sense of normality.

'Yes, next week.' She gripped his arm for a moment, looking up eagerly. 'Come on, Ray. Go through the cockpit drill for a Mark V Spitfire. They obviously won't ask me that, but I can drop it in somehow — and think how impressive it'll sound.

Fuel, rad., flaps, ailerons, rudder, tabs — that sort of thing.'

Raymond performed for her, the sequence occasionally broken by their laughter.

'Now the Typhoon. Come on.'

'No, no, no — that'd be excessive. You just tell them about Tiger and her cockpit drill. They won't let you fly Spits for a while, anyway.'

Rachel now spoke dead seriously: 'Don't you believe it — you just see. I might even be the first woman *operational* pilot.'

Raymond, slightly puzzled yet also impressed by her intensity, remained silent for a while as they continued slowly along the path. Above all, he did not want to sound patronising, so in the end he said, 'Well, I've no doubt you'll do very well, Rachel. And why not? There are hundreds of women pilots flying operationally with the Russian Air Force.'

He broke off and peered into the fog, which was again so thick that they could see only the lower branches of the trees. 'Do you know where we are, Rachel?'

'Of course I do, silly. I got top marks for navigation in my B Licence exam.' She giggled. 'How's *your* navigation, Ray?'

'Terrible. Always getting lost.'

'I don't believe it ... Jack says it's terribly important. His good navigation saved his life in Burma — several times.'

'Tell me about Jack in Burma,' said Raymond. 'He never talks about it to me. A pretty hairy business, I guess.'

'Yes, he has told me once or twice. He tells me everything. We're very close.'

'I can see that.'

Rachel stopped still beside the stream. The fog wrapped about them. Even the lapping of the water seemed hushed.

'The Japanese Zeros were too good for the Hurricane. He lost one pilot after another, and no replacements at his remote airstrip. And if you were shot down and baled out, the Japs would shoot you as you came down. If you did manage to land and they picked you up, you were shot anyway — probably after torture. And if they didn't catch you, the jungle got you. That's what Jack told me.'

Rachel dropped a twig in the water and it span out of sight on the ripples. 'You just disappeared, like that,' she said. 'He's

113

never admitted it, but the strain must have been ghastly. Then he bought it. Somehow crash-landed in a clearing behind the Jap lines. They were all around him but he managed to get through, shooting two of them with his .38.

'It was three weeks before he got to safety, living on roots and heaven knows what. "I was always a wizard navigator," he said. But he was half dead with starvation and malaria. And then he learned that only one sergeant-pilot had survived, of all his team.'

Rachel broke off to whistle up the dogs, who had strayed off into the fog. 'Their navigation's awful,' she said, then returned to her brother's Burma crisis. 'Poor Jack, he was at death's door — in a coma for days. Eventually they managed to air-lift him out, and got him to a base hospital. He still looked ghastly when he arrived back here — and not quite himself, if you know what I mean.'

'I'm sorry he still hasn't managed to throw off his malaria,' Raymond said. 'It must be terribly debilitating.'

'Yes, he gets so depressed with it, and then everything that he sees as dark in his life gets even darker. Papa especially worries about him.'

Rachel took Raymond's arm in just the same way her mother had, and marched him back along the path. 'I think the dogs have had enough exercise.'

'They don't look as if they're enjoying themselves much.' He picked up Bonz and then dropped him quickly. 'You're like a *sponge!*'

Raymond handed to the 69 Squadron adjutant, Flight-Lieutenant George Lubbock, the letter Jack Boland gave him before he left the vicarage. Jack had been sweating heavily and his hand shaking so badly that he had difficulty writing the adjutant's name.

Lubbock glanced at the envelope and interpreted the situation correctly. 'I suppose the CO's having one of his "gos", as he calls them.' Lubbock was an ex-RFC pilot from what he called 'the '14-'18 business', with a faded ribbon of the DFC (the old horizontal stripes sort) under his wings. He was the most modest of men and had never been heard to talk about his flying experiences, which must have been eventful.

114

'Yes,' Raymond confirmed. 'He says he hopes to be back in two or three days, and meanwhile there are instructions in this letter.'

Lubbock opened the envelope and extracted the letter. He appeared to read it through once, put it down on his desk, lit his pipe, then read it again. 'Do sit down, Ray,' he said. 'This is a bit tricky. I think you'd better read this and see what you think.'

Raymond read it through once quickly, and then again slowly, just as George Lubbock had done. 'The boss didn't know what he was doing when he wrote this,' Raymond said, outraged. 'It was a bad malaria attack, and struck him quickly. What do you think we ought to do?'

Jack Boland's letter laid down in the clearest terms who was to fly with who on operations in his absence, the section leaders and the names of reserves in case of sickness, absence or casualties. It made perfectly good sense and was expressed with complete clarity. But the last paragraph ran. 'As to the overall command of the Squadron until I am able to resume my duties, I wish Flight-Lieutenant Raymond Cox to take my place, with full powers and responsibilities, and with Flight-Lieutenant Eccles as his deputy. Flying-Officer Wileski will take temporary command of B-Flight.'

'This is ridiculous,' Raymond said. 'What d'you think we ought to do? Should we take it up to Group, and not even mention it to Tubby?'

The Adjutant pressed down the burning tobacco in his pipe with his thumb and thought for a moment. 'No, I think Jack would throw a fit if he found out. And we don't want to upset his health any more. I think we ought to get Tubby in here and talk it over. Thank God he's a gent.'

Tubby Eccles had sensibly given himself the day off as soon as he learned that there was no chance of the weather clearing, and it was not until late in the evening that George Lubbock was able to convene a meeting of the three of them at the far end of the officers' mess bar. Tubby was heavily-built rather than fat, a big man, six feet three and sixteen stone, a perfect match, it would seem, for the aircraft he flew with such skill and élan. He had a remarkably smooth skin, a soft beard that only had to be shaved every two or three days,

115

and a prematurely receding hairline. He had been in the front row of the rugby scrum for Oxford, and sported the almost statutory broken nose as a result.

Tubby Eccles was as amiable on the ground as he was ferocious in the air, and was as popular with the ground crews as with his fellow pilots. His good nature was clearly being pushed to the limit as the Adjutant gave him the gist of Jack Boland's letter, and then handed it to him. Tubby's eyebrows lifted quizzically as he turned the letter over and read the last paragraph.

'You go over to his place quite a lot, don't you Ray?' he asked pointedly.

'Yes, I've been there a few times since I belly-landed near the family home — the vicarage. But, honestly, Tubby, all this comes as big a shock to me as to anyone. He's obviously temporarily off his rocker, but what are we to do?'

Tubby took a long draft from his pewter mug of beer, wiped the froth from his lips and grinned at Raymond. 'I'm not suggesting any collusion, Ray. In fact, *nobody* could have plotted a scenario like this for himself. It just looks too obvious. Almost as if the boss wanted to queer your pitch with the rest of us — I mean, you being the new boy and all that.'

The Adjutant said, 'I've got the answer.'

They both turned on him and Tubby said, 'What? There isn't one.'

'Oh, yes, there is. Tubby, you're off on an engine course at Napiers. Everyone has to do it some time — and your time is now.'

'But I don't *want* to go on a bloody engine course at Napiers. I don't understand how a car engine works, and I'll certainly never learn how a Sabre works — all those sleeve valves and things. I want to go on flying with the boys. Especially now we've got these drop tanks.'

'It's only for four days,' George Lubbock insisted. 'And it'll solve everything. I'll fake an urgent signal, and off you go in the morning.'

Raymond smiled sympathetically at Tubby's misery as they exchanged looks. 'I really am bloody sorry. But that does seem to be the answer.'

Tubby Eccles departed for his unwelcome engine course at Acton on 1 July, the day after Jack Boland had succumbed again to his malaria, and on the same evening instructions from Group announced a hundred per cent fighter support effort for bomber operations on the following day. American 8th Air Force heavies were to mount their strongest attack so far. Against the heart of Germany's industry, in the Ruhr — as a follow-up to RAF Bomber Command's night attack on Cologne on 28-29 June, when over six hundred aircraft had done immense damage to that city, killing almost ten times as many as the German Air Force had killed in Coventry on that terrible night in 1940.

At nine o'clock in the evening of Raymond's first day of duty as temporary Squadron-Commander (and after just ten days on the Squadron), he found himself standing on the platform at briefing, alongside the Spy and a blackboard showing the route the American bombers would take to the Ruhr valley the following morning. His determination not to show his nervousness and apprehension barely overcame his conviction that it was really impossible to conceal what he was feeling as he now faced the dozen faces, some of which were still scarcely familiar after the short time he had been at Horning.

It was another letter, received on 22 April 1936 (a day engraved on his memory for all time), which had thrown Raymond into his first position of responsibility. It had arrived on the last day of the Easter school holiday, with the school crest embossed on the back of the envelope. 'What on earth do they want to write to me about, May?' he murmured to his aunt. 'I'll be back at school tomorrow.'

'The answer won't be difficult to find,' she practically said as she began her morning ritual of tidying up the flowers.

As he opened the envelope he saw that it was printed '*From the Headmaster*' at the top.

'Hey, Maintree's not coming back this term, and I've got to take over the House.' An awful emptiness suddenly formed in the pit of his stomach. 'I can't do it May. I'm not ready for all that. There're lots of chaps older than me in the House.

They'll give me the most awful time.'

May put down her scissors and marched out into the hall. 'Come on,' she said firmly. 'We're going for a long walk.'

'But it's pouring.'

'Doesn't matter. Get your mac on.'

They walked for miles, across Clifton Downs and beyond, while May gave him a kindly lecture about responsibility and rising to it, about fear and courage, concealment of your feelings, humility, keeping your head, and the other qualities that make a man worth anything. It did not sound in the least like a lecture, however, and she had him laughing many times as the rain continued to pour down and they paddled through muddy fields.

They ended up at a country pub, and for the first time May offered him a whisky and soda. 'Just to signify your new manly status,' and she gently slapped his cheek in her standard token of affection.

And now, seven years and fifteen hundred hours of flying later, George Lubbock had taken on May's mantle. 'I'd just keep it low-key and light,' he advised. 'You know, matter-of-fact. Stick to what matters, that's all they'll want to hear, and for God's sake don't even *mention* the CO or Tubby. They know what it must be like for you — and they'll be on your side all the way so long as you show you're confident of doing the job.'

So Raymond was brisk and brief, beginning, 'This is our first do with long-range tanks. We've never used them before, but the Tiffy is so strong and powerful you'll hardly notice the difference. Until you drop them, that is. We'll fly on these tanks for the first hour, unless we meet any Huns, and when you see *me* drop, let 'em go.'

Raymond indicated a point twenty miles off the Dutch coast. 'Our escort duties will start there. There'll be three squadrons of Spit IXs with a drop tank each, too. They'll be above us at twenty-five thousand, we'll be close escort at twenty thousand, and we'll keep with the big boys as far as Nijmegen — here. Then two American Groups of Thunderbolts will take over and stay with them to their target, and out again. They've got drop tanks too.

'Bob Jackson will lead A-Flight, and Wicks B-Flight. OK? Any questions.'

How had he done? He had no idea. He wished he could ask them *How was that? Did I show the right self-confidence?*

Instead, he looked over their faces, glancing at each pilot in turn, hoping there would be at least one question. How many times had he himself been down there looking up, and — with the exception of one short-lived CO on 21 Squadron — always with total confidence in his leader, whose authority seemed to fill the briefing room.

Then Wicks spoke, thank God, in his thick east European accent. 'What will happen if we see ze Hun over the sea — do we keep our tanks, or do we fight zem?'

'If they're going for the bombers, we drop tanks and go for them. If your name is Wicks Wileski, you'll go for them anyway.' This led to laughter: it was well known that the Pole's enthusiasm to get at the enemy was uncontrollable.

There were no more questions, and the briefing broke up in what Raymond hoped was the right spirit. The pilots all adjourned to the mess bars.

On 2 July 1943 the thirty-four-month-long World War was raging east, west, north and south, in the Pacific, the Mediterranean, China, Burma, Russia, the Atlantic — the greatest and most widespread war of all time.

As a minute contribution to this massive effort by millions of Allied soldiers, sailors and airmen to defeat a national and racial tyranny that threatened the world, Raymond Cox led out all the ten serviceable Typhoons of 69 Squadron to the head of the east-west runway at Horning at 0830 hours on 2 July. The planes had taken on an entirely new configuration with their long cylindrical extra fuel-tank under each wing, and any anxiety about taking off and flying encumbered with this extra weight was more than offset by the reassurance of seventy extra gallons of fuel to draw on.

They pounded down the runway in pairs, finding the lift-off point scarcely any longer than normal, and formed up over Lowestoft at ten thousand feet with two other similarly equipped Typhoon squadrons. There was broken cloud, but very little at this height, and far to the east Raymond could make out the mass of white contrails — almost another cloud layer — made by the heavy bomber groups heading for their targets. Keeping the engine revs below 3,200, he waggled the wings of his Tiffy to indicate that the squadron should engage S-ratio for the supercharger to give them the extra power needed at high altitude. Then the three squadrons formed up, still keeping radio silence, and set off after the B-17s.

Half an hour later, with the Dutch coastline looming ahead, Raymond positioned 69 Squadron on the starboard flank of the bombers, with himself and his number two in the lead, and behind and a little below were the two 'finger fours' of A- and B-Flights led by Bob Jackson and Wicks Wileski.

The American bombers in their stacked formations of four and six, designed to give the most effectual fire cover for their guns, made the most massive display of air power any of them had ever seen — an armada stretching over square miles of sky, the whole like an arrow speeding towards the heart of Germany. But the first puffs of heavy flak began sprinkling the sky about the B-17s even before they crossed the coast — a multitude of black puffs fading to grey, then losing their tight shape and blending into just another stain across the sky astern of the formations.

'As night follows day,' Raymond told himself, 'as soon as that flak stops, we can expect the Huns to arrive.'

The responsibility for this squadron of the most lethal fighters in the world had instilled in him a sense of power and seriousness of purpose unlike anything he had experienced as a section or flight leader in the past. It was as if he had been elevated to a new level of self-confidence and skill in his trade, a feeling that — with himself in command — there was nothing they could not accomplish, no enemy so powerful that it could not be destroyed.

Yes, and here they came, half a dozen 190s, stubby, twinkling, darting like summer swallows, up-sun and high, ready to come down on this solid phalanx of bombers, but (or was he imagining it) holding off at the unexpected sight of Typhoons at this height, and in this rôle of escort. Waiting for reinforcements, were they? Temporarily deterred?

'Buttercup leader calling,' Raymond transmitted. 'You've all seen the bandits at three o'clock high. There'll be more.'

And so there were. The Spits high above spotted and reported them first. 'Many bandits twelve o'clock. Get amongst them.'

They looked at first like fistfuls of gravel hurled head-on at the bomber stream. In less than a second they had formed into rough shapes, then clearer shapes, some twin engined — Ju88s and Me110s — but mostly 109s, clearly the fastest, barrel-rolling in at a closing speed of 600 mph or more.

The Spits came down vertically, a wing of them, turning and twisting, struggling to get amongst the enemy before they could open fire; while tracer from the nose and belly ball turrets and top turrets of the B-17s trailed a thousand lines amongst friend and foe alike. Here, in breathtaking grandeur and at heart-stopping speed, was the opening act of the drama, air combat on the heroic scale.

And act two was the responsibility of Raymond and his squadron as the enemy came out and re-formed for the next attack. Raymond had no need to transmit a single word of order. He waggled his wings once, glanced at Cobber James, his number two, and took them down into the cauldron of writhing, climbing, diving, twisting fighters, every one hell-bent on getting back up into an attacking position again.

Take your bloody pick. No shortage of targets. Only, for God's sake, you had to remember your tail — remember it every five seconds or sooner, for things moved so fast; relative positions could be reversed in the time it took for a cannon shell to leave the muzzle and strike the target.

Never had the killing-urge swept over Raymond so strongly. When he spotted the twin engine 110 at 11 o'clock and climbing fast, black smoke pouring from the exhausts, he kicked left rudder as if it was the flank of a charger and heaved his machine round, the turn-and-bank gone momentarily mad. Waste of ammunition to open fire like this, but half a second later it was not a waste of ammunition. Deflection twenty degrees. Steady. Pull the dot through.

All Raymond's skill and experience of those tumultuous years of air combat, with their accumulation of bitterness and determination — all this and the new enhancement of all his fighting qualities which promotion had given him — with this he knew he could not fail.

The burst was no more than one second long. His shell explosions danced as innocently as fairy-lights from halfway along the Messerschmitt's fine fuselage to the cockpit, to the port wing root, settled there like a celebration, flickered lightly to the port Mercedes-Benz engine. And, fifty yards in front of him, Raymond's enemy dissolved in an instant cauldron of flame, black smoke, white smoke, vapour and more flame.

Raymond jerked back the stick, failed to avoid all the debris, and did not glance again at his victim. Cobber James, five hundred feet above, shouted in his distinctive Australian voice, 'Good on you, Skip. You fucked him all right.'

'Green Two, shut up and break — now!' Raymond replied as he saw a 109 closing in on his number two.

Not since the Battle of Britain had Raymond been involved in such a tumultuous, prolonged and widespread dogfight. With the battle now over their own country, as it had been for the RAF back in 1940, the Luftwaffe fought with unbelievable ferocity, holding their nerve-shattering head-on attacks on the bombers until the last split second, before diving away, and then being set on themselves by Spitfires and Typhoons.

For as far as the eye could see, distantly over the German and Dutch countryside etched by the winding Rhine, the swirling, diving, climbing, fantastically fast individual combats continued. From time to time, a winged bomber, engine smoking, would fall out of the formation, and like a maimed animal of a fleeing herd, would be set upon by the jackals of the sky. Twice Raymond saw B-17s drop from their formation and spiral down, wingless or tail-less, trailing smoke, while far below a parachute or two blossomed open, signifying a miraculous escape from the death-trap.

A double kink in the Rhine, and the dark stain of a town, told Raymond that they were over Nijmegen. He was sorely tempted to continue the flight for another few minutes, but he knew that to do so would risk his Squadron ditching in the North Sea for lack of fuel.

'Buttercup aircraft from Buttercup leader,' he transmitted. 'Break off and re-form over Hertogenbosch, angels one-two. Out.'

High above he could see the distinctive silhouettes of many Thunderbolts taking station in front and on each flank of the surviving bomber formations. The Germans would be back, and there would be more attacks, more dogfighting, more shattered bombers before they began their bombing run.

Seven of the 69 Squadron Tiffies made the rendezvous, and Raymond at once began leading them back over the dykes and ditches and winding rivers of Holland. They were picked at by heavy flak once or twice, and they jinked and ruddered when it got close, but there was no serious trouble; and calls from Bob Jackson and Cobber James reassured Raymond that he had lost no aircraft on his first mission as temporary CO. 'For which relief much thanks, O Lord!'

They were a few miles off the coast with fuel gauge needles nudging zero when control called them up. 'Base U/S, Strawberry leader. Pancake at Hector' — the codename for Stiplowe.

'Roger,' Raymond replied. 'Hope they're cleared ready for us.'

Their route took them over Horning. There were two crashed B-17s, one on the east-west runway, the second at its intersection with the other runway, with crash crews and trucks by them both. Raymond surmised that they were from the earlier diversionary raid, which had met with misfortune. But the broad runway was clear at Stiplowe, 382 Group's Thunderbolts being still airborne and with the bombers, by now leaving the Dutch coast behind them.

Raymond landed 69 Squadron rapidly in pairs, coming in last himself with nil fuel showing for all tanks on the gauge, and they were ordered to park on the tarmac by the control tower. Here Colonel Schneider greeted them personally, congratulating Raymond on his promotion and asking how they had got on.

'Busy, sir,' Raymond said, hanging his helmet and goggles on one of the projecting cannon of his Tiffy. There were black blast stains round the muzzle, and several scars from the 110's debris on the leading edge of the wing. 'They were throwing everything they had at us.'

'And we threw it right back, sir,' added Harry Hobbs. 'I got a 109 and damaged another.'

The Squadron's total score, to be confirmed by cinefilm later, was six in all. 'Guess that's pretty good,' commented the Colonel, who was distributing his fiery cigars to anyone who wanted one.

'And how were my boys doing when you left?'

'They looked as if they were going to have the time of their lives,' Raymond said, causing laughter from his pilots. 'There'll be plenty to talk about when they get back.'

There was a group of officers standing about the Colonel's car when he led Raymond over to it, some already scanning the eastern sky for the first signs of the returning fighters. Among them, seen with a tug of instant recognition, was the tall figure of Louise Daintree. She stepped forward, smartly saluting the Colonel.

'You'll remember Flight-Lieutenant Cox from his previous visits here,' said the Colonel, returning the salute with a sly smile, and then leaving them together. They walked back towards Raymond's Tiffy, which was now being refuelled from a massive bowser. The air was heavy with the stench of oil and high-octane petrol and hot engines, overwhelming her scent of roses.

'My God, how wonderful to find you here!' exclaimed Raymond. 'I've never wanted to see you so much as now ... and here we are, diverted from Horning, and here you are.'

'Just like a wife greeting hubby home from the office.' She laughed and fleetingly touched his hand. 'And I see he's been working so hard he's been promoted.' She glanced up at the massive Typhoon. '*And* he's got a bigger plane.' Her grey eyes searched his face. 'How was it Ray? A tough one?'

'It was OK. But I had to stand in as CO, and it's the first time I've led a squadron.'

'Well, gee, that's great. And you didn't lose anyone, either. Oh, why can't we celebrate?'

The men with the bowser had finished, and one of them cat-whistled at her as they drove on to the next machine.

'We *must* meet one evening soon,' Raymond said. 'I'm aching for you — I never stop aching for you. Not just for your body — for *you*.' He smiled at her and said, 'It's bad for my flying not to see you.'

The faintest sound of approaching aircraft could now be heard, echoed by a rising murmur of voices, broken by cries and orders. The drivers of the two ambulances and crash wagons started their engines and drove out to the edge of the apron.

'Here they come. Can you see them?' Raymond held Louise's hand, directing her gaze towards the approaching dots in the sky.

Louise said, 'I'm going to be busy for a while now, Ray. I'll call you up tonight. I want to see you just as much.'

All the elaborate machinery of this air-base was grinding into action, preparing to receive three squadrons of battle-scarred fighters. The flying controller and station commander were on the control-tower balcony with their staff, a splash of khaki and brass, binoculars trained on the approaching aircraft. Down at the dispersals, the mechanics in their peaked caps had emerged like termites from the huts, and stood ready to take over their aircraft. A mixed collection of officers, non-commissioned officers and enlisted men (including some of the kitchen staff in white aprons) had collected on the edge of the camp. How had their boys done? How many would come back?

Raymond watched the lead aircraft on its final approach. It had obviously been given priority because of damage. Only one wheel of the undercarriage had fallen, and an ambulance and crash-wagon roared forward as it lost height, heading for the grass alongside the runway. The Thunderbolt touched down, the pilot holding the big machine on one wheel and the tail-wheel for a short distance, before it dropped a wing and began spinning in a cloud of dust.

The others quickly landed in pairs, Raymond counting thirty in all, with no sign of further damage and a great deal of waving of arms with thumbs raised by the pilots as they taxied fast towards their bays. As the last engine cut out, the sound level at Stiplowe suddenly reverted to the normal day-long murmur of jeeps and trucks.

But not for long. A lieutenant shortly approached Raymond, saluted and said, 'The Colonel says to tell you your base is clear now, and you have permission to take off.'

Raymond thanked him, called out to the other pilots, and climbed up onto the wing of his aircraft. He settled into his cockpit in contemplative mood, brought on partly by sheer weariness. He had led his squadron into battle, he had fought and killed, he had returned after almost three hours, and to find here — by some brilliant stoke of fate — the woman who meant more to him than anyone since May had died all that time ago.

Suddenly Raymond realised that as May had been to him in his childhood, so Louise was now to Ray Cox the man — the fighting man — meeting all his emotional needs, but also the changed needs of a grown man: cerebral, social, sexual.

It was true — of course it was true — but what a moment for this sort of introspection! Pulling himself together, he reached out with his right hand, pulled the toggle to select a cartridge and pressed the starter and booster coil buttons together. The Sabre burst into roaring life and he raised his hand to the rest of his Squadron and led them out in single file to the end of the runway.

126

Chapter Eight

THE HEAT OF the air war over Europe in July 1943 was matched by the summer itself. Long, hot days down at the dispersal — with the Squadron sometimes on readiness from 5 am until after sunset — were broken by alarms and exercises, scrambles after tip-and-runners, urgent calls for escort support for the medium bombers over France and the Low Countries, and even more sudden calls for strafing attacks on German E-boats harrying coastal shipping and trawlers.

There was longer notice for American 8th Air Force bombing attacks, and there needed to be, as these always called for long-range drop tanks and rendezvous pre-planning. On 4 July they celebrated Independence Day by penetrating deep into France to bomb factories at Nantes and Le Mans. Then there was a series of attacks against German airfields, followed later in the month with even more massive attacks against German industry — Hamburg and Hanover and Kiel.

One hundred and nine of these great four engine American machines, each with a crew of ten, were shot down in July in spite of all the efforts of the escorting fighters, and many more were damaged and their crew members killed or injured. The sight of these maimed or burning machines falling from the sky with their crews struggling to get out, and all too often failing to do so, haunted Raymond's dreams.

Other sights flitted across his mind half-subconsciously as he lay in his bed recovering the strength of will and purpose he needed for another day's flying: E-boat sailors twisting and spinning through the air as they were torn up by his cannon fire; the fleeting glimpse of a pilot's pale goggled face staring back at his Typhoon before the shells tore him asunder; the memory of Charlie Farrell of A-Flight jumping out too low and hitting the water at 300 mph, 'chute half open; the unheard spread of concussive explosions, each circle with its petals of dust and detritus, as the heavy bombs spread across the target twenty thousand feet below; and always that close black enemy, the puffs of heavy flak which sometimes seemed to fill the sky and rocked you like a boxer's punch, rattled you with fragments, and, when very close, could even be heard above the roar of your engine — *whooomph, whooomph.*

The sun shone with the same heat as during the Battle of Britain. The riggers and fitters, radio technicians, electricians and armourers, worked shirtless, grease stains on chests and backs, whistling 'In the Mood' and 'Elmer's Tune', cursing a great deal, downing mug after mug of hot sweet tea, and lighting Woodbines from the glowing tips of their mates' fags. The pilots remained silent about the pressure and escapes, and those who did not come back; they spoke laconically of their successes, without 'shooting a line', and scathingly about almost everything else — the flying of other squadrons, the blunders of high command, or the food in the mess. WAAFs and civilian girls were referred to, individually and generally, in prurient terms, until they married (and two pilots of 69 Squadron married that month) when they suddenly attracted hushed respect.

Jack Boland came back on the same day as Tubby Eccles, and Raymond relinquished command with much relief, but also (he had to admit to himself) with some regret. As if making up for his absence, Jack seemed to be everywhere at the same time, giving orders and making comments in the air and on the ground, in the mess and at the dispersal, leaving behind a trail of half-smoked cigarette ends, the sound of his high-pitched laughter creating an uneasy sense that the man was sometimes uncomfortably close to hysteria.

The CO led every show, and in the brief lulls had them on air-to-air gunnery, driving Chiefy and his crews almost to the point of mutiny with his demands for serviceable aircraft. His only relaxation was to invite Raymond home with him to the vicarage for a meal or an evening, always travelling in Delilah with Bonz on his lap.

It was on one of these car trips that Jack suddenly told Raymond that he should take some leave. He repeated this instruction at the family supper round the kitchen table. John Boland was half asleep after several whiskies, Dorothy was bustling about serving food, Arnold on long leave from Eton was fully occupied in eating, and Rachel was helping her mother.

'As I mentioned, I think you need a week's leave, Ray,' Jack said.

'What can I do with a week's leave?' Raymond asked. 'And where am I supposed to go?'

'You can do absolutely nothing for seven days and nights. You've been under pressure for long enough, and you'll be more useful to the squadron after a rest.'

'And where you can go is *here*,' Dorothy Boland chipped in. 'We'll look after you, won't we Rachel? Breakfast in bed. Potter about, take a few walks ...'

Again it seemed to Raymond that they had already discussed this matter between them and that it was a part of some prearranged plan, a *fait accompli*.

'It's terribly kind of you,' said Raymond. 'But I can't hang about here while I'm needed at Horning.'

John Boland suddenly opened wide his heavy-lidded eyes and sat up as if from a posture of prayer. 'You are weary, my son,' he said. '"Come unto me, all that labour and are heavy laden, and I will give you rest." Matthew 11:28, I think.'

'Quite right, Papa,' said Rachel. 'Of course Ray must do as he's told.'

'Yes, it's an order, Ray,' Jack insisted. 'And I'll tell you another thing, though I shouldn't really, before it's promulgated. I put you in for a DFC and it's been approved.'

Raymond looked at him in amazement. 'But what on earth for, Jack? I haven't done anything special.'

'Oh, yes, you have. You took over the Squadron at short notice and made a bloody good job of it. Especially on that Yank raid on the Ruhr, which brought your score to nine.'

He turned to his mother. 'I think the moment has come to produce that bottle.'

'Hear, hear!' exclaimed his father predictably.

For the first time Raymond noticed a tray of champagne glasses on a corner of the kitchen sideboard. A bottle of Mumm's Extra Dry was produced from the fridge, and Arnold attacked its foil and wire with enthusiasm.

Raymond looked at them in turn, wondering what to say. 'You're blushing,' said Rachel, laughing. 'I've never seen you blush before.' She bent towards him and kissed his cheek, and Dorothy put her arms round his shoulders and laid her cheek against his. 'Congratulations, dear Ray,' she said. '*I* think you deserve a VC.'

Jack watched all this with the utmost satisfaction. He raised a brimming glass in Ray's direction. His father, wide awake now, said, 'Bless you, my boy.'

They all sipped in silence, but Raymond knew he had to say something. So he stood up from the table and raised his own glass. 'It's all of you who should be toasted, not me,' he said, glancing round. 'For all your marvellous kindness and hospitality. So — to the wonderful Bolands.'

They finished a second bottle of champagne in the study after supper, and as the talk and laughter became louder, Dorothy proposed a game of charades. It was just the right thing for this sentimental and somewhat alcoholic occasion.

Louise ran down the platform, breaking away from the crowd of service men and women just off the train from Norwich, and she fell into Raymond's arms. As he held her tightly, she whispered in his ear, 'Oh freedom, wonderful freedom! Three days and nights of it.'

He picked up her suitcase before they were overwhelmed by the torrent of passengers, and they made their way, arm in arm, to the side exit of Liverpool Street station. Here Raymond had reserved a cab for them, far from the long queue which stretched from the regular cabstand day and night.

'The Ritz Hotel, please, driver.'

'Gee Ray, the Ritz! Aren't you the smart boy.'

Louise looked out of the cab window in horror as they drove through the devastated city, past St. Paul's Cathedral standing in magnificent surviving isolation in a wilderness of rubble. 'This makes Norwich look like a picnic,' she exclaimed.

'At least we can get through the streets,' said Raymond. 'I think that's more than they can do in Cologne right now.'

Life in London appeared normal in spite of the ruins. Bowler-hatted businessmen and top-hatted messengers hurried along the pavements, and as they approached the West End there seemed to be more Americans than any other Allied servicemen on the streets, hanging about, picking up girls, or heading for the cinema or Rainbow Corner, the recreational headquarters for the American Army in London.

Louise was disappointed by Piccadilly Circus. 'It's so small!' she exclaimed. 'And where's the famous Eros, Ray?'

'Under that shelter.' He pointed to the protective box built around the statue. 'We didn't want the god of love to be damaged by those wretched Huns.'

'And talking of love,' she said, 'I think I really go for you, airman.'

She was wearing a neat little pillbox hat perched just off centre and a blue light cotton skirt and jacket, very simple and just right. He met her eyes and they smiled at each other, lightly touching hands.

'Well, that's a good start,' he said. 'I rather go for you, too.' His eyes caught the simple ring she had slipped on her wedding finger, and he added, 'Mrs Cox.'

The cab stopped and a commissionaire was soon holding open the door. Raymond paid the five-times fare he had agreed previously with the driver, and climbed out after Louise. Their room overlooked Green Park, and Louise drew back the net curtains so they could look out. There was a big air-raid shelter below them and, more distantly, anti-aircraft guns. High above, barrage balloons spotted the afternoon sky. But there were also trees and bushes and green grass, and the Ritz had provided them with a window-box of red and white geraniums. The war was indisputably and evidently all around them, but this summer colour offered promise — and they had this room, and three days and nights, and each other.

Louise said, 'I guess I'm ready for everything to stop still so we can keep it just like this.'

'Well maybe we can move about a little.'

'Just a little.' She put her hand on the back of his neck and gently ruffled his black hair. 'Like we could make some love on this great bed. And have some tea. And make just a little more love.'

'And have a cocktail or two,' he broke in, his head full of her scent of roses. 'And just a little more love. And then some dinner.'

'And so the lovely evening will wear on.'

Louise let drop the net curtains and turned to him and pulled his head to hers. They kissed for a long time, brushing lips slightly then pressing firmly, and in the most leisurely way they started to take off each other's clothes, letting them drop at their feet.

'Trousers are such a damn nuisance!' Raymond complained without much conviction. 'They have to be stepped out of.'

'I can help there,' she said, pushing him onto the bed and laughingly dragging them off.

Later he said, 'It can never be as good as this again.' He could only just get the words out as they moved in unison.

But Louise was able to say, 'Oh yes, it will, darling. You'll see . . .'

Of course she was quite right.

Louise got up at six o'clock the next morning. 'I feel so marvellous I must go for a walk.'

Raymond groaned and buried his head in the pillows, but finally pulled himself out of the bed. 'We could go and feed the ducks in St James's Park,' he suggested.

So out they went into the clear dawn, unwashed, unmade-up, unshaven, feeling as if they owned not only London but the world.

Several times on those days and nights together, Raymond wondered just what made Louise such easy and pleasant company. Apart from the sisters of some Bristol school friends, he had previously had little contact with girls. Then the exclusively male world of public school had been exchanged for the exclusively male world of the RAF. Even WAAFs had been a rarity in those early days of the war, and he had developed no close relationship with any of them since.

Raymond had realised he was awkward with women — as incapable of judging their nature as their moods. For this reason they made him nervous and unnatural in manner. Was it because she was American that none of this applied to Louise? he wondered. She was neither coquettish nor patronising, neither aloof nor self-conscious and hoydenish. She was straight and direct, brisk and uncomplicated, absolutely without guile: someone to whom he could say anything without fear of shocking her, just as her own responses would come equally unwrapped and unvarnished. Raymond felt entirely relaxed with her, and their unity of mind and body was amazing. Even more remarkable was the speed at which they had found it.

On the afternoon of their second day they were lying on their backs in Hyde Park, staring up at the sky. Over towards the Serpentine there was a crowd round the bandstand and they caught snatches of music from Gilbert and Sullivan while in the opposite direction more serious figures moved among the sandbagged redoubts and their skyward-pointing anti-aircraft guns. There was a faint hum of traffic from Park Lane and distant cries of children and barking dogs, all combining in a strange symphony of war and peace.

Raymond dreamily quoted Marlowe. '"Stand still you ever-moving spheres of heaven,/ That time may cease, and midnight never come./Fair nature's eye, rise, rise again and make/Perpetual day, or let this hour be but/A year, a month, a week, a natural day."... How's that?'

Louise did not answer at once. Then she said rather solemnly, 'Yes, very good. In fact, perfect. Just let's have our natural day, and be content.'

As Raymond lit her a cigarette, she said, 'All the same, I have to go back tomorrow night. Then what will you do with the rest of your week off?'

'I'll come back with you.'

She laughed. 'To Stiplowe? That'll be swell. I'll call for another bed in my hut. The Colonel's very tolerant.'

'Yes, that'd be nice, but maybe not very practical. I think I should go to the Bolands. They're expecting me.'

Louise propped herself on her elbow, looking at him quizzically. 'Who exactly are these Bolands? Why are you always going to the Bolands?' She pronounced their name as if it was two distinct words — 'Bo-lands'.

'They're very kind and hospitable. You met the daughter along with Charlie Dee at that dance — when we first met.'

'Yes,' she said slowly. 'That girl . . . Her name is Rachel.'

Raymond squeezed her hand. 'It's OK. She's scarcely more than a schoolgirl. Her father's the vicar, and an old Great War pilot — with one leg. And there's a younger boy still at school. And my CO, Jack, who's terrific. And of course their mother, Dorothy, who's kindness itself.'

'You certainly have got entwined in their lives, haven't you? Or the other way round . . . What did they say when you told them you were coming to London?'

To his surprise he saw anxiety in her grey eyes. 'Why do you ask?'

'Well, perhaps they were hoping you would spend your leave with them, you know.'

Raymond felt momentarily uncomfortable and wished Louise had not reminded him. 'Yes, they were a little upset. That's why I promised I'd spend the last couple of days with them.'

'Did you tell them about me?'

'No, of course not. I just said I was going to meet a friend in London.'

Louise stubbed out her cigarette in the grass and lay back again, smiling up at him. 'Well, you listen to me and have a good story ready. Because I'll bet my last dollar they'll want to hear about every minute of every day.'

'Don't take against them before you've even met them, Louise,' he said. 'They really have been grand. So generous. And Jack, who seems to know everyone, got me transferred to his squadron — and then gave me a flight. Even put my name in for this.' And he put his finger on his new mauve and silver striped DFC ribbon.

'OK, sorry, I'll let it alone. Shall we talk about New York instead?'

'Yes, please. Go ahead.'

134

'Well, it's big and noisy and not at all like London. All the streets are straight and you're liable to get pushed off the sidewalks in the crush of people. Privately they're the nicest, warmest people in the world, but publicly they don't seem to give a damn. The skyscrapers ... well you know all about them.'

'But what about you. I'm interested in *you* — and how you live.'

'Well, I live at home, it may surprise you. Very chaste and well behaved I am, nearly all the time. My parents have an apartment on East 68th Street near Central Park, which is nice. My father works in oil and my mother does charity work, and we entertain quite a lot and go to the theatre — but not the opera, which always makes us giggle. Let's see, what else?'

'Do you spend all your time in the city — at weekends and in the summer?'

Hands clasped behind her head, Louise was staring straight up into the full-leaved plane tree beneath which they lay.

'We're a pretty city family, Ray. We haven't got a house on Long Island or in Connecticut, or anything like that. But we go visit friends when we need a change of scene and smell. Two brothers, by the way — both older, both married and both darlings. Then there's me and that's about it.'

She smiled across at him, then struggled to her feet and put out her hand to help him up. 'Let's go back to the Ritz for tea. Tea at the Ritz — I still can't get over it all. And maybe we can take in a show tonight. My treat.'

That night Louise sobbed quietly again, after they had made love. 'Why do I have this effect on you?' Raymond asked, wiping her eyes. 'Why do you feel so miserable? You know how damned innocent I am, but does lovemaking really always do this to women?'

'No, you sap.' She crushed him close to her body. 'Don't you understand? I'm so goddamned anxious for you. I shouldn't let you know that, but I can't help it. It's you doing what you're doing, and me being so near and hardly ever seeing you, and wanting you so much.' She pressed her wet cheek against his. 'Don't you understand, you goof? I'm crazy about you. I really

135

do love you, and this is just like some scene from a goddamn Hollywood war movie — *This Above All* with Joan Fontaine and Ty Power.'

Raymond laughed and kissed her. 'I love you, too, my darling. And perhaps we really are in a movie — in which case there's bound to be a happy ending with a lot of heavenly music and us fading into the sunset together.'

Louise sniffled and took the handkerchief he was holding. 'Or maybe the movie will be called *Faustus*, and "time may cease, and midnight never come".'

'Too late,' said Raymond sleepily looking at his watch. 'It's already gone.'

Jack Boland greeted Raymond a touch coolly. 'How are things at home?'

Raymond set Bonz down and moved towards the mess with his CO. 'They're fine. Rachel's got her uniform and is ready to leave for training. Think of that, Rachel an ATA pilot.'

At the mention of his sister's name, Jack turned and looked at him sharply. 'Maybe that's just as well.'

Raymond had no idea what he meant by that comment, and he also knew this was no time to enquire. Instead he enquired how things had been going over the past week, and learned that 69 Squadron had done only three ops and had been engaged in a good deal of liaison flying with 382 Group.

'Incidentally,' Jack added, turning on his heel, 'I'd like some shop talk in my office at 6 o'clock this evening. I've got something for you.'

'Right, sir,' Raymond said, saluting Jack's back as he strode off. He was left feeling faintly uneasy, not so much about whatever task Jack might have in mind, but about Jack's mood itself.

When the hour arrived, Raymond found the CO's office in its usual state of chaos and disrepair, just like his home at West Aitcham. Jack was seated behind the cluttered desk, signing papers. Two cigarettes, one only slightly shorter than the other, were burning on a pile of stubs in his tobacco-tin ashtray.

At length, Jack pushed the papers aside, adding further confusion to the desk-top, and said in exasperation, 'If I did all the paperwork they throw at me, I'd never fly. Or even talk to my men, for that matter.'

As usual, the words were rattled out with much nervous tapping of his cigarette before the ash grew too long. 'Colonel Schneider over at Stiplowe is sending some of his pilots on an op. with the heavy kites so they can see their problems at first hand. Also to experience what it's like having half a dozen 109s coming in at you from all sides at once.' He gave a high-pitched nervous laugh. 'Should be quite interesting. I think we ought to do the same.'

'All of us or some of us, sir?' Raymond asked.

'You to start with. Good example for the other types. Now, it so happens that there's a wizard show coming off next week.' He fixed his eyes on Raymond. 'Feel like a holiday in the sun?' the CO asked with a sly grin.

'Yes, sir,' Raymond answered promptly, determined not to be tempted into asking what Jack meant.

The CO ran his hands through his fair hair, then occupied them in reshuffling the papers on his desk. 'Colonel Schneider will give you the gen when you arrive,' he said, closing the subject. 'Adj. will give you the time and day ... But that's not all for you, Ray, and I hope you'll feel that the Yank job and this other one, which is urgent, are a reflection of my trust in you.' Jack fumbled among his papers again, and this time pulled out a map of north-west Germany.

'While you were living it up in the West End instead of keeping my family company, I was up at Air House having a few words with the Intelligence people.'

'What about, sir?' Raymond asked, ignoring the hint of criticism.

'Secret weapons. German secret weapons.'

Hitler's secret weapons had long since assumed the status of a national joke, and had even been the subject of cracks on the wireless.

'You're not serious, sir?'

'I bloody am. It looks as though there are now two of these *Wunderwaffen* — miracle weapons. One of them a long-range rocket and the other some kind of self-propelled bomb. Reports are coming in from our people in France and Denmark and we've got some PRU photographs of something we can't identify properly at a German experimental base at Peenemünde. We've also got reports of these being assembled at an underground factory north-west of Cologne.'

Jack spread the map flat on an adjoining table, as there was absolutely no clear space on the desk. With a pencil he pointed at a small village called Minch, lying off an autobahn. 'Just about here. Intelligence have some high-level pictures which identify the position of the factory, but they need a detail low-level shot.'

'You're not suggesting that I . . .'

'Exactly that,' Jack interrupted. 'Just exactly that. On the deck, all the way in and out. Drop tanks. A stripped unarmed and unarmoured Tiffy with a boosted engine. Nothing'll be able to get near you.' He smiled, looked up briefly, drew a pencil circle round the target area, then looked up again. 'Piece of cake, Ray.' He had been talking so continuously that for once enough ash had accumulated to fall from his cigarette. It hit the pencilled target.

Raymond sighed sardonically. 'So — two trips to Germany. And both "interesting" — that's the word you like, isn't it, sir?

'Both pieces of cake,' Jack repeated.

'And which first?'

' *Wunderwaffe*. The day after tomorrow, if the weather's OK.' He bent down to the lowest drawer in his desk and drew from it a bottle of whisky. 'It's for Papa, really, but he would approve of us taking a nip.' He poured out two very generous measures and raised his glass. 'Well, here's to your DSO next.'

Jack put his feet up on the desk and looked hard at Raymond with his clear blue eyes. 'I hope you don't mind taking on this recce, Ray. You're my most experienced pilot, and you're better at navigation on the deck than anyone else here, too. Spy'll give you a hand later on the areas to avoid when going in and out. There may be a spot of flak at the target itself, but with any luck you'll only need one run over it.'

The 69 Squadron Intelligence Officer was very different from the austere, precise Spy of Raymond's last squadron. Dick Latchmere was a veteran ex-bomber pilot who had flown

Whitleys in '39 and '40, a rare survivor of those early raids, who had lost an arm over the Ruhr and been grounded. Dick was a peacetime airman and a very punctilious IO. He had spent an entire day working out Raymond's route, marking identifying points — a violent bend in a river here, a railway interception there, a big cement works with a tall chimney a half mile to the right, a large reservoir — best marking point of all — and so on. Heavy flak areas were chalked blue, and given a wide berth by the thick red line that marked Raymond's route, and balloon barrages were shown as a number of small circles.

'I've taken you a mile to the south of your target, here,' Dick Latchmere explained, 'so that you can do a tight turn to the left here — but watch the overhead cables. This way you'll come in from the south. One run over the target at two hundred and fifty feet — snap, snap, snap, — and out again.'

'And the flak? Where's that?'

'Believed to be mobile. It doesn't show on the high-level photo, as you can see.'

Raymond thanked him. 'That's marvellous, Dick. And it's off at 4.30 am from Manston, so there'll be a bit of light when I cross in.'

Dick nodded, and Raymond said, 'Leave me with this, will you? I want a quiet look at it all for an hour. Then a look at the kite.'

It was early August and the nights were already closing in. The Tiffy had been flown in that morning and was in one of the B-Flight hardstandings guarded by a couple of RAF Regiment aircraftsmen who saluted him when he identified himself.

It stood like a naked woman, stripped of everything except small roundels on each wing: no identification letters, no red, white and blue stripes on the tail, no projecting cannon from the leading edges of the wings. A silver ghost in the half-light of dusk. When he examined the wings he saw that the rivets had been hand-filed and polished, and even the radio mast had been dismantled to provide, perhaps, another mile an hour, while the camera set into the underside of the fuselage was completely flush-fitted.

He climbed into the cockpit where his parachute had already been laid out. Pampered ... There would be *two* eggs and bacon for breakfast. Nothing too good for the patient before the operation, or the victim before the execution. He sat still for a moment, not even touching the controls. Everything smelt unfamiliar, like a newly decorated room. No character. Tomorrow it would smell of sweat, not of cordite, because he had no guns — nothing except the Smith and Wesson .38 he always carried on ops.

On the windscreen where the reflector sight would have been, he saw in his mind the map he had been looking at so intently, learning his route so that he would never have to consult it again ... In at Nieuport, then Thourout, south of Ghent, hit the railway track south-west towards Brussels, but keep north of that city, marshalling yards on the right, then due east 90 degrees on the compass to Maastricht, sixty miles, ten minutes exactly (unless someone's on your tail, when it would be more like seven minutes). Ten degrees port, note rising land to the south, hit and follow the Aachen-Krefeld railway line five more minutes, over the frontier into Germany and due east again to a little place called Bedburg where the church was on the south side of the main road. And the final approach to the target area.

Raymond felt strangely elated as he took off for Manston where, once again, he had topped up his tanks, made the familiar drop over the cliffs down to sea level, and headed across the Channel. There were several reasons for this elation. He always loved the independence of a lone mission, and in this case the importance of it added a further spice. And the challenge of flying into Germany in a machine so fast that no other plane could match it provided a schoolboy excitement that set the adrenalin flowing fast. And the light was right for the occasion: a three-quarter moon sparkled silver on the waves to match his silver Tiffy, while the eastern horizon revealed the faintest hint of a golden dawn.

Raymond had long ago trained his mind not to linger even for a moment on the odds for a safe return. Had he done so on this op the figures must have made grave reading. But he just took each mile as it came and went — every ten seconds

140

or so — concentrating on keeping no more than twenty feet above the flashing waves, while darting a glance first at the instrument panel and then at the rear mirror.

The sandy beach at Nieuport went past in a blur of grey — the beach defences of rolled barbed wire, pillboxes and anti-tank obstructions leaving an impression no sooner registered than it was erased. It was the same over the next half hour as he shot across the low farmland of north Belgium at 350 mph and +4 boost, gently lifting the nose over a line of poplars, glimpsing livestock scattering before him in the fields as he cut a swathe of panic.

Minute after minute, mile after mile, sweeping over villages and empty roads, and still not a human being to be seen, as if the continent of Europe had been denuded of population. Then at last a man on a bicycle, wobbling uncontrollably as Raymond flashed over him, and a few minutes later two women in black talking outside a cottage, their heads suddenly turned in a fearful white-faced reaction, then gone. There on the right was the big triangular-shaped forest of fir trees he had noted on the large-scale map.

The daylight was matching the moonlight as the outer suburbs of Brussels loomed up to the south. Raymond ruddered onto 090 degrees, checking the clock, and began more seriously searching the sky. Dropping his tanks put the speed up 20 mph and he opened the throttle at the same time, ASI indicating just under 400 mph. There was plenty of traffic on the Aachen railway line, great black locomotives, double-banked and drawing numberless coal wagons, black smoke trailing lazily behind in the still dawn air.

Then the worst happened. The next landmark never showed up. It should be Bedburg but it was not there, and the time to turn was past. 'Do *not* panic!' he told himself firmly. Just a little altitude and carry out a square search. At five hundred feet he could see off to the right the towering spire of Cologne cathedral, as magically spared as St Paul's in London ... and at the same time the flak opened up. Instead of four hundred bombers in the dark as target, they had one fighter sparkling in the first light of dawn, and the sky was instantly pockmarked with black splashes and criss-crossed with light tracer from every point of the compass.

Raymond kicked the rudder pedals savagely and jinked with the stick, dropping like a stone back to the comfort of the treetops. At the same time he picked up a main road going north-west, and when it turned into a four-lane autobahn he knew he was all right and reorientated. In less than a minute he saw the little hamlet of Minch, and to the right the woods in which the factory lay.

He was going so fast he overshot his target, catching a glimpse under his starboard wing of many low camouflaged buildings, a large open area with olive drab trucks and a scattering of small aircraft, one of them on what looked like a narrow-gauge railway line.

So, there they were, neatly lined up and waiting for him, like guardsmen on parade. Could these little toys be *Wunderwaffen*? They looked so innocent, yet . . .

He aileroned steeply, almost clipping the treetops with his wingtip, switching on the camera, completed a 180 degrees turn and, with light flak whipping up at him almost horizontally but underestimating his speed, he raced over the centre of the factory at two hundred and fifty feet, concentrating on keeping straight and level while the belly camera did its work.

Then he was back on the autobahn and set his compass on 283 degrees, the lines of the day's first shadows, of isolated trees and telegraph posts, a village water-tower, the steeple of a church, all the shadows pointing left now but soon towards home and safety and (as he fleetingly permitted himself to recall) towards Louise Daintree. At the same time the great red ball behind him offered blinding cover for pursuing fighters, and every airfield in Belgium and north-east France would by now have been alerted to the presence of the lone silver enemy machine streaking west.

Flying on the deck was a tiring business, every split second requiring an adjustment, and it had been like this for ninety minutes or more, lifting, dropping, turning slightly to right and left to achieve the maximum protection by hugging the ground. At the same time he had to cover the sky from horizon to horizon every few seconds. East of Maastricht he caught sight of a *Schwarm* of 190s flying in the opposite direction at about two thousand feet. They were almost out of sight when he saw one of them peal off, followed by the other three. He had been spotted, and the radios would be crackling. Raymond opened the throttle to give +7 boost and his Tiffy thrust forward like a hunter given its head. With the advantage of their dive, the 190s held him for a while, then fell back, unable to match his 440 mph ASI.

But at this speed he was using a lot of fuel, and Raymond throttled back as soon as he felt safe. He saw nothing more — just a desultory display of flak as he went out again at Nieuport — and in mid-Channel he pulled up to four thousand feet and switched on his identification signal to reassure the radar controllers and gun crews.

Over the fields of Kent he could see the first reapers cutting into the corn harvest, and the fruit-pickers in the orchards — horses and men and women all in for a hard day's work. A party of hop-pickers paused to watch the unfamiliar silver machine above, as it circled before lining up to land. Without radio, Raymond waited for a green Very flare to shoot up from the control tower at Manston, then he throttled back, dropped the undercarriage, flaps and radiator flap. He had about ten gallons of fuel left, and very little power of concentration: just enough to see him safely down and to taxi in.

He switched off, the big three-blade prop stopped, kicked back, and was still. He sat in the cockpit savouring this moment of peace and tranquillity, the silence caressing his nerves. He was wearing no more than battledress but his shirt was soaked, and when he took off his helmet the sweat flooded down from his hair and over his face.

'Are you OK, sir?'

Raymond eased himself out and allowed himself to be helped onto the wing. 'Yes, fine. I just feel I've been away a week.'

'They'll be just starting breakfast in the officers' mess,' said the rigger. 'I should think they might find you an egg, too.'

The photographic crews were already at work, removing the big camera from the plane's belly. 'Did you get it all right, sir?' one of them asked.

143

'I hope so,' Raymond replied, lighting a cigarette and filling his lungs with relief. 'An awful waste of time if they don't come out.'

But they did. Prints reached Horning late that afternoon and Dick Latchmere and the CO called Raymond in to view them. It was evident that he had not flown dead centre over the factory yard, but three of the planes were clearly visible, and the fourth on the ramp could just be seen at the edge.

Dick said, 'I've had a word from HQ and they're very pleased, Ray.'

Raymond looked at them closely through a glass. 'What the hell are they? They're like nothing I've ever seen.' By matching them to the length of a lorry, they were very small, and they had stubby wings set halfway along the fuselage, with a vestigial tail at the tip of the tapering body. They each seemed to be carrying what looked like a small torpedo at the stern.

'That's it,' said Jack. ' *Wunderwaffe.* It's not a miniature fighter. It's some sort of guided missile. A flying bomb, and we think that's some sort of jet or rocket engine at the rear. A few thousand of those on London will make a mess of the place.'

144

Chapter Nine

IT HAD RAINED continuously since before dawn, and it looked as if this would go on all day. At Horning, Dick Latchmere gave both flights a talk on the strategy of the war and its likely future shape. He was a well-informed officer who had completed a thesis on military history while at Cranwell before the war, and there were a surprising number of questions for him. Jack Boland had ordered an hour's run for the afternoon, and clay-pigeon shooting if the weather eased. Down at the dispersal, the ground crews in capes and sou'westers caught up on maintenance of their complex and temperamental Tiffies.

Raymond was standing at the bar with Tubby Eccles when the steward came up to tell him he was wanted on the outside telephone. He guessed it was Louise and his heart lifted when he heard her voice. 'It's five days since I've seen you and I'm starving to death,' she said. 'Please, can we meet?'

'So am I. I can't get away till seven, but let me pick you up then, and we'll go to the Nelson. At least we can talk.'

It was still raining when they arrived, and the pub was almost deserted. Bonz hated the rain and refused to leave the car. They sat up at the bar and Raymond ordered a pint of beer for himself and a shandy for Louise. He lit her a cigarette and brushed her cheek with his hand as he put it between her lips.

She said, 'I'm sorry about my uniform. I know you like me better in a dress. But I'm working again tonight.'

'You can be dressed in what you like — or not at all.'

145

They talked then about their future, as if one day they would be together for life, but without actually mentioning marriage. Somehow that did not seem to be necessary.

One or two locals came in. Outside the sky was lightening from the west, with the cloud breaking up and letting through flashes of low sun. Louise broke off telling him about her peacetime career, doing research for a big advertising company before Pearl Harbor. 'I want to tell you something about my current work now,' she suddenly said. 'But I can't talk about it here, so let's go outside.'

They carried their glasses to the car, and released Bonz who was now showing signs of agreement that the weather was at last becoming tolerable. Together they walked along the bank of the broad to the willow tree where they had stood on that night when Raymond had been thrown into the water.

'What is it? What's so hush-hush?'

'We had a file this morning from the Air Intelligence Branch,' she said in a low voice. 'It was marked "Most Secret" and was restricted to the base commander, Colonel Schneider, and me.'

She explained that it was a memorandum on the enemy's new weapon developments: some form of pilotless aircraft and a long-range rocket, both intended to be used against British cities, and primarily London.

'Yes, I know about them, Louise, but why are you telling me all this?'

Bonz was up to his usual game of chasing birds, barking excitedly when they flew up and settled in a tree or bush. His antics added a comforting commonplace touch to the doom-laden nature of their conversation.

'It was my job to file away the papers and photographs in the safe. There were several of Peenemünde, a German experimental site on this Baltic island, showing something that looked like winged rockets lying about.'

Louise sat down on a low branch, drew on her cigarette, and took a sip from her glass. 'There was also a more recent photograph taken at a plant near Cologne. On the back it was dated 2 August — that's last week. Then the code number 69SFLRCO627. What do you think all that stands for?'

Raymond saw Louise's grey eyes watching him keenly. 'You know, don't you, Ray?'

'Good God!' Raymond exclaimed. 'Fancy you spotting that! No wonder you're queen of the 8th Air Force's Intelligence.'

'Not very difficult if you know the guy and the number of his squadron. But what in God's name were you doing over Cologne at twenty-seven minutes past six in the morning at nought feet?'

He laughed. 'Taking pretty pictures.'

Louise slipped off the branch and stood close beside him, her voice low but intense. '*Who* ordered you off on this mission, Ray? Fighter Command didn't authorise it. You've no photographic experience, and there are dozens of specially trained photographic pilots who should be doing this sort of job. You know perfectly well, for Christ's sake, that this was an op for the photographic Mosquito at thirty eight thousand feet — not some crazy daredevil operation at zero feet on a target as heavily protected as that secret weapon site.'

Raymond shouted at Bonz to stop him barking. Louise was clearly very angry, and for some perverse reason he too was feeling guilty and angry at the same time. Why was she getting at him like this? 'Bonz, come *here*!' He picked up the recalcitrant little dog and looked warily at Louise, who was waiting impatiently for him to explain things.

'Well,' he began, 'I don't see why I have to go into all this. I came back, didn't I? Here I am ... and I don't want to fight you, of all people, heaven knows. There's quite enough damn fighting going on. My Tiffy was specially stripped so I could get away from anything the Hun put up. I wasn't even touched, the whole way.'

Another couple came strolling onto the lawn, and Louise took Raymond by the arm and walked him out of earshot. 'Darling,' she murmured, squeezing his arm, 'I'm not angry with *you*. I love you dearly, and you did a swell job. But whoever ordered you to do that was either nuts or had criminal intentions against you; *and* he wanted the glory for himself without risking his own life.'

Louise pulled a cornflower from a patch of long grass and slipped it through his top buttonhole. 'It was Jack Boland, wasn't it?'

'Yes, of course — he's my CO. And certainly *he's* never shrunk from taking risks. He takes orders from Group, and Group takes orders from Fighter Command, and in this case from Air Intelligence, or so he told me. We've all got jobs to do. Just don't worry, darling. I've survived three years of this and I'm getting better all the time.'

'I know, Ray. Of course you're going to survive. But I happen to know that your CO seems to have a finger in every pie and he got some undercover intelligence that PRU — you know, the Photo Reconnaissance people — were going to be put on this job, and he short-circuited and short-cut everything and fixed this all himself — for the greater glory of Jack Boland. And he picked *you* because he always picks you for the dirty stuff. Goddamn it, Ray, you *must* see that.'

'No, darling, you're imagining things. We're very close. He's always telling me I'm like part of his family.' He led her back towards the pub. 'You've got to get back to base, and so have I. And thank you for worrying about me — but please don't.'

The sun was going down over the broads, a wet brilliant sun casting the long, last shadows of the day. They kissed for a long time in the car and whispered their love.

Raymond drove fast, hood down now, back along deserted roads, the cool evening air cutting through their hair. They caught glimpses of 382 Group's Thunderbolts nestling in their pens, radial engines tarpaulined, like warriors resting for the night. A guard with white puttees saluted smartly as they halted by the gates of Stiplowe.

Louise passed Bonz from her lap to Raymond, and said to the dog, 'Now you just stop your master from being a sap, OK?'

In turn, Raymond turned to the dog and said, 'You just tell the Lieutenant here it's OK, because I'm off on liaison duty with her lot for a couple of weeks. With the 100th Bomb Group — how's that?'

Raymond blipped the accelerator and let in the clutch. He took his left hand briefly from the steering-wheel and blew her a kiss. Moving away, he caught the briefest glimpse of Louise's face and was puzzled to see an expression of dismay. Why? he wondered. Surely he was less likely to get the chop in a B-17 than doing a PRU in a stripped Tiffy?

Raymond arrived with Bonz at Thorpe Abbotts on the afternoon of 12 August 1943, creating a small sensation he never intended as he brought Delilah to a halt just outside the officers' mess as they were assembling for lunch. A bunch of 100th Bomb Group aircrew gathered round, curious, wanting to know all about the Alvis. Was it supercharged? How fast did it go? Could they take a peek at the motor?

'I have to report to your Colonel,' Raymond interrupted them. 'Can anyone tell me where to find him?'

He was somewhere there in the crowd. 'Hey, Colonel, the English officer here wants to meet you.' And the Colonel emerged, a tall man with a Ronald Coleman moustache and black eyes. He smiled genially.

'We've been waiting for you, Lieutenant. We're told the RAF wants to know what it's like at the receiving end.' He ushered Raymond towards the mess door. 'Colonel LeMay said you're to do a couple of missions with us as an observer so that you can see our problems first hand.' He ordered Raymond a beer, sat him down at a table, then called over a captain from the other side of the room.

'Bill, this is Lieutenant Raymond Cox' (He pronounced it Lootenant.) 'He's a veteran fighter pilot of the RAF.' He turned to Raymond. 'Meet Captain William R. Strang. He's from Pennsylvania, and you're assigned to his ship.'

They shook hands, and Raymond studied the craggy-jawed captain who looked like the hero of a Western film — someone who should be leading a sheriff's posse instead of the crew of a B-17 bomber. He had slicked-back greying hair parted in the middle, and eyes almost as blue as Jack Boland's. Strang took a packet of Camels from his top pocket and flipped out one for Raymond.

Soon another officer joined them — the crew's bombardier. Lieutenant James O. Watson was a fair-haired rather aesthetic-looking young man, light in weight and light on his feet — as Raymond noticed when he came over to meet him — like a dancer or a featherweight boxer. They smoked a couple of cigarettes over their beers before Bill Strang finally said, 'Time for chow, fellows.' He turned to Raymond.

'We're doing formation practice — the whole Group — this afternoon. You'd better come with us.'

Knowing how good Americans were at remembering names, Raymond did his best to memorise those of the other eight men making up the crew of *Grable's Legs* — the B-17 named after the popular Hollywood star Betty Grable.

After lunch, as they were driving down to the dispersal in their jeep, Raymond asked if Bonz could team up with the crew. He had proved a great social asset.

'You mean *fly*?' Bill Strang asked.

'He's a veteran,' Raymond replied, holding up the dog so that his face was into the wind. 'He really prefers an open cockpit but I expect he'll make do with a B-17.'

Raymond had never been close to one of these bombers on the ground. On both sides of the nose the name 'Grable's Legs' was painted in flesh pink alongside an unnaturally long female leg ending in a high-heeled shoe. The machine was awe-inspiring in its size, with its four great radial engines, and the wheels coming up to a tall man's chest. The other most striking feature was its defensive armament. Designed to look after itself against fighter attack, the .5-inch guns sprouted from the bombers fuselage like a porcupine's spikes: from a twin-turret above the cockpit, from the chin, from both sides of the nose and the extreme tail-end, from above the radio-operator's cabin, from each side of the waist, and from a ball turret suspended beneath the fuselage.

Although Raymond had seen German fighters attacking B-17s as if they were sitting targets, he could now imagine the nerve required to face the combined cross-fire of a tight formation of these bombers. He had already been introduced to one of the waist gunners, a small ginger-haired enlisted man, Staff-Sergeant Glenn R. Mackenzie ('Mac'), and before boarding the plane he asked Mac if he had shot down any enemy fighters on their missions so far.

'Yeah, Lieutenant, we've done five missions and I know we knocked down a couple of krauts on the second. It's not always easy to tell, when you're in tight formation with everyone shooting in all directions.' He grinned and made a circle of his thumb and finger. 'But that time we were lagging and no one else was in range, and we socked two 109s, OK. One a flamer; the other guy got out.'

Dressed in full American Air Force gear, except flak jacket, and already feeling as if he had been transferred to a different world, Raymond now waited with the others for the arrival of the Captain. Glen Mackenzie offered him some gum. 'Keeps the eardrums clear,' he recommended.

As they stood around talking, Raymond found himself being shown cherished photographs of American families posed in front of clapperboard houses, or photographs of pretty girls standing selfconsciously for the camera — underlining the reality that these men had been dragged from comfortable civilian life thousands of miles to participate in a war that must seem nothing to do with them, and with great risk of injury and death.

The tail gunner called out, 'Here comes the boss-man,' and a jeep with Bill Strang driving turned fast off the perimeter track into the blast bay where 'Grable's Legs' was parked. He jumped out before the jeep stopped moving, leaving it to run on until it gently nudged some sand-bags.

'Engines in five minutes, men,' he announced. 'Stow your-selves aboard.' Like the rest of them, the Captain was wearing a standard-issue one-piece flying suit, belted round the waist, a leather helmet, goggles and combined R/T mouthpiece and oxygen mask — though they could not need oxygen on this relatively low-level exercise. Gauntlets, zip-up fur-lined leather boots and body webbing straps for the clip-on parachute completed the outfit.

Strang turned to Raymond. 'The first thing you and your dog must learn is how to get into this crate.'

The bombardier, Jim Watson, took over and explained to Raymond that it was easier to get out ('Thank God!') of a B-17 than get in, unless you were the ball gunner. He pointed to an open hatch under the plane's belly, and over six feet off the ground. 'Mike,' he called to a gunner, 'show the Englishman the cupid's leap.'

This was accomplished by two men hoisting a third until his head and shoulders were above the level of the bomber's floor, when he could get leverage from the lip of the hatch to haul himself in — the last men being pulled up from above like sacks of coal.

The inside of the B-17's ribbed interior at first seemed vast, but by the time the crew of ten were accommodated there was not much room for moving around, and even without any load in the bomb-bay amidships, or the ammunition for the guns, there was a tremendous amount of clobber about, from radio and navigational equipment to oxygen bottles for all the crew and elaborate first-aid equipment.

Raymond was asked to take a seat between and slightly behind pilot and co-pilot for take-off, and from here he got a good and remarkably high view of the whole Group assembling for take-off, as well as the pilot, Bill Strang, and the co-pilot, Lieutenant 'Stuff' Musoski, at work. A Typhoon's cockpit appeared simple by contrast with this four engine Boeing's, and Raymond watched with interest as the two men went through the pre-flight checklist and the co-pilot primed and started each engine in turn, warming them up at 1,000 rpm, checking the prop feathering, the magnetos and turbos.

The first bombers in the Group were already taxi-ing past, and as soon as Bill Strang spotted K-King, the letter painted white on black on the tail, the co-pilot released the parking brake and unlocked the tail wheel lock control on the floor of the cockpit. Then, with the inboard engines idling at 800 rpm, Bill Strang opened the outer engine throttles and used them to control the direction of his plane.

A green Very was fired from the jeep parked alongside the runway while they were in the queue on the perimeter track, and Raymond saw the Group leader's plane starting to move forward from the end of the runway. Thirty seconds later, as the B-17 lifted off the ground halfway along the 4,400 feet runway, the second plane took its place, and in turn its big wheels began to rotate.

A few minutes later it was their own turn. Stuff Musoski gave the thumbs-up sign to his captain, who at once eased forward the four throttles through their quadrant; the props became four blurs, and the thunder of the engines filled the cockpit. Musoski, Raymond noticed, watched the engine instruments until maximum power was reached; then he took over the throttles from his captain, who kept the big bomber dead-centre on the runway, and pulled back on the wheel when the ASI showed 115 mph. As they skimmed over the hedge at the end of the runway, Bill Strang called out on the intercom, 'Gear up', at the same time confirming by hand signal that the undercart should be raised. Musoski then touched the brake pedal to stop the wheels spinning, before operating the hydraulic lever. As soon as the undercart had clunked home, and Bill Strang had eased back the throttles to give them a steady climbing speed of 140 mph, Raymond felt them both relax, and the rest of the crew felt free to use the intercom if they had anything to say. Raymond released Bonz so that he could wander freely about the plane, taking a look in turn through every aperture — from the bombardier's in the nose to the gunner's cramped quarters at the extreme tail end of the bomber.

'Hey, Englishman,' the tail gunner called out a few minutes later, 'your dog kinda likes it in here with me.'

While the B-17 continued to climb towards the Group's assembly area and buncher beacon, Raymond unhooked his R/T and made his way down the bomber, squeezing past the waist gunners sitting by their big .5 machine-guns, round the retracted tail wheel housing, until he was crawling under the bomber's huge fin. The tail gunner was sitting on a seat like a bicycle's saddle, with a marvellous wide-open view beyond the twin barrels of his guns. Bonz, who clearly favoured this position for its view, was sitting on the lap of the gunner, who turned and grinned when he saw Raymond crouched beside him.

'What's it like with a 109 coming in from dead astern at 350 mph?' Raymond shouted.

'I guess there's no time to think. All you know is he's probably as shit scared as you are.'

It took almost an hour for the twenty-one aircraft of the Group to assemble over an area north of the London balloon barrage. Raymond settled back in his position behind the cockpit and plugged in his R/T again to hear the Group leader giving his orders to form up in seven Vs — or vics — of three. 'Pull in there tighter, Charlie,' he heard him say. 'Paul, you're lagging back there. Sitting duck when the krauts come down from 12 o'clock.' Then, 'Let's have it all tight and hunky-dory, you Knights of the one hundred Nights!'

Once settled in their battle formation of two groups of six aircraft, and one of nine, all covering one another with the potential cross-fire from over two hundred guns, 100 Group made an awesome spectacle as it flew serenely across the English countryside at eight thousand feet, each plane rising and falling independently by no more than a few feet, but maintaining strict station. If one plane fell back a little, it soon pulled up again, and only a couple of times did the Group leader have to rebuke a pilot for slipping out too far from his formation position. Bill Strang's eyes were constantly switching from the plane ahead and above to those on either side, his right hand always easing the four throttles to and fro with the delicacy of a surgeon.

The Group crossed out over the Wash into the North Sea, then after fifteen more minutes turned through 170 degrees to head back to base. Far below, through broken cloud, Raymond could make out one airfield after another scattered like fallen leaves over the green landscape of East Anglia — North Creake to the left, Alconbury and Docking under the right wing, Sculthorpe and West Raynham, Swanton Morley and Wendling with a scattering of Liberator B-24s, Shipdham, the familiar configuration of Watton, at present being taken over by the Americans from the RAF; and finally, Thorpe Abbotts came into sight ahead, the newly completed runways of Tibenham just north of the village of Diss.

Now, under orders from the Group leader, the formations began to break up and form independent line ahead for landing. Twenty minutes later, *Grable's Legs* was eased carefully back into her blast bay, Bill Strang turned her through 180 degrees with her starboard engines, Stuff Musoski threw up the switches, and a soothing silence filled the B-17's cabin.

The Captain unstrapped himself and turned in his seat. 'Well, Ray, what do you make of that?'

'Very impressive. I wish I could teach my boys to fly formation like that.'

'It's more difficult when the flak's popping around and the krauts are coming in from every goddamn point of the compass.'

The hatch was opened and Raymond and Bonz followed the two pilots through and down onto the tarmac.

'When are we going to see that?' he asked.

'You won't have to wait long.'

In the event, Raymond and the senior officers and squadron-commanders of 100 Group had to wait just three hours between landing from their formation exercise and the initial briefing for an operation the next day.

The Group Intelligence Officer and the Group Commander officiated at this briefing in the Intelligence Office at 5 pm. From talk he had overheard among other officers Raymond was not surprised when the Colonel, sitting informally behind a large table, began, 'This is the big one, gentlemen. Tomorrow we're going into the heart of Germany, to a target I guess the men are going to relish.'

The GIO unrolled a large map covering southern England and northern and central Europe, pinning down the corners. On it a line had been drawn across the North Sea, across the southern tip of Holland, across Belgium, into Germany south of Cologne, then south of Frankfurt and deep into Bavaria, where the target was ringed and the name Regensburg was heavily underlined in red. An arc cutting across the route just south of Liège showed the pathetically short limit of the range of fighter cover.

There was absolute silence in the office until someone scraped a match to light his cigar. Another officer muttered, 'Christ!'

The Colonel finally asked, in a conversational tone, 'Do you know what they do at Regensburg?'

'It had better be important, sir,' said Bill Strang amidst some forced laughter.

'They make goddamn Messerschmitt 109s — that's what they do. And we're going to level that plant tomorrow afternoon.'

Raymond glanced at the faces of the officers around him. Two were smoking cigars, two more were chewing gum, and all of them stared at the map expressionlessly. But it was not the cigar smoke that Raymond could smell. It was a smell he was familiar with — one he had often smelt as men slipped on their Mae Wests before a shipping strike or other critical ops. It was the smell of fear, as from dogs before a scrap.

'Colonel,' asked one of the squadron-commanders, 'on the rash assumption that one or two of us get there, which way do we come home?'

'You don't,' rapped the Colonel — and, before he could go on, the same officer said, 'You ain't kidding, sir.'

Ignoring him the Colonel indicated a short dark line, almost invisible, pointing south from the target. 'You go to Africa. So pack your suntan oil and swimsuits.'

So — Africa, Raymond was thinking. Holiday in the sun.

Every officer in the room knew that the big one was coming up. The coming and going of senior officers from HQ, the build-up of cypher traffic, the frequency of exercises like the one that morning, the intangible threat that hung in the air — all these factors had built up until they pointed irrevocably to 'a big one'. Inevitably, they had believed Berlin would be 'the big one' — at some time — and the place was mentioned often during the long hours leading to every major briefing: Berlin, the most heavily defended of all cities, 550 miles distant — and most of them without fighter escort.

But a one-way ticket to Regensburg: that had never been considered during all the hours and hours of speculation about future targets. 'You can't be serious, sir?' repeated one of the squadron-commanders.

'No, it's 8th's big joke,' said a captain who was sitting, legs wide apart, on a reversed chair. His cigar now looked as if he had tried to eat it for breakfast.

The Colonel still ignored both remarks and continued with the briefing. Primary target: Messerschmitt factory at Regensburg, which makes two to three hundred 109s a month, thirty per cent of the total output. Secondary target: FW-190 engine plant at Munich. Last-resort target: centre of the city of Munich. There will be seven bomb groups on the operation. Another twelve bomb groups will be going to the ball-bearing plant at Schweinfurt 'right there.' and *they'll* be coming back to England. So the krauts' defence will be divided, and there'll be more diversions and bombing of German fighter airfields. The route had been picked to avoid the worst of flak batteries.

The Colonel listed them, and the number of guns, concluding with Italy — 'Seventy-five heavy guns at La Spezia, thirty at Bolzano ...' The mere mention of these places in southern Europe added an air of total unreality to the proceedings, but the men were all listening alertly now, scribbling notes.

'If you're forced down near the target, head for Switzerland — and be sure to say you're escapees not evaders, otherwise the Swiss will lock you away under international law. If you're forced down over Italy, hide up until Italy surrenders. And, if possible, surrender to Italians and not Germans. They'll ship you back to Germany, and you won't get away from there.'

And that was it. The GIO read out the timetable and then pinned it on the board: *Breakfast* 2.00 am, *Briefing* 3.00 am, *Stations* 5.00 am, *Alert* 5.25 am, *Taxi out* 5.35 am, *Take-off* 5.50 am.

As if still not believing what they had just heard, 100th Group's senior officers hung about in the Intelligence Office, staring first at the map, then at the timetable, then, like sentenced criminals, at each other. Raymond found himself standing beside Bill Strang, who repeatedly whispered to himself the timetable details, as if memorising them. Then he turned his bright blue eyes on Raymond and uttered one word: 'Horseshit!' Slowly he pulled out his pack of Camels and flicked one for Raymond. 'Gee, Englishman you don't want to come on *this* one, for Christ's sake.' His mouth was set in a sideways smile that was not generous on mirth.

Raymond took the cigarette and lit for both of them. 'Well, Bill, you don't really suppose I could skip this because it's a dodgy do, even if I wanted to? Anyway, I've always wanted to see Tunisia.'

By 9 pm the officers' mess at Thorpe Abbotts was empty. Raymond lay on his bed smoking a last cigarette, staring at the corrugated roof of the nissen hut in which he had been assigned a bunk. He was feeling apprehensive, he could not deny it. But it was apprehension about being involved in a scrap solely as an observer, and having nothing to fight with. He had been given a camera to take photographs and he had a notebook. He knew it was more likely he would be using the first of these.

Before he drifted into sleep he recalled Louise's expression of dismay at the news that he was off to join 100 Bomb Group. Could she have known in advance about this Rogensburg raid? Yes, he was damn sure she did. But, then, it was her business to know — just as it was *not* Jack Boland's business to know.

It was pitch dark when Raymond emerged from the hut, freshly washed and shaved and carrying his flying gear, but he could feel the dampness in the air and knew from long experience that mist and low cloud hung over the airfield. The 8th Air Force's biggest ever raid was due to be postponed or cancelled, of that he was sure.

To the sound of several testing engines from distant dispersals, he walked to the officers' mess, barely feeling his way by the dim lighting. He was not hungry at this unnatural hour, but he knew it would be a long time before they had their next proper meal, so, like the others, he ordered two fried eggs and bacon from the cooks behind the ranges — no food shortages for these Americans. There were forty or fifty officers at the tables, a subdued crowd intent on eating rather than talking, and mostly sitting with their fellow crewmen.

But Jim Watson called out cheerfully, 'Come and sit here, Englishman. I guess you don't get up this early in Fighter Command. Now you know how *we* suffer, even before we start.'

Raymond sat down with his plate and poured himself coffee. 'Have you heard the met. forecast?' he asked Bill Strang.

'Yeah. It's lousy. But we'll have the full briefing — want to come?'

There was an officer standing under the shaded lamp which identified the entrance to the briefing tent, with a big box of cigars on a table beside him. 'Good luck!'. . . 'Give 'em hell!'. . . 'Shoot straight!' — dishing out these exhortations with the cigars to every man who passed.

'They all know what that means,' Bill Strang muttered to Raymond.

Inside, the big tent was packed with some two hundred officers and NCOs, their cigar smoke rising like grey cumulo-nimbus clouds towards the naked lights hanging from the top — reminding Raymond of the first circus May had taken him to outside Bath, with its rough, ribald audience.

But there was only one item on this programme, and it was a show-stopper. In front of them all was a big screen covered by a curtain. The Colonel then stood on a platform, holding up his arms and calling for silence. 'OK, men, listen to this. And listen hard — because your lives may depend on your memory.' He turned to the GIO. 'Right, Jack, let them have it.'

An orderly pulled the curtain aside, revealing the map, twelve feet by ten feet, but like no other map they had seen before. There was a stunned silence as two hundred pairs of eyes stared unbelievingly at a map comprising the whole of central and southern Europe, the central Mediterranean, and the coast of North Africa.

Then the hubbub broke out — protest, disbelief, outrage, rebellion. And all expressed amid a hailstorm of curses. It took a full five minutes for the shouting to die down, and it would have been longer if their curiosity had not been aroused when the CIO began pointing at the numerous subsidiary lines drawn on the map, including those to German fighter airfields and the long, lone one to Schweinfurt, while he mouthed his briefing in detail.

At last it was quiet, and the Colonel and the GIO repeated the briefing they had already given to the senior officers. The rallying speech from the Colonel at the end — 'and just you remember, men, that every goddamn bomb we drop on that plant means fewer 109s to attack us in the future' — seemed to inspire them with some confidence, and with less concern for the dangers of this operation.

After that they all had too much to do, and no time to worry and complain. The gunners hurried to the armoury to draw their ammunition, as always trying to grab more of the long belts of .5-inch bullets than their entitlement according to the load capacity of the B-17 . . . the navigators to their charts . . . the bombardiers to a special briefing which Raymond also attended.

Photographs taken by high-flying PRU Mosquitoes showed the town of Regensburg nestling in a big loop of the River

Danube, with the scattered Messerschmitt factory to the east, and adjoining a large sports arena. If met. was correct and it would be clear all the way all day, then the location of the target was a piece of cake. But other aspects of the operation, Raymond reflected, might not prove so edible . . .

Down at the dispersal the air still smelt of low cloud and mist, and in the dimmest light of early dawn you were aware that visibility could not be more than a hundred yards. Jim Watson was supervising the fusing of the bombs by the armament sergeant. Suddenly the hooded lights of the jeep driven by Bill Strang sprang out of the gloom like the eyes of a tiger.

They had been sitting around on their parachute packs, exchanging wisecracks and licentious stories, chewing gum and smoking. Now they got to their feet as their Captain drew up beside them. Strang did not even bother to get out. 'Postponement,' he called to them as if it was an invective. 'One hour, maybe two.'

Hey, sir,' the navigator protested, 'It'll be dark when we get to Africa.'

'Good thinking, Glen. That's why it'll be two hours or nothing. Climb in and we'll have another breakfast.'

The bacon and eggs tasted better second time around. Raymond noticed that his fellow officers ate slowly, as if drawing out the minutes.

Once Jim Watson went to the window and drew aside the blackout curtain. He returned to the table grinning. 'Still thick as a nun's hood,' he told them.

Chapter Ten

ON 14 JANUARY 1940, early on one of the coldest mornings Raymond could remember, he had taxied the Tiger Moth towards the watch office, thinking with relief that the lesson was over, he would soon be able to beat some life into his frozen limbs and get a mug of tea from the NAAFI van. Instead, his instructor in front told him through the Gosport tube to stay where he was and not switch off. Then he got out, re-clipped the straps that had been securing him and walked away, waving his right arm to indicate that Raymond should turn and take-off.

The action took him entirely by surprise. He had not yet completed seven hours' instruction dual, and although two cadets on his course had already soloed, he did not feel he was yet ready for it.

Taking off had never worried him. The little Moth would bounce about a little on the grass, then her tail would come up at about 30 mph and she would lift herself off the ground a few seconds later, pleased to be airborne and doing it all herself.

But, Raymond had to admit, the absence of a head and pair of shoulders in the cockpit before him was slightly alarming confirmation of his aloneness. Now, he told himself, he was the sole arbiter of his fate, like that juvenile eagle he had seen on a flickering nature film at school, launching itself into space from its nest for the first time.

At five hundred feet he had levelled off and felt again the bitterly cold wind biting through his layers of flying gear. Bank and rudder left, then left again, the grass patch of the aerodrome appearing disquietingly small. When the right lower wing revealed a farmhouse, he knew it was time to turn again, and then once more for the final approach.

He could see another Moth taking off, and there was another close behind. Oh, the humiliation if he was forced to go round again! He was too high. No — he was too low. Should he open the throttle? He had been taught how to sideslip to lose height, but he certainly wasn't going to try *that* on his first solo, thank you.

The little engine was ticking over nicely, the prop just turning, as he let the Moth take him down in a steady glide, a touch of rudder to keep him into wind. Back on the stick, back, hold it, the snow-flecked grass whipping past ten feet below. Would she never stall?

Then with a sickening thump he was down, and he would have been thrown out of the cockpit if the straps were not tight . . . But he was down and taxi-ing.

His instructor did not appear until he had switched off. Then he sauntered out, very casually, and nodded. 'Not bad — not very good either. But you'll do.'

Later, in the privacy of the public phone-box, Raymond told May that he had just soloed. He could hear her rich laugh. 'There's my intrepid birdman! Well done, my darling.'

He sneaked out, looking to right and left as if he had committed some crime. But almost at once he felt a slight swagger taking over his step. He was a pilot now, wasn't he?

Grable's Legs nudged her nose into the cloud at two thousand feet. There was a brief moment when you could see the fields below intermittently through flecks of fleece. Then they were wrapped up and cocooned, the interior of the bomber's cabin a world private to eleven men, the sound of the labouring engines signifying their only means of escape.

It took an effort to accept that almost two hundred more of their kind were also groping their way upwards like blind men seeking the salvation of vision — and it needed only a glancing blow to topple any of them into eternity.

This was, they had been told, a risk that had to be taken. The cloud was not thick, and irrevocably the complex machinery of the biggest daylight air operation ever was already in motion — with feinted blows and diversions, fighter cover and dive-bombing attacks en route ...

So, ninety minutes after their scheduled time, 100 Group had taken off, every officer and man, every captain and bombardier, every radio-operator, navigator and gunner all nerve-strung for the ten-hour-long flight across a hostile continent and two seas.

They were out of cloud again at just above four thousand feet, suddenly into a brilliant, white, sun-drenched world. On every side, at distances from a half-mile to five miles, B-17s could be seen emerging, bringing friendly life to the emptiness, like the cast of an opera leaving the wings and filling the stage for the first act.

There was a majesty and grace about the assembly of the Regensburg force high above the cloud, over the unseen English countryside. Laboriously, almost one hundred and fifty B-17s gained altitude, and at the same time manoeuvred themselves into their tight formation patterns at between seventeen thousand and twenty thousand feet: the 94th Bomb Group from Bury St Edmunds, the 385th from Great Ashfield, the 95th from Horsham, the 390th from Framlingham, and 388th from Knettishall, the 96th from Snetterton Heath, and, taking up the rearmost position in the low group (notoriously the most dangerous), the 100th.

Raymond had never met the 4th Bombardment Wing's Commanding Officer, Colonel Curtis LeMay, but in his short time with 100 Group he had often heard talk about 'Old Ironpants'. He was apparently very tough, dedicated and ruthless, with an unsmiling demeanour and, as one of the first senior officers to arrive in Europe, unsurpassed in experience of heavy daylight bombing.

By 9.20 am the entire Regensburg Wing was at operational height and in operational formation, seven groups in twin line ahead, high groups to the right and low groups to the left, with LeMay's lead group in the van and tucked in between. Raymond took photographs with the Leica he had been lent for the occasion, from the starboard waist gunner's aperture and the upper gunner's turret, using a small mobile oxygen bottle when he moved about the aircraft. *Grable's Legs* was in an ideal position, almost at the tail end of the lowest squadron of the Group, the entire armada stretching ahead and above in tight formation.

As they crossed the coast at Lowestoft like a giant skein of migrating geese, the cloud disappeared, leaving clear blue skies and unlimited visibility across the North Sea. As met. had forecast, it would be ideal bombing weather, though nothing was said about it being ideal fighter weather, too.

With a strong following wind bowling the Wing along at over 200 mph, it took a mere twenty-five minutes to span the North Sea. Far below, but crystal clear as if seen through reversed binoculars, were four familiar islands set among the complex winding arteries of the Dutch rivers. In another ten minutes the leading group was already over mainland Holland. Raymond settled himself in his old place just behind Bill Strang and 'Stuff' Musoski and plugged in the intercom just as Strang was alerting his crew: 'Test your guns, men. Expect bogies any minute now. But don't forget our little friends should be around, too.'

Sergeant Mike O'Donnell in the belly turret called out, 'Flak 3 o'clock below.'

By craning his neck, Raymond could see the black blobs staining the sky like spattered ink. Not very menacing. The bomber shuddered as one gunner after another fired off a few test rounds.

'Fighters one o'clock high.'

Yes, there they were, four of them, closing in at the unnatural speed of oncoming aircraft. But these were no threat. Quite the reverse. Raymond at once recognised the fat configuration of Thunderbolts.

'OK — little friends,' Musoski called out.

The Wing had been five minutes late at the rendezvous with their escort, which had doubled back on its course. More groups of fighters appeared, some dropping their tanks as they swept past, dividing into two groups some three thousand feet above and close in on each flank, weaving to stay with the much slower bombers.

The great city of Antwerp was below, flanking the winding Scheldt, the biggest port in Europe in peacetime, now with a mere scattering of ships like matchsticks at the wharves. The flak was heavier now and the groups began weaving and losing and gaining height. It was heavier still over the airfield at Woensdrecht, but no bomber appeared to be seriously hit and the formation remained tight.

'Where're the krauts?' Glen Mackenzie asked from his waist gun position.

'Don't ask stupid questions,' rebuked the skipper. 'Just keep looking.'

To Raymond the escort seemed very thin, and the most he ever counted was seventeen P-47s. Some of these high up to the right appeared to be drawn away, and he caught a distant glimpse of wildly manoeuvring fighters in a dogfight. A few minutes later, with awful inevitability, a group of Focke-Wulf 190s came out of the blinding sun, banked to the right, and came in head-on at the leading bombers of 94th Group.

Raymond darted to the radio-operator's window and tried to photograph them as they flashed towards the B-17s ahead and above to the right, but the distance was too great. The tracer from the bombers' forward gun positions streaked out to meet the 109s like firemens' hosewater. The fighters, apparently unharmed, raced through the formation, some of them inverted and all of them miraculously missing head-on collision.

It was the 94th and 95th Groups that took this first attack, and the fighters left two of the bombers with smoking engines, while the end B-17 of 94th Group took a dead-eye burst of cannon fire right in the nose. The effect was devastating. The bomber bucked, and then buckled like a misused toy, the whole tail section coming adrift. As the awful wreckage passed by and fell below, four bodies fell out in turn, and — as Raymond counted — one, two, three, four parachutes opened. But that was all. The fore part of the bomber fell fast, diminishing in size until it became invisible against the farming landscape three and a half miles below. And then suddenly, by now far astern, it reappeared — but only as the yellow and red centre of a shockwave from its exploding bombs, fuel and oxygen.

Two or three minutes later Bill Strang warned, 'Twelve o'clock high — it's our turn now!'

Raymond slipped under the cockpit and, bent double, eased his way forward to the nose. Jim Watson was operating the chin turret guns; the radio-operator and navigator the two single .5s. Raymond kept clear, but from the navigator's table had a clear view forward and above, which allowed him to photograph the first *Schwärme* as they raced towards them. The nose guns opened fire on the 109s while they were no more than dots, hoping that their tracer would throw them off their line. Then Jim Watson joined in, his two .5s making a thunderous clatter, spent shell-cases flying about like shrapnel and rattling onto the floor of the nose.

The 109s concentrated on the lead planes, sweeping up after their pass at breathtaking speeds, or slicing straight through the tight formation, somehow avoiding a collision. Raymond caught no more than a glimpse of mottle-brown camouflaged fuselage and wings, a black cross, a yellow spinner, and then they were all gone. One of the bombers in the leading squadron was smoking from an engine, but it kept in formation for the time being, and another was yawing as if with aileron trouble.

Seconds later a second and then a third *Schwarm* concentrated on 100 Group. This time one of the 109s blew up and swept through the entire formation, the whole plane alight, like a comet. One of the gunners shouted, 'Chr-r-i-st! Let's have more like that . . .'

But, for the present, that was all. Suddenly they were surrounded by P-47s, the relieving 56th Fighter Group, who were taking over to the end of fighter range. The nearest squadron carried the 'LM' of the 62nd Squadron on their fuselage, but somewhere out there, almost for sure, would be Charlie Dee, and Raymond felt strangely comforted by this.

The savage German answer to this relief from fighter attack was a sudden intensification of flak, heavy 88 mm stuff that got the range with amazing speed. Raymond photographed the blackened sky about them, holding tight with one hand as the bomber was thrown about the sky, and Bill Strang jinked evasively.

Raymond had the camera on one of 100 Group's element leaders immediately ahead, and clicked the shutter just as it received a direct hit on the port wing. The bomber lurched up as if struck by a giant invisible fist, then fell away to the left, passing terrifyingly close and revealing the name *Alice from Dallas*. The port wing's fuel tanks were blazing, but the pilot still seemed to have some sort of control because *Alice from Dallas*, after completing a left turn, suddenly banked in the opposite direction and appeared to be attempting to regain her position in the formation. But now the fire had spread, reaching the fuselage and starting to run along the length of the plane, just as the B-17 was closing back to her squadron.

But the squadron did not want her. This beserk bomber was like some maniac, a terrifying threat to all of them. The two nearest bombers flinched away; another shot up as if hit by flak in order to avoid her. The B-17 was yawing about more and more convulsively and, at last, falling away. Raymond got one photograph of her before she disappeared below, with the crew bailing out like shot-away fragments of their own stricken machine.

It was past noon and the sun was at 2 o'clock, a dazzling furnace without heat at this height, from which, like sparks from a fire, the enemy fighters would inevitably spring. But not yet, not just yet. The last of the Thunderbolts had left for home, rocking wings in regretful farewell. The flak had faded astern, too, and not a German fighter was in the sky, though evidence of the ferocity of the fight could still be seen far behind: fires from fallen bombers, smoke rising high, funeral pyres to the dead American airmen spread across Germany, miles below, one here, another there, a particularly big and black fire where a hayfield had also been set alight.

The surviving B-17s had closed the gaps, filling in to keep the pattern secure. And 100 Group alone had already lost three aircraft, and two more were trailing and surely doomed.

Below, the flat plains of northern Germany and then the Rhine valley had changed to the severe contours of the Eifel mountains, the roads winding, the villages nestling amid valleys and forests. Raymond could imagine the puzzlement of the Luftwaffe and High Command at this unprecedentedly deep penetration, the scarcely deviating line of the armada. The range of the B-17 was well known. *How could they get back?* the Germans must be asking. Should the *Geschwader* in northern Germany, the Low Countries and north-east France be preparing to attack them on the way home? Yet, already another force, even bigger than this one, had been reported over the North Sea and heading for the Fatherland.

There was a spirit of optimism in *Grable's Legs* now, as no doubt in many other planes. They had fooled the Germans, they had been told there was little in the way of defences at Regensburg, and after the target — well, it was little more than consuming gas — on to North Africa.

'How're things back there?' Raymond heard Bill Strang call the tail gunner.

'Quiet as the goddamn grave, skip.'

'OK for ammunition?'

'Sure. About three hundred rounds left.'

The other gunners reported the state of their ammunition. 'Not that we'll need it now — except for potting at Mussolini as we pass,' Mike O'Donnell cracked.

'Don't you be too damn sure. We've got a long way to go yet,' Strang warned. 'So keep your eyes open.'

The massive 4th Bombardment Wing continued implacably on its course, the German hills and valleys and villages rolling below. Still not a fleck of cloud. And only when you took off your gauntlet's were you aware of how cold it was up here, and how thin the air when you switched off oxygen to relieve yourself or grab a sandwich.

Raymond was eating one of these when he saw the radio operator turn in his seat and switch to intercom. 'Wing Leader reports bogies coming up, sir.'

'I can see them — Christ, the whole Luftwaffe,' the ball gunner said.

From Raymond's position he could see nothing, until pressing against the radio operator's window he caught a glimpse of 109s spiralling up, fast, difficult to spot against the forest land at first, but growing in size all the time.

Raymond made his way down the fuselage, where the gunners were preparing for the new assault, spinning their guns on their swivels, checking the free run of the ammunition belts, pulling down their smoked-glass goggles — the top gunner with his head in his perspex turret; the radio-operator with his rearward-firing single; the ball gunner sunk beneath the fuselage in his cramped private world, spinning his inverted turret; and the two waist gunners at their windows almost back to back, clutching the butt handles of their .5s like two duellists.

Raymond settled himself on an ammunition box behind the starboard waist gunner, Staff-Sergeant Gus Melini, a thin, olive-complexioned, neat little man from Chicago who had shared a beer with Raymond after the previous day's exercise. There was no socket for Raymond's R/T and, instead, Raymond tapped him on the shoulder and indicated he would not obstruct his movements. The sergeant gave the thumbs-up.

The whole crew, the whole Squadron, the Group, the Wing — everyone knew with absolute certainty that the attack would come from the right — dead out of the sun. Even the timing was predictable within one minute. Every gun that could be brought to bear, including Melini's, was already steadied on that blinding orb — some fifteen hundred machine-guns poised to blast off a million and a half rounds a minute, twenty-five thousand a second, at targets travelling at a relative speed of 600 mph.

'Three o'clock high.' The skipper might have been intoning the number of the next psalm in church. But the congregation murmured not a word. The bomber's music droned on, a one-note funereal background. Raymond glanced down at the open box of bullets, linked neatly like greasy frankfurters ready for the eating. Then his gaze turned to the rear of Melini's head, leather helmet close to the fore sight of the gun's long stock, and barrel waving easily to and fro, to and fro, on its swivel as the gunner searched the dazzling sky.

And there they were, in *Schwärme*, four in close line abreast, then another four above, another four behind to the left, another behind to the right, a hard seasoned bunch, Raymond recognised. They came down first on the 390th, the lead high group on the right. It was much too far to photograph, but Raymond could see the first 109s concentrate on the right squadron, at once setting on fire the number three in the first element. Then the fighters swept past under 94 Group and 95 Group, some of them upside-down though still keeping loose formation.

Melini followed them round with his gun but they were way out of range, sweeping up again at an incredible speed, turning to gain height for another pass. But already a fresh bunch were coming in, free now of defending fighter intervention and the need to cover each other's tail. Raymond could not see them for Melini's crouched figure, but suddenly *Grable's Legs* was vibrating from the fire from every one of her guns, the cacophony silencing the sound of the engines and the clatter of thousands of empty cases as they began piling up around every gunner.

It was all Raymond could do to keep on his feet, one hand clutching a fuselage frame, the other the camera. The idea of using the camera had become ridiculous. The two waist gunners were moving from side to side, swinging their guns and giving short bursts at flashing targets that offered no more than a brown-grey blur and black cross ... though one was slower, much slower, and trailed a line of smoke like a faltering rocket. When their own fire momentarily ceased, with no target in range, they could hear a new, uncanny sound like hailstones beating on a tin roof — metal hailstones, spent shells and shell cases from the hundreds of guns filling this sub-stratosphere sky with hate and defiance.

What the hell am I doing here? Raymond asked himself. What could he report at the end of it all? Except that life is pretty good hell in a B-17 under attack. If only he had something to do!

He started to crawl back towards the tail gunner. He was sitting in his little perspex booth, knee deep in spent shells, swinging his twin .5s in search of a target. He noticed Raymond out of the corner of his eye, raised a hand from his gun in a gesture of greeting, then reopened fire, following a plummeting 109 as it spiralled down, seemingly untouched. Then the bomber gave a huge lurch, which threw Raymond hard against the side of the plane.

He squeezed his way back to the waist gunners, aware through all the thicknesses of his flying kit of a new low level of cold, and feeling a blast of icy wind against his face. Then he saw the hole in the left side of the fuselage just forward of Glen Mackenzie's station. The metal had been punched asunder like a badly opened can, leaving a three-feet hole with jagged edges. There was a smaller hole, at an angle and rearward of Melini's station. Between them Mackenzie lay dead, his head half blown off by the blast of a rocket. He was stretched awkwardly across his shell cases, his blood spreading among them. The big pivoted gun was swinging from side to side in the gale.

Melini, a few feet away, had either not seen or was too preoccupied with survival and the battle. And there was still plenty to shoot at. *Grable's Legs* had been hit in the port outer engine, which was streaming vapour, and they had fallen out of formation. Strang had feathered the prop — and to German fighters a B-17 with a feathered prop was like a small boy to school bullies. Raymond pulled Mackenzie's body aside, plugged in the R/T and seized the handles of the gun.

The steady voice of the skipper was calling out the attacking positions of the 109s: 'Ten o'clock high ... two o'clock low ... two at 12 o'clock, coming in NOW!'

The continuous rattle of the guns was ear-splitting, and as soon as Raymond could line up the open sights of the .5 he recognised how the vibration was an added handicap to accurate shooting. But then he spotted the two o'clock low 109 coming in, spinner and wing leading edges sparkling with cannon and machine-gun fire. Ball turret and upper turret were already pouring in steady lines of tracer, and now Raymond, activating the trigger, added his contribution, following the line of the banking fighter with deflection shooting that was not bad for first time.

He could not take any credit for it — or maybe he made a modest contribution — but the combined fire was too much for the 109, which suddenly shot up like a kicked dog and began streaming smoke.

'Get down, you bastard!' someone called out. And the Messerschmitt obeyed, turning over on its back and dropping. As it fell astern a blast of flame broke from the stricken machine, and at the same instant a dark shape like a foetus detached itself from the craft, assuming human form only when the pilot streamed his parachute. It opened like a white flower and sent him swinging gently down towards the earth three miles below ...

There were a couple of twin engine 110s among their tormentors. Raymond spotted them far out of range and transmitted a warning: '9 o'clock high. Two twins. Probably more rocket carriers.'

Bill Strang came back, 'Where are you, Englishman?'

'Left waist gun, skipper. Mike's had it and I've taken over.'

'Nothing we can do?'

'Not a thing. He's really dead.'

'Poor bastard.'

The radio-operator broke in, 'They're coming, Bill.'

Raymond saw the 110s banking steeply about a mile away and closing in on them, isolated and still falling behind the main formation. Far beyond the range of machine-gun or even cannon fire, the big fighters launched their rockets, each streaming a tail of smoke. Bill Strang at once dropped the plane with a lurch, which sent Raymond and Melini sprawling, first into the air and then half onto the pile of cases on the floor and half onto Mike's sprawled corpse. *Grable's Legs* was shaken again several times as the rockets exploded above, and for several seconds the plane was out of control.

Once straight and level again, there was another head-on attack. Raymond swung his gun round to the limit but could not bring it to bear. He caught the sound of a few expletives, and then once again the fuselage of the bomber thundered to the sound and shook with the multiple recoil of the guns. A more violent kick told of more hits. The 109 shot past under their belly, pursued by streams of tracer. Raymond got in a short burst but his gun stopped with his fingers still on the trigger, the drum empty.

The plane yawed and steadied. They were still flying. How? Raymond wondered, and as he steadied himself, and began to feed in another length of .5 belt, he suddenly caught a mental picture of Louise.

Why think about her now? he asked himself. Get on with your job. He had watched Melini reload, and now Melini himself swung round and checked that Raymond was doing it right. But Louise was still there, grey eyes watching him with tender concern. A dying man is supposed to relive his life in his last seconds. *And all I'm doing is looking at the face of the woman I love.* She would be in the Intelligence Office at Stiplowe, surrounded by clattering teletypes, taking in and recording reports from 382 Fighter Group, which would be almost home, and from Colonel LeMay of the 4th Bombardment Wing. Louise would be the first to hear of the casualties: how many had survived, how many had turned back, how many had littered the countryside with their fragments. Raymond sent her a silent message — *OK — we're OK, my darling, or most of us are. We're half an hour from the target, and the attacks have stopped.*

And so they had. It would not be because of the defence they had put up, nor the casualties the fighters had suffered. They were so far from the usual targets, so deep into Germany, that they had left behind the main fighter bases. And the 4th Bombardment Wing would not be returning this way — by God, it wouldn't!

Raymond locked the gun and called out to Bill Strang, 'There's a hole you could walk through back here, skipper. And it's colder than the North Pole.'

Bill Strang ordered Melini and the tail gunner forward, and Raymond pulled Mackenzie's body out of the blast of icy air and then stripped off his outer leather jacket, revealing the flak suit that had failed to save his life. The head was a terrible sight.

Raymond knew that he could do no more ... Then he decided that he must and could. So he took the jacket and placed it over the ruin of a face, and tucked it under the shoulders of the little red-head whose head was no more — or almost no more.

There was worse to come. Melini and he were working their way forward when Melini paused by the hatch to the ball turret. Raymond realised he was checking that Mike O'Donnell was OK. Melini began to crank round the turret until the exit was facing the inside of the plane. Raymond and he both looked in and saw at once that it was half filled with blood, with O'Donnell crumpled like a baby in a womb. Wrong

173

simile: this was not the beginning of life; it was the end.

As they pulled him out, they saw that two cannon shells had pierced the perspex of the turret and struck the gunner in the centre of his body. They stretched O'Donnell along the floor of the plane, like Mackenzie, covering his face with his leather jacket. Then Melini plugged in his R/T and reported to Bill Strang.

Raymond worked his way further forward, across the narrow gantry through the bomb bay, fearful of finding the radio operator and engineer dead, too. But they were all untouched here. He ducked down under the cockpit, back into the nose. Raymond could see that *Grable's Legs* and two other stragglers were some way behind the Wing, which was attempting to reform, filling the gaps, for the run-in to the Initial Point of the bombing run. They were over open hilly country, the old city of Würzburg twenty miles to the north. All the enemy fighters and all the ugly black-grey flak had disappeared from the clear blue sky, as if a cleaner had wiped away the stain of combat. There were many fewer of the 4th Bombardment Wing, but they were on their own at last. LeMay had evidently ordered the lead groups to slow down, for *Grable's Legs* was now catching up in spite of her dead engine.

It was 11.30 am. The Wing, still a formidable and majestic force of some one hundred and twenty B-17s, had taken up bombing formation at the Initial Point, each group forming into line-ahead behind the next. The pilots of the lead bombardier planes had switched to automatic flight control, leaving the final guidance to the bombardiers with their Nordern sights, which had been pre-set for wind, speed and altitude. The other planes in each formation would bomb visually in conformity with their leaders.

They were ten thousand feet below their usual bombing height, in order to ensure accuracy, and this must have accounted for the inaccuracy of the opening rounds of flak. The gunners here had had little practice anyway, unlike the Ruhr valley gunners and those of other popular targets like Hamburg, who were on to the target with their radar-guided guns from the first round. This was as well, for these were the critical minutes when evasive action was out of the question.

The few defending fighters, flown mainly by factory test-pilots, showed their lack of experience, too, and Raymond saw them flinch away as soon as the tight-packed formation opened tracer fire.

There, in front, was the big loop of the Danube, enclosing the target town; and on this side the prominent semicircular race-track, the airstrip beside the factory buildings. Every crew member who could see them on that morning of 17 August 1943 must have felt a special relish at the thought that, after all that they had suffered and the terrible price they had already paid in men and machines, they were about to complete what they had set out to do. Through the thick perspex nose windows Raymond could see the lead aircraft of the 96th Group, bomb doors open, followed by the 388th and 390th Groups.

One, two, three, four — ten in all — the black objects fell from the belly of this first B-17 in rapid succession. Raymond clicked the shutter of his camera and glanced at his watch. It was precisely 11.46 am. The other seventeen bombers in the Group released their bombs almost simultaneously, the black dots speeding down and becoming lost against the relative darkness of the target areas.

There were people down there, hundreds, perhaps thousands, looking up in terror at the massed formation of bombers twinkling in the sun, intruding in a sky that had never previously known an enemy plane. And, three miles above them, Americans of the Eighth Air Force who had been through the gates of hell on their journey here, looked down and awaited the awful consequences of their arrival.

Captain John L. Latham, lead bombardier of the 96th Group, had done his work well. His ten 500-pounders danced in a dead-straight line through the factory buildings, each explosion a sudden pulse of flame and circular shock waves. The vivid spots of light had not yet faded, nor the debris and smoke begun to rise, before the next stick, and the next, and the next, spotted their bright pattern of explosions like a Broadway neon display in a fever of short circuits.

As the other groups sailed over behind the leaders, the area of the explosions spread, some sticks falling on the race-track, a few in the residential area of the town. But it was already clear that terrible damage had been done. Two groups ahead of the 100th had failed to position themselves accurately, and suddenly they broke to the left from the long line-ahead formation, and began the painfully slow and dangerous swing-round for a second run.

Only Jim Watson of *Grable's Legs*'s surviving crew had a clear view of the run-in from the Initial Point. In the lead plane ahead, *Beauty Girl*, the bombardier with the Nordern gunsight, Captain Mike Malvern, searched for an aiming point. The smoke and rubble dust were thickening and rising, obscuring details of the targets. It was the price of early success. The explosion of later bombs appeared now as ruddy glows through the dust and smoke cloud, and these made the only aiming point. The lead bombardier in *Beauty Girl* pushed a switch. The bomb-bay doors opened, and Jim Watson and the other bombardiers conformed almost simultaneously.

A voice over the intercom said, 'Make it a good one, Bill. It's been a long ride.' Bill did not reply. He was delicately moving the knob on the AFCE which brought the sight indices together, while the pilots watched the tiny movements of the wheel they had temporarily surrendered. Then he pressed the control button . . .

Back in *Grable's Legs* Raymond had felt the slight shudder as the bomb-bay doors opened, then felt the rush of a new draught. Just two minutes later, Jim Watson conformed to the lead bombardier, and the bomber lifted in a scarcely discernible series of leaps of relief, the bombs tumbling from their bay like boulders in an avalanche.

'Bombs away!' Jim Watson called out, his voice high in mixed relief and triumph. Bill Strang at once gripped the wheel again, banking *Grable's Legs* steeply to the right, while the navigator called out the new course. For the first time since it had come to Europe, 100th Group was not heading back to base after a bombing run, through the flak zones and the replenished and re-armed fighter *Gerschwader* of the Luftwaffe.

'Steer 183 degrees, skipper,' the navigator called out over the intercom.

'Switzerland, here we come!' a voice chipped in. And there was a brief yodel from another crew member, cut short as if he had suddenly remembered their two dead companions lying close to them.

For a while there was silence in *Grable's Legs*. The wind whistled through the big hole midships, and a glance through the navigator's window showed the dead engine with feathered prop and the cannon and machine-gun holes in the wing. The Captain called the tail gunner to come forward: 'I guess you won't be needed back there for a while, Hank.' Then Bill Strang summarised their situation in these words:

'You can see the 4th Bombardment Wing's gotten scattered and the two groups that went round again will be bombing about now. And, fellows, we can't keep up with the Colonel anyway. So we'll be on our own. In fifteen minutes we'll be out of Germany, but we've got nine hundred miles and nearly five hours flying ahead of us. I reckon we'll make it OK. And just look at that scenery coming up . . .'

The white-topped Swiss alps were spread out dead ahead, a magnificent sight with the sun glinting on the saw-tooth mass of mountains and deep valleys. After the bombing run, *Grable's Legs* had lost height, and Bill Strang, rather than using precious fuel to regain fifteen thousand feet, was going to give them a sightseeing trip through the Austrian Tyrol to Innsbruck. Ten minutes later, with Munich far behind on the right, the Captain was heading for the higher mountains which, in the clear air, already seemed to tower above them.

There were people on the streets of the toy-town of Innsbruck below, Austrians far from the war who had never seen an enemy bomber. But today for the first time they had already seen evidence of enemy air-power as more than one hundred Flying Fortresses had laboured overhead, south towards Italy — all many thousands of feet higher than this solitary bomber with only three of its engines working.

'Take a look at that. They're getting in the goddamn harvest!' someone exclaimed. 'And all by hand.'

Three thousand feet below, on the lower slopes of the valley, figures in long rows could be seen scything the corn with wagons drawn up nearby. This medieval scene was in strange contrast to the sights of twentieth-century danger and bloody destruction that the crew had so recently experienced. Raymond found himself succumbing to the breathtaking vista of peace and beauty. Then he remembered Mike O'Donnell's body lying just feet away, twisted into its unnatural posture, head covered, on the floor of the plane, and his mind took a sickening lurch back to the present.

During the next thirty minutes, Bill Strang flew the bomber up the Brenner Pass, the wingtips from time to time seeming to brush the rock-strewn slopes. It was almost as if they were driving up the pass on a cushion of air, following the contours of the winding road, up through the snow-line, banking steeply right to conform with a sharp deviation in the shape of the valley, up higher and higher, an eleven-thousand-feet peak on the left towering like a massive white sentry over the Brenner summit.

There was a small gathering of military vehicles at the top of the pass, and Raymond saw soldiers hurrying to swing their rifles and open fire. But *Grable's Legs* was quickly beyond their range, and ahead of them was the city of Bolzano and the Italian alpine foothills. They had now passed over the spine of central Europe, and the afternoon sun beat down on the bomber to fill it with a warmth they had not before experienced. Thorpe Abbotts, and the chill cloud and mist of England, seemed as far distant as the other side of the world. Was it possible that only this morning they had taken off from that airfield?

Then, at 12.10 pm precisely, the bomber's starboard outer engine began misfiring.

Chapter Eleven

'YES, SIR, WE bailed out about here. We were the first out when the Captain gave the order. There was no great rush. We were at eight thousand feet and losing height, heading for the south of France but not very fast. The Captain at first thought we might make it to some flat land north of Albenga, here, and belly-land — but the wind was a bit stronger than he thought.'

The Wing-Commander turned to Gus Melini. 'Did you see the others get out, Sergeant?'

'There were two dead crewmen, sir, so that left seven after we'd gone. I think we saw two for sure in their 'chutes. I guess the rest got out, too, but we were busy thinking about ourselves after that.'

'Pretty rough terrain, was it?'

Raymond took over the narrative and told the debriefing interrogating officer how they had landed on the lower slopes of a mountain, and in accordance with evasion practice had got out of the vicinity as quickly as possible.

'We slept rough the first night and then we made contact with a farmer with some goats, who took us to his cottage where his wife gave us some much-needed food and a litre of rough — very rough — wine. Luckily Gus speaks Italian.'

'Where did you learn that?' asked the Wing-Commander in some surprise.

'Talked nothing else as a kid. My Mom and Pop talk nothing else now.'

'It really saved us, sir,' Raymond said. 'They were one hundred per cent for us. We stayed with them for a week, with their friends in and out until they got us papers through the local mayor, and I signed a chit for some cash and we took the train into Monaco.'

The Wing-Commander laughed. 'That sounds cool. How about the frontier?'

Gus said, 'Here they come,' and Raymond bent down and studied the contents of the old canvas bag they had been given. It contained a ten-inch-long salami sausage, half a dozen cold mutton chops (tough as hell) and half a loaf of coarse bread; and at the bottom, wrapped in a rag, his Smith & Wesson. He hoped to God he would not need it. He could hear Gus chattering away to the official, no doubt wildly gesticulating — though he never did so talking English.

Raymond handed up his papers without raising his head, and Gus took them from him. He was saying something about the Hôtel de Paris, the only words Raymond understood. It had been agreed that they would claim to be waiters there, returning after two days with their families in the village of Pirazia. They had been told before they set out that Italy was on the verge of surrender, but that the Germans occupying the country were showing a new viciousness to their one-time allies. They had seen no sign of any Germans at any of the stations they had passed through on this coastal line, but Gus and Raymond were certainly not going to chance their luck with Italian officials either. It was far too early for that.

The official passed on. Gus handed Raymond his identity papers and indicated it was all clear. The previous year Italy had occupied the coastal strip of France as far as Nice, so there was only one frontier to cross — that into Monaco, which was a mere formality.

The moment they stepped out of the station at Monte Carlo they entered a new world, a world of clean boulevards and gardens of exotic flowers, of white mansions and apartments in Third Empire style with geraniums falling from window-boxes, and the residents lying in the hot sun on lawns and along the promenade. A scattering of carriages and one or two buses constituted the only traffic.

They were soon walking up the steep hill from the station towards the towering casino and the Hôtel de Paris, both looking like great iced wedding cakes perched on the slopes of the Principality. Gus suddenly stopped, and with hands on hips looked about him in wonder, and then at Raymond. 'Pinch me, Ray,' he exclaimed. 'This isn't goddamn real. Can't be.'

Raymond pushed him along. 'Real or not, we've got to find work — so let's see if our cover story can be real.'

But by the time they had reached the Hôtel de Paris they had begun to suspect that this was no island paradise in war-ravaged Europe. Most of the food shops were closed, and looked as if they had been closed for years. One or two that were open had only a few scrawny-looking vegetables for sale, and Raymond had noticed that, for all the apparent opulence, the people they passed looked pinched with that miserable look of the really hungry.

'You got jobs in the hotel kitchen?' the Wing-Commander exclaimed. 'And they paid you?'

'Sure,' said Gus. 'Not much, but enough to pay our bus fares. Food was our big problem after we quit the toytown of Monte Carlo. I won some dough at the casino, enough to buy some black-market bread as we headed along towards Marseilles.'

'Don't forget Madame de Rousillon,' put in Raymond.

It did not have much relevance to the art and craft of 'evasion,' which is what their interrogator wanted to hear about, but their week in a villa behind Antibes could not be missed out.

'She was one hundred and ten years old — or looked it,' said Raymond. 'Claimed to be a cousin of the Comte de Paris, and really fell for Gus. Rich as hell and with all the black-market food she wanted. That bit was fine. But we had to move on.'

'I don't see why,' said Gus. 'I'd be there still if I'd had my way.'

'After that it did get a bit rough.'

When the two old ladies got out of the bus just before Cuges-les-Pins, Raymond and Gus slipped into their seats just behind

181

the driver. They had been warned that the Gestapo was very hot around Marseilles, and they intended to avoid the centre of the city and find a way out through the northern suburbs. They had also learned that buses were safest, but had fixed a prearranged plan if there should be trouble. And there was — just west of Cuges.

From a distance it looked as if there were a lot of people at the next stop, but as the driver slowed Raymond saw that they were all men and wearing singularly and sinisterly long overcoats and trilby hats — in spite of the warmth of the day. They might as well have had 'HUN' emblazoned on their lapels, and their intentions were of a suspiciously enquiring nature.

'You look after the passengers, Gus,' Raymond said quietly, and left his seat with the canvas bag clutched in his left hand. The driver was starting to slow when Raymond pulled his Smith & Wesson out of the bag and placed the muzzle within inches of his head. '*Continuez, mon ami,*' he said without raising his voice, '*Vite, vite!*'

The driver, a pale-faced fellow with a straggly moustache, turned only his eyes, not his head. He might have said, '*Mon Dieu!*' Raymond did not much care whether he said it or not. What he did do was to put his foot hard on the old Renault's accelerator pedal, and the bus's speedometer showed an unspectacular increase in speed to 35 kph and then to almost 40.

Raymond did not take his eyes off the driver, saw nothing of the reaction at the bus stop, and guessed that Gus was having no trouble, for the only sound he heard was the straining gas-fuelled engine.

When they were round the corner and over the level crossing, which conveniently lowered its barrier behind them, Raymond ordered the driver to halt. When he had pulled on the enormous handbrake, the man looked up at Raymond like a dog expecting the lash. '*Pardon Claude,*' Raymond said, smiling. '*Maintenant, s'il vous plaît descendez.*'

The passengers were already getting out at the back of the bus, with great speed considering the quantity of their luggage, which included some rabbits in cages. Within two minutes they were alone in the bus, Raymond in the driving seat trying to find first gear.

'How did *les paysans* react to all that, Gus?' Raymond asked as he at last found some forward motion.

'Very well, really. But I think they might have been on our side. They've had a rough time from the krauts round here.'

'And the gentlemen in the long coats?'

'Bung full of hate, and running like crazy.'

'They've only got to run to catch up,' said Raymond through gritted teeth. They were facing up a hill, which did not help. But at length the Renault gained some momentum. They passed several bus stops, where waving passengers mouthed curses at them, then Raymond turned off the main road and headed north.

'You know, Gus, we've got to have something faster, and less prominent. What do you think?'

'I guess we let the cops find us — or the bus.'

Later they parked the vehicle prominently on a main road close to a derelict barn, and settled down, well concealed, to wait the inevitable outcome. But it was dusk before a low, unmistakable 15 Citroën came fast up the road, headlamps blazing, and drew up just in front of the bus. Two uniformed gendarmes got out and, with guns drawn, walked cautiously back to it.

'Damn it — they're not the Gestapo. We don't want to shoot them if we can help it.'

Cicadas were in full song in the field behind them and there was a strong smell of hot stone and dried grass in the ditch in which they lay. Raymond was trying to remember the position of the controls in the Citroën. He had driven one of them once before the war, and vaguely remembered a very crank gear change and very heavy steering at low speeds because of the front-wheel drive. One of the gendarmes had now entered the bus through the rear door, and the other was standing, keeping an uncomfortably thorough look-out, in front of the bus's radiator.

Raymond whispered, 'I'll go first and you follow in about five seconds.'

'You'll never make it while he's there. We'll have to use our guns.'

The other gendarme must soon emerge and return to the car. He did that about one minute later, just as Raymond was steeling himself for a dash, with Gus to give covering fire.

The man called out to his mate, '*Viens ici, Maurice.*'

As Maurice began to walk back the length of the bus, Raymond got up and raced the twenty yards to the Citroën, yanked open the door and threw himself across into the driving seat. He was still looking for the ignition switch when Gus hurled into the passenger seat. Neither had been seen, and just as Raymond was beginning to panic he realised that the engine was already running. His hand fell for the gear lever, but Gus was saying, 'Christ — it's there, look!' pointing at the dashboard from which protruded a horizontal chrome lever with a bakelite handle set at 45 degrees.

That was it. Typical French logic. Why clutter the floor with the gear lever? Raymond stamped on the clutch and slipped the lever through the gate, pressed the accelerator, let in the clutch and the car leapt forward. Above the roar of the four-cylinder engine they heard the crack of revolver shots and the tinkle of smashed glass. The gendarmes were pumping bullets into the back of the car at near machine-gun rate. Raymond and Gus flattened themselves, and felt the hail of broken glass as the windscreen was smashed. Other shots hit the dashboard, but in a few more seconds they were out of range, as the gendarmes proceeded to re-load.

Raymond switched on the headlamps as Gus punched out the remaining glass in the wind screen frame. He was bleeding, but only from a sliver of glass. 'You OK, Ray?'

'Fine. Nice car.'

Gus was laughing in reaction to the crisis. 'Think of those poor guys when they get back to their precinct in an empty bus! How about that, Ray?'

The Wing-Commander was smiling as he made notes. He put down his pen and said. 'I suppose the joke wore off eventually.'

'Yes, but it was still a good night's work. Gus found a map in the back, and the big fuel tank was almost full. Driving steadily we made over two hundred miles to Carcassone. No one tried to stop us, and we met only about a dozen cars.'

'Next?'

'We dumped the Citroën in the River Aude. It made a hell of a splash and I was sorry to see it go, but there was nil chance of getting any more fuel without violence.'

'And then?'

It was Gus's turn. He lit another cigarette, sat back in his chair and with his feet on the Wing-Commander's desk. 'For the first time we hoofed it. The weather was swell, the scenery was pretty, and the people were nice to us.'

Raymond, watching him as he spoke, knew how much he was going to miss this cheerful American with his freckled face like a boy's — and how familiar it had become over the weeks! — and the way his friendliness and openness had achieved a response from all the people they met along the way.

'We were near the frontier, sir, and during the escape lectures we had back at the base we'd been told about an escape route that passes through the extreme south-west of France and into Spain.'

The Wing-Commander nodded, and noted, and asked, 'Did you have any trouble finding the link?'

'No trouble at all,' said Raymond. 'And they'd never picked up any evaders as close to the border. It wasn't all plain sailing — or walking — though. We had two tough nights getting over the Pyrenees. We came down through a small town called Camprodon and walked most of the sixty miles to Barcelona, though we hitched one or two rides in carts. They may not be at war any more in Spain, sir, but, oh boy, they live very close to the bone.'

'Our man in Barcelona look after you all right?'

'Yes, the consulate knew how to deal with us. There were four more there — three of them Americans shot down in northern France. We all travelled to Algeciras by train. Took four days and we played poker the whole way. Then over the frontier into Gibraltar. Another week in the sun, filling up with food again, and a bumpy ride home in the bomb-bay of a Liberator. Worst part, really.'

The Wing-Commander smiled and pulled a bottle from the bottom drawer of his desk. 'Calls for a small Anglo-American celebration. And thanks for your help.'

The next day they both signed the fifty-five page report.

'Right, you can go now, but mum's the word about all this. And, by the way, I've got good news for you. We've just heard that the rest of your crew — those who weren't already dead — are all safely in the bag. The Red Cross let us know, so I'll be sending off cables to their next-of-kin.'

The Colonel himself was at the railway station to meet them, a tall dark figure in impeccable uniform, together with his WAC secretary. Raymond and Gus, each in the style of his own service, saluted him as they stepped down onto the platform. Then the Colonel shook them warmly by the hand, congratulating them, and as they walked to the car he asked how they had got on in London.

So much had happened since Raymond had left behind this East Anglian theatre of war — of wide-open skies full of the sound and sight of warplanes, of airfields and uniforms, of the new scent of oil and aviation fuel blended with the old scent of harvest and hay — that to come back there was like magically returning to a strongly remembered but irrecoverable past.

And yet here was the reality: a B-17 low overhead on its final approach to Thorpe Abbotts, the big left-hand-drive, camouflaged staff car, the welcoming Colonel — 'It's a great day for us to have you back!' The only living link with the past was Gus himself, as irrepressible and cheerful as on the first time they had met all those weeks ago on this same airfield. And the figure of the WAC officer as she stepped into the back of the car, tucking in her skirt to make room for the Colonel, was a haunting reminder of the flesh and soul of Louise Daintree.

By now, Louise must have learned of his return, but every effort to contact her by telephone had been thwarted, first by the initial strict security which had kept Gus and himself *incommunicado*, and then by their failure to get through to Stiplowe from London on the public phone system.

Once they were installed in the staff car, the Colonel offered Raymond a cigar and, while lighting it for him, said, 'I can reassure you about your private possessions, Lieutenant. We felt responsible for your kit and your automobile ... although when we heard you weren't coming back — at least not for a while — there was a lot of competition to buy your Alvis sport car.'

'And my dog, sir?' Bonz was a gregarious fellow but Raymond knew that he would have been moping for him. On his travels through Italy, France and Spain he had often sadly imagined the little dog with his head between his paws, the whites of his eyes showing only disappointment when anyone came near him, and perhaps only alert and running to the door when a plane taxied to a nearby hardstanding.

'Your dog, Lieutenant? Everyone turned up to look after him.' The Colonel turned to his secretary. 'Eleanor, didn't you say some WAC officer came over from Stiplowe to claim him?'

'That's right, sir. She said she had been specially asked to look after the dog if anything happened to his master. It was Lieutenant Daintree — the senior Wing Intelligence Officer's deputy.' She turned to Raymond. 'I do hope that was all right.'

'Yes, that's a great relief,' he said, thoughtfully.

The Colonel lit a cigar for himself and said, 'Eleanor, didn't you say that some other woman turned up to make the same claim? You were rather confused by that.'

The WAC looked at Raymond with an anxious expression. 'Yes, that one was an Englishwoman. I guess she didn't care to leave her name. Then only a few days ago, if you remember, Colonel,' she continued, 'Lieutenant Cox's Commanding Officer called up and enquired about his clothes and his automobile and said we had no business to let anyone take the dog.'

'That's right,' confirmed the Colonel. 'I had to speak to him myself and explain that while you were flying with us, you were our responsibility. He was more excited than abusive, but ... And then I had the pleasure of telling him that you were OK — that you had evaded capture and were back in this country.'

'What did he say to that?' Raymond asked, his mind racing with speculation and anxiety.

The Colonel's face creased. 'He didn't say anything at first. I guess he was a mite put out that he didn't know already. Then he just said, "Oh, that's wizard."'

The guard at Thorpe Abbotts opened the gate and saluted smartly. A B-17 taxied past on the nearest length of perimeter track. Gus Melini, looking about him from the front seat, exclaimed mischievously, 'Well, it's great to be back, Colonel. I guess there'll be a mission for me this afternoon? Schweinfurt, sir? Will I have time for lunch, sir?'

'No, Sergeant, you're on your way home — next week. We couldn't find another crew willing to have you, so General Eaker thought maybe three months' furlough was due.'

Melini's eyes were wide open in only half-believing joy. 'You really mean that, sir?' Then he leapt out of the car, slapped Raymond fondly on the cheek, almost forgot to salute, and ran off towards his quarters.

The driver stopped the car in front of the officers' mess. 'We've a bottle of something special for you, Lieutenant,' said the Colonel. 'It's too bad Bill Strang and the rest of his crew can't share it ... I just hope those krauts are looking after them properly.'

In Raymond's mind, time may have stood still since he had last seen Louise Daintree. Those weeks in the heat and anxiety of southern Europe were as if encapsulated all in one brief dream, but here the sun and the seasons had proved inflexibly faithful to their timetable. The fields of Norfolk had long since lost their last cereal crops, and the sun was low in the sky when Raymond set off from Thorpe Abbotts in Delilah for the Nelson Arms. The gulls were wheeling and settling, wheeling and settling behind the ploughs, and the last of the day's standing fighter patrol along the coast was winging its way towards Southwold. Soon the Bomber Command night heavies would be going out. Another winter of war lay ahead. And there would be no three months' furlough for Raymond Cox.

Louise had said she had the use of the Colonel's car, and would meet him at the pub. It was before opening time when Raymond arrived, and he parked Delilah beneath some alders where it would be almost invisible in the failing light, and waited for her. It was a windless, silent evening, with — for once — not a plane in the sky. Raymond became conscious of the steady thumping of his heartbeats.

'Don't be ridiculous,' he told himself. But he saw that the knuckles of his hands clutching the Alvis's steering-wheel were white with tension. He took them away, lit himself a cigarette, and leant back in the seat, willing himself to relax.

Raymond heard the car before he saw it. Then he spotted the twin hooded headlights through the trees, and the big white star on its side. It drew up close to the pub's darkened porch.

He saw Louise get out of the driver's door and walk round the car, her head turning enquiringly. Bonz followed her on a lead, and she stood still on the gravel, listening, a tall figure with her cap in her hand.

Raymond gave the double whistle he always used for his dog and Bonz leapt in his direction, front paws high at the limit of the lead. When Louise bent down and released him, Bonz rocketed across the car park whining and whimpering with excitement.

Raymond got out to welcome him, crouching down. The dog threw himself at his chest, wriggling and licking his face with a fierce passion. Louise ran towards them both, calling out, 'Oh Ray, oh Ray!' She, too, threw herself into his arms, while Bonz leapt at his legs.

She held him close as if he might be suddenly snatched away again. 'Oh, God, Ray, you're back! You're safe. Don't ever go away again . . .'

He passed his hands over the curve of her waist, up her straight back, cupping the softness of her neck, savouring her scent of roses. She was sobbing gently, as he knew she would, and then she held both hands against his cheeks. 'Oh, look, you're crying, too,' she choked.

'That's Bonz's tongue, you ass. But I *might* start crying if you go on like this.'

They laughed, looking into one another's faces inches apart. And they kissed, with her tears a salty accompaniment to the love he felt for her, while Bonz trotted round and round their linked feet, seemingly pleased that they were together again.

Arm in arm they walked past the pub, from which came the sound of voices and clinking of glasses as preliminaries to opening time, across the lawn by the water, past the big willow, and then along the path that followed the banks of the broad. They talked quietly, as if anxious to avoid breaking the spell of this magic, and then they lay down together in some long grass, seized with hunger for one another's body.

It was too cold to undress fully, but this only seemed to add spice to their touching and caressing. And later he buried his face in her partly uncovered breasts.

'How did I live all this time without this?' Louise asked fiercely, pressing her cheek so hard against his that the contact hurt.

Bonz had departed in embarrassment, and came back only when they were on their feet again, repairing the damage to their clothes. They laughed at the wet patches on their uniforms. Louise said resignedly, 'I guess we'll just have to say we fell into a ditch.'

'And who'll believe that?' Raymond pulled her by the arm. 'Come on you need a drink to warm you up.'

'Honey, I've never been so hot in my life.'

They were not alone in the bar for long. Some locals came in first and Raymond bought them pints of beer. 'Been over Germany, 'ave ye?' One of them asked, and Raymond grinned and said, 'I'm not allowed to say, am I? Careless talk costs lives.' And he wondered how they would respond to knowing where he had really been since he last bought them a pint at this bar.

Louise had invited some of her friends from the base for an informal celebration. They were Joan and another small dark Southern WAC officer called Olivia, who was very cheerful and friendly but almost incomprehensible, so strong was her accent; and four pilots including Charlie Dee.

Charlie threw his arms round Raymond's neck. 'You made it, Ray — by God you made it!'

Louise was playing darts with the determined concentration of an eager learner. She was not managing badly with a double twenty as Raymond came up behind her.

'This is a great game,' she said, turning round excitedly.

Later they teamed up against Charlie Dee and Joan, who beat them five-three. Then the landlord cried. 'Time, ladies and gentlemen,' and they all wandered out into the pub's forecourt, their voices and their smoke drifting away into the darkness.

'Charlie's agreed to take the Colonel's car back,' said Louise, picking Bonz up in her arms. And Raymond said, 'Well, what good luck for me!'

'For me Delilah's more like a home than an automobile,' she remarked as she climbed into the front passenger seat. 'It's sort of grown that way. It's all that we have just to ourselves. I mean, hotel bedrooms are OK, but they're not *ours*.' She put her hand over his as it rested on the gear knob. 'Do you think we'll ever have one together, Ray?'

'You mean a home? Of course we will, darling. And I'll tell you where it'll be: halfway up a hill behind Antibes, on a patch of land next to a villa where I spent several comfortable nights not long ago.'

He stopped the car part of the way back to Stiplowe, at the entrance to a field that smelt of autumn dampness and newly ploughed soil. They kissed for a while and then sat still, letting their love and compatibility lap silently about them.

The only sound was of distant bombers streaming out to Germany, and the only light came from fine white search-light beams fingering the sky to the south — but these were such long established features of each night that they made no mark on their consciousness.

Jack Boland was at his crispest, and greeted Raymond as if he had just returned from tea-break. 'I told you you'd get a holiday in the sun,' he said with satisfaction, looking up from the ocean of papers on his desk. 'You'll be ready to tell the Squadron what it's like flying in a B-17 when the heat's on, will you? And any useful tips about evasion? Not that any of them are likely to be baling out as far south as you did.'

'Of course, sir, whenever you say.'

Jack lit a new cigarette from the half-smoked one topping his heaped ashtray, and he leant back in his chair. 'What I'd like you to do before anything else is to run over and see my family. They've been worrying themselves sick over you.'

Since Jack had telephoned ahead, the three Bolands were already at the door to greet him. Dorothy threw her arms round his neck and hugged him. 'Oh, Ray, how wonderful that you're safe again! We've been worrying so much.'

John Boland grasped Raymond's hand with great firmness, and Rachel kissed him on the cheek. Then they all went into the house. It seemed just as when he had first seen it, with the great banked-up fire in John's study, and the two elderly labradors thumping their tails in greeting. The cats slid off at the sight of Bonz, and the vicar began pouring triple whiskies from a bottle ready on the tray.

John handed Raymond his glass. 'Like the desert, we "shall rejoice, and blossom as the rose",' he said. 'That's Isaiah 36, of course.'

'Can you make his safe return the subject of your sermon tomorrow, darling?' asked Dorothy jokingly.

'Yes, dear. As we were waiting for Raymond I thought I would use Jeremiah 8:20. You know, "The harvest is past, the summer is ended, and we are not saved" — but Raymond, our brave boy, is saved, and by his efforts and Jack's and those of all who are fighting for freedom, we shall all in the end be saved. How about that?'

'Excellent, dear. Very patriotic. But perhaps we can now put aside the Good Book for the moment and hear about Ray's adventures — all that he's allowed to tell us, that is.'

Raymond found himself wishing that Louise could be there so that she could witness the warmth of the Boland hospitality. It would surely dispel all her suspicions. For who could be more reassuring than the sensible, down-to-earth, kind-hearted Dorothy Boland, or the old warrior himself, sucking on his pipe and nodding his head as he listened keenly to Raymond's self-censored account of his adventures.

And Rachel? Well, who could be more innocent than this sweet young girl who had helped him from the cockpit of his crashed Spit all those months ago?

The walk they took after lunch — certainly the last before Rachel went back on Monday to her flying school — was as fixed a part of the ritual at the vicarage as matins at the church. Because it would be their last for a while, they strayed further than usual — so far that the two labradors went on strike. 'Just look at those lazy old things!' Rachel exclaimed as they prepared to cross another wide field, heading for a wood on the far side. The two animals were sitting firmly on the path, not even prepared to look in their direction, and were obviously not intending to go a yard farther.

'Go on, Bonz, go and tell them to hurry up,' Raymond ordered, to no effect, so they headed on without them. They had almost reached the wood and were sitting on a grassy bank for a rest when suddenly a Typhoon sprang from the sky, low down, and steeply banking some distance away. Then, as if it had spotted them and was determined to put on a show, the big fighter came straight towards them, so low that the prop would allow no room for anyone standing in the plane's path.

For the first time, Raymond saw that Rachel was frightened when she clutched his hand, calling out in terror, her words lost in the roar of the Sabre engine scarcely ten feet above their heads as she lay flat against the ground.

'He's gone mad!' Rachel screamed, as the Typhoon went into another steeply-banked turn on the far side of the wood. 'He'll kill us, Ray!'

'Don't worry, he's just showing off,' Raymond tried to reassure her, though he felt like remarking too that if the pilot killed them he'd also kill himself — which seemed highly likely as the plane careered across the newly-ploughed field straight towards them. This time, Raymond, too, could not resist the urge of panic to fall back flat on the grass beside her.

The Typhoon raced a few feet overhead at full boost and revs, if anything lower than ever, the sound deafening, the slipstream tearing against them like a hurricane as the plane climbed away.

'You're right — he *is* mad,' said Raymond, raising his head. He had to admit to her that he had never seen such low, low flying, and there could be no possible doubt that *they* were the deliberate target of this beat-up.

The Typhoon was now climbing almost vertically, spiralling at the same time, three complete gyrations as neat and compact as any Raymond had seen. But he had also seen, briefly — distantly but clearly — the identity letters on the Typhoon's fuselage: 'RE-H' – 'H for Harry'. *His own plane.*

'Is he coming back again?' asked Rachel in a voice shaking with fear, and muffled because her face was still buried in the grass.

193

'No, I don't think so.' The fighter was already a dot in the distance. 'But, my God, I'm going to have that pilot court-martialled.'

What made him more than ever angry was that the noise had sent Bonz scuttling off somewhere for cover. Raymond called him again and again, but the dog did not appear. Taking Rachel's arm, he said, 'Come on, let's get you home. I'll come back for him later.'

Raymond was not at all confident that the mad pilot might not return. And was it just coincidence that his own plane had been used for this deliberate attack? He realised that H-Harry would have been taken over by someone else during his absence, but it did add another edge to the insult that the very plane he had flown so often against the enemy should now be turned deliberately on himself.

Bonz had sensibly rejoined the Boland dogs, the three of them making their own way home with much desultory sniffing and snuffling in hedgerows and long grass. Raymond and Rachel caught up with them just before they reached the stream leading back to the end of the garden.

'One of your chaps practising a spot of low flying?' John Boland asked when they reached home. 'I went to the back door to watch the kite. Did he come anywhere near you?' There was concern in his voice.

'He did indeed,' Rachel said emphatically. 'And they don't fly like *that* in the ATA. I suppose he thought he was being clever.' Despite her bold words, she looked pale and wretched after their alarming experience.

An hour later, after some tea, Raymond said a special goodbye to Rachel. 'Good luck. I'll keep in touch with your progress through John and Dorothy,' he said. 'And when you get to Tiffies, remember there's a lot of torque at take-off.'

Rachel laughed and kissed him briefly. 'I expect I won't get any further than Tiger Moths. But even that'll be fun. I've been grounded for too long, haven't I, Papa?'

The Bolands stood together at the door, just as they had done to welcome him that distant morning — a neat group who between them had made the vicarage at West Aitcham seem as close to a real home as anything he had known since his aunt had died and 'Montrose' had been levelled.

The Flying Control Officer at Horning was an able and amiable flight-lieutenant called 'Pip' Mandrake. Raymond quickly cornered him in the mess and offered him a beer. 'Can you remember who was flying my old kite, H-Harry, this afternoon, Pip?'

'The Squadron was stood down at noon, Ray. There's been no flying since then.'

'Are you sure?'

The Flight-Lieutenant paused before replying, filling the interval with a good swig of light ale. 'I'd have to consult the records to be certain, I suppose.' Then, 'Ah, someone did an engine test — no more than fifteen minutes as far as I can remember. About five o'clock.'

'That's it. Do you remember the pilot?'

'No, the CO just rang me and asked if it was OK to send off someone on an engine test. Naturally, I said OK.' He paused, frowning. 'At the time I assumed it would be you . . . but obviously it wasn't so I really don't know.' He shrugged with obvious embarrassment.

Raymond thanked him, and steered the conversation to more casual topics.

Chapter Twelve

On 14 October 1943, five days after Raymond's eventful visit to the Bolands, the American Eighth Air Force laid on another giant raid on the heart of the German ball-bearing industry at Schweinfurt. It was the first on this target since the Schweinfurt-Regensburg joint raid in August, which had led to such a catastrophic loss of heavy bombers, including *Grable's Legs*. The range of the escort fighters had not increased since then and heavy bomber losses were expected again. But the Allied High Command judged that the destruction of this plant, deep in the heart of Germany, was so crucially important that the risks had to be faced.

Mission 115 involved almost three hundred US heavy bombers, supported for as far as they were able to fly by over one hundred Thunderbolts and several RAF fighter squadrons.

On the evening of Wednesday 13 October, Dick Latchmere and Jack Boland addressed the pilots of A and B Flights, 69 Squadron, down at the dispersal ops room, where the coke stove was beefed up for the occasion. It was a chilly, damp autumn evening, which promised low cloud and fog for the next day.

It was Raymond's first briefing since he had returned to the Squadron. Life had been relatively quiet since 17 August, and they had lost only two pilots, with another two completing their tour of ops and going on leave. But Robby Simpson and

Wicks Wileski, Barney McQueen, Cobber James and the two sergeant-pilot brothers of B-Flight, Roly and Harry Hobbs were welcome familiar faces to Raymond, as was Jamie Miller, who always seemed so ridiculously young to be flying at all, let alone to be going on ops.

For a moment Raymond glanced at Jack Boland standing beside his IO, one hand running through his long fair hair, the other, as always, busily employed with a cigarette, tapping off non-existent ash, putting it to his lips for a swift, deep inhale, lighting a new one from the glowing tip of the half-smoked previous one . . . In the eyes of all his pilots, Raymond knew, Jack seemed the hardened warrior, the leader who had brought them safely through so many hazards: not much loved maybe, but greatly admired as a leader.

But as Dick Latchmere revealed on the blackboard 69 Squadron's operational plan for the next day, Raymond suddenly realised a subtle change in his own feelings about the veteran fighter pilot to whom he had always felt he owed so much. For sure, Jack Boland had never been comfortable company, but since Raymond's return, he had felt a growing sense of unease about the man. There was no doubt about the continuing warmth shown by the rest of the Boland family towards Raymond, but he sensed a certain ambivalence in Jack — a faint awareness of threat. Was it only a flattering trust in Raymond that had led the Squadron-Leader to send him on that low-flying photo recce . . . and then on the Regensburg raid as an observer? And was it possible that it was Jack Boland who had so terrified Rachel and himself that last Saturday afternoon? Surely not — his own beloved sister? But, if so, why, in the name of God?

Boland himself was speaking now. '. . . and for heaven's sake, hold onto your tanks for as long as possible. We'll need every bloody drop of fuel. The Hun'll certainly put up maximum strength.'

Then he turned to look directly at Raymond. 'Ray, old boy, do you mind flying number two to me? No demotion . . .' — he brayed like a donkey and everyone turned to look at Raymond, some of them laughing along with their CO — 'no demotion, of course, but you may be a bit rusty after living it up in the south of France.'

A-Flight, with Tubby Eccles leading the six serviceable Tiffies, was to hover around Schipol hoping to catch the *Staffeln* as they took off and landed; while the CO would lead B-Flight to reinforce the Thunderbolts on their final leg, together with three squadrons of Spit IXs, including his old squadron which had at last got rid of their Vs.

'There's a riot on here!' This was as far as Louise was prepared to go on the open telephone line, to hint of the next morning's raid. 'How are you, honey?'

'It's good to be back at work,' Raymond said. 'But I miss you no end. Let's make it soon.'

'Oh, darling — yes. But got to go now. Just ...' she pleaded, 'just keep your eyes open tomorrow.'

'You bet.'

Raymond could imagine the hectic state of the Intelligence Department at Stiplowe: the weather reports coming in all the time, along with new instructions and new queries from General Eaker at 8th Bomber Command HQ at High Wycombe; the red scrambler telephones ringing, the tele-types clicking. And, cool and ordered within all this confusion, Lieutenant Louise Daintree.

Raymond replaced the receiver and went into dinner. He sat down next to Jamie Miller, who had brushed his hair for the occasion and was actually looking smart. Raymond suspected that he was regarded with some awe by this comparatively raw pilot officer, who did not look as if he had the strength to handle a Tiffy — though in fact he did so with great skill and élan.

Raymond did not want to talk shop, and because he liked Jamie, who was clearly a good deal more refined in mind and manner than the general run of aircrew, he persuaded him to talk about his home background, his family, and the school he must have left less than a year ago.

Jamie came from the Border country near North Berwick. 'A Lowlander,' he said ruefully. 'The Highlanders despise us, as you know, but we, too, have to be fairly tough to get through the winters sometimes. We were snowed in for three weeks in 1940 ...'

The Scots boy outlined for Raymond a life of shooting and fishing, with much riding across the moors, and a style of living that had changed little in hundreds of years, with his father's men and his tenant farmers enjoying between them a sort of benevolent feudalism.

'All that must seem a long way from a fighter pilot's life in east Norfolk — what do you miss most?' Raymond asked.

'Aye, it's different in some ways, but not as different as you might think. Look how dependent we are on the ground crews, yet they're no different from the men who make my father's estate tick over and see to the grouse.'

'Ah, the grouse,' said Raymond with a laugh. 'So that's why you're such a good shot. You just watch my tail tomorrow, will you? Come on, I'll buy you a brandy.'

Jamie smiled back, his brown eyes on Raymond's 'Do you think I might have a malt whisky?'

The clock on Raymond's instrument panel showed five minutes to five when Jack Boland called out, 'Bogies 11 o'clock below. And it looks a hell of a donny.'

Familiarity made the scene to the south-east of them, where Mission 115 was on the last leg of its homeward flight, no less impressive and appalling. It was at once evident that the bombers had taken a terrible pasting all the way from their distant target. Their stepped V formations had been broken up, and the B-17s had assembled themselves extemporaneously into groups of four or five, or even pairs, in a desperate attempt at mutual self-protection. A number of stragglers, like walking wounded behind an army, were being harried by the jackals of the sky, and seemed to have little chance of surviving the return flight.

As Jack Boland took them down in a swallow dive, Raymond could identify one type after another of enemy attacking planes, from 109s to 190s to Ju-88s, 110s and even some converted Dorniers, the bigger machines launching long-range rockets in an attempt to break up the formations from well out of range of the bombers' machine-guns. The fleeter enemy fighters were using their usual tactics, tearing in from dead ahead or from an acute angle, making lightning attacks before diving out of range.

The CO ordered them to switch radios to Channel C, on which the Americans were operating, and the ether was at once shattered by urgent shouts and warnings and claims — 'Two bogies coming in 1 o'clock' ... 'Jesus, just look at that kraut burn' ... 'Watch those rocket-throwers at 3 o'clock' ... 'Oh Christ, watch that B-17, out of control' ... and then cutting through it all a long, blood-curdling scream from a jammed mike of a doomed pilot with a background muffled chorus of multiple machine-gun fire, reminding Raymond of his fated time nearing the target at Regensburg two months ago.

A bomber with one wing torn off at the root was spiralling at an impossible speed, falling towards the earth three miles below, with no chance of the crew getting out, the severed wing like a falling leaf. Another, luckier, was in a 45 degree dive, three engines trailing smoke, the crew dropping out like litter thrown from a car.

Jack Boland was heading for a straggler and the three 109s pestering it with nipping dog-like attacks from both sides and dead ahead. No tracer spat back from the B-17 and Raymond, holding tight to his CO's tail, guessed they had shot off all their ammunition. Jack went in with his usual *brio*, making the Tiffy do things it was never designed for, and making Raymond's task of watching his tail almost impossible. Two of the 109s saw them coming, flicked onto their backs and were gone towards the scattered cloud ten thousand feet below. The third stayed for one more pass at the half-crippled bomber. He paid the price.

Raymond saw Jack streak down on it, throwing the Tiffy into a steep turn at over 400 mph, and with breath-taking accuracy put a short full deflection burst dead into the Messerschmitt's cockpit area. Raymond had once shot a hare in mid-leap, and this 109's reaction was the same, celebrating death with a massive twitch, and falling like a projectile — in this case the little 109 breaking first in half, then into smaller fragments that fell behind and at once out of sight.

But this episode was only the preface to the main contest into which the half-dozen Tiffies were now thrown. The action was already over the coast, and the enemy was holding on more tenaciously than ever, knowing that in another five

200

minutes or so the bombers would be beyond reach. Usually the Luftwaffe dropped out of sight when the escort began ripping into them, aware of the unacceptable risk of pressing home an attack with the enemy on your tail. But this afternoon it was different, and the sky was alive like an advancing locust plague as far as the eye could see, with whirling, diving, climbing, spiralling 109s and 190s, Thunderbolts, Spitfires and their own contribution of Typhoons.

In all his long experience, Raymond had seen nothing like this fight in its intensity and density, flak, tracer fire, contrails, black streaks from fires, white vapour trails from leaking glycol, and, here and there, the little white monuments to survival: the gently falling parachutes — the whole massive panoramic canvas of conflict filling the sky.

Raymond had lost Jack Boland in the mêlée, and no one on either side was making co-ordinated attacks any more. It was a time of instant and spontaneous reflexes, of lightning opportunism, a burst here with its shuddering recoil and stench of cordite; flickering visions of a crazily tilting machine, friend or enemy, ahead or to either side, or fleetingly in the rear-view mirror; of piercing darts of terror and elation or final annihilation.

Suddenly, 'Break, Ray — break, break, *break!*' a voice was screaming, and he stamped on the left rudder pedal and tore at the stick to throw himself into a violent left-climbing turn. There had been a Junkers-88 dead ahead, at that very moment of warning, releasing four rockets that etched four parallel white lines towards a group of stacked B-17s. He had already glanced into his mirror preparatory to pressing the gun button, but in that split second, someone had got in behind him.

Raymond blacked out and saw nothing for several more seconds. When the veil was drawn aside again, he saw briefly a stubby 190 and two Tiffies on parallel courses flashing past. Perhaps Jack was right and he had got rusty. Thoroughly shaken by the narrowness of his escape, Raymond climbed higher, feeling the peculiar imbalance of his plane, and feeling furious that he had allowed himself to be damaged and nearly destroyed in such an elementary way.

There was a massive gash in his left wing, which had ripped off the aileron entirely and exposed the two gunbays. He was now as helpless a cripple as the B-17 which he and Jack saved from ultimate destruction. Far ahead and below, like a fleeing horde, some fifty bombers were halfway across the Channel, free now from further danger as they headed for their airfields. One or two fat Thunderbolts spotted the sky, making their own way home, the pilots, like Raymond, no doubt still stunned by the sights and sounds of combat.

The Tiffy was a beast to fly, needing hard opposite stick all the way, to keep level. The Sabre engine sounded healthy enough, but there were no hydraulics for flaps or undercarriage. Ten minutes from Horning, with tanks almost dry and his arm aching painfully, Raymond switched radio channels and called control. 'Red Two coming in on my belly.' His machine was damaged Cat. B anyway, and he wasn't risking a dangling undercart — no, thank you very much, not after that lot.

H-Harry touched down fast on the grass beside the runway, bounced heavily, and spun to a halt in a cloud of dust. Bonz was first out of the crash-wagon, which arrived with the ambulance in less than a minute. Bonz had never reconciled himself to the sound of a Sabre engine after the familiar Merlin, and he expressed his disapproval by making no attempt to jump into the cockpit.

They waited half an hour longer, then Dick Latchmere rang Group. 'Has Squadron-Leader Boland put down anywhere, do you know, sir?' he asked. He gave 69's reference letters and, 'Yes, A-Apple. We've all been back for nearly an hour, and B-Flight's back from Schipol.'

There were half a dozen of them in Latchmere's office, where the IO had the red scrambler phone to his ear. There was a long pause, then Latchmere said, 'Thank you, sir. Will you let us know if you hear of any crash landing? And perhaps you would be kind enough to try 11 Group?'

Raymond said, for something to say, 'I don't believe it. Not after all he's been through.'

Latchmere asked, without any hint of accusation, 'When did you last see him, Ray? You were his number two.'

'I managed to stay with him after he caught a 109 — and, my God, that was the best bit of shooting I've ever seen. After that, as you know, it all became a shambles.'

He was thinking: they're going for a burton all the time, and have been for years. That massed array of dead faces — like a school photograph — had grown too long to register any longer. Charlie Russell, the first that he could remember, back at OTU — Charlie who never saw the enemy, only the ground rushing up to meet him because he tried to spin a Hurricane too low. And 'Boy' Peters, and ... oh, let it be! Isn't there enough grief already?

But Jack Boland! Surely *someone* must be inviolate. And he knew, just as sure as debriefing follows an op, that it would be his task to break the news to Dorothy and John — and, worst of all perhaps, to young Rachel.

Wicks Wileski was *the* veteran at concealing all feeling. As you would expect, he now sat stony-faced, reading an old copy of *Esquire* from which the colour centre-spread girlie had long since been removed. Dick Latchmere drummed his fingers on his desk, playing out silently Chopin's 'Death March'. Cobber James stared for long at an identity silhouette of a Dornier-17 on the wall, then broke the silence suddenly with 'Oh, fuck it!', his Australian twang more than usually evident.

Barney McQueen said, 'No use mooning here. I'm going to have a drink. I'm going to have *many* drinks.'

They had nothing more to say to Dick Latchmere, and he had nothing more to say to them. 69 Squadron claimed four enemy destroyed and three probables (the cine film might confirm those) and three damaged. Raymond's plane was a write-off, but no one else was damaged. And Squadron-Leader Jack Boland was missing. That's all there was to it. Quite right — 'No use mooning here.'

After dinner, George Lubbock suggested inviting the Sergeants' Mess over for a noggin. Only the pilots came, knowing that according to tradition there was always a mighty piss-up when a CO went missing. Raymond tried to enter into the spirit of the evening, fearful, as always, of being thought standoffish. But after a while he went outside, craving for Louise and the words she would say which would be just right.

A heavy mist was building up, fed by the broads and the nearby sea, and the chill was more winter than autumn. For once, the only sound was local: raised voices from the mess, a passing Commer van, singing from the distant airmen's mess. Jack Boland must be dead — Raymond was sure of it. They had been over the sea when he was last seen, and no reports had come in from Air Sea Rescue. It would be weeks before he was reclassified 'Missing Believed Killed'. But he was dead all right.

Someone came out of the mess. There was a momentary glimmer of light and then the door was shut. A match struck for a cigarette revealed the dark face of Jamie Miller, and Raymond called out to him.

'Taking a break from all that, Jamie?'

'No. To tell you the truth, Ray, I was looking for you.'

'Is that good news or bad news for me?'

'A bit of both, I suppose. But I don't think I can sleep until I tell you.'

'This all sounds very hush-hush. Let's go and take my dog for a walk.'

They had rooms in the same nissen hut, and Bonz came racing out of Raymond's doing his jumping-up-to-be-caught act and barking with joy until Raymond threw him his ball. They proceeded in dense darkness down towards the perimeter track, Raymond occasionally flashing a torch to check their position and feeling the damp air like a flannel over his face. 'Harry clampers tomorrow, Jamie. I could do with a lie-in. Now, tell me . . .'

'Before I do, it's you who's got to decide whether this should be passed on to higher quarters, Ray. I hope not — but you *have* to know.'

'All right, spill it.'

'When I shrieked at you to break this afternoon —'

'Oh that was *you*. Well, thank you very much. It was a fairly dodgy do. Was it that 190?'

There was a pause. Then Jamie spoke, softly.

'No, it wasn't the 190 — it was the CO.'

Raymond felt shock — then disbelief.

'You mean Jack Boland was shooting at *me*? Oh, come off it, Jamie! You must be mistaken.'

204

He could see nothing but the glow of Jamie's cigarette, which faintly illuminated the Scotsman's face when he drew on it.

'If there was the slightest doubt I wouldn't be talking about it at all. You *must* understand that.'

Raymond longed to see Jamie's expression instead of having to make judgement on a disembodied voice. But he knew the Scotsman was as straight as a runway — and why should he make up such an accusation? The implications were so shattering that he found it hard to take in what he had heard.

'He must have misidentified me,' Raymond protested with waning belief in what he was saying. 'He'd never do a thing like that. We're old friends.'

'He didn't know it but I wasn't fifty yards away. I could see exactly what he saw. He deliberately turned in for a 10-degree deflection burst at under two hundred yards' range. When I saw the streams of smoke from his guns I knew he wasn't playing about. He would have blown you to pieces if you hadn't reacted so quickly. He obviously thought that either his attack wouldn't be noticed in that crazy ding-dong or would be seen as an accident. But it was no accident, I can tell you that for sure. It was a deliberate attempt to kill you.'

Raymond turned and began to walk slowly towards the watch office, though with no destination in mind. The crunch of shoes on the path behind told him that Jamie was following him. He flicked on his torch and played the beam on his companion.

'I don't see any point in letting this go further,' Raymond said. 'I believe you, Jamie. And you'll have to believe me when I say I know of no reason why he should try to kill me.' He sighed wearily, then spoke, half to himself. 'I suppose it simplifies things that the man is dead.' Then to Jamie: 'What the hell would we have done if he hadn't been killed?'

Jamie said, 'Let's not speculate. I've got a bottle of malt whisky in my room. Want a drop?'

'Thanks for the thought. And thanks for saving my life. But I don't feel much like a party — not even a private one. I just want to go to bed and forget that today ever happened.'

205

By the light of the torch they saw Bonz ahead. Sensing Raymond's decision almost before he made it, he was streaking away home. It was no night for dogs to be out either.

Group had appointed Tubby Eccles as temporary Squadron-Commander, and Raymond was the first pilot to be called to his office on that foggy morning of Friday 15 October. Tubby grinned as they shook hands. 'What you might call rôle reversal,' he said. 'It's just as well we two get on all right. And I'm *not* going to send you away to Acton on an engine course!'

'How did that go for you?' Raymond asked.

'I didn't understand a single bloody word from start to finish — all about H-configuration and sleeve valves and supercharger speeds. I mean, for pilots like us either the damn thing works and then we fly, or it doesn't and we land or we crash-land or we crash.'

Raymond asked, 'No news of Jack, I suppose?'

'Not a word. The only clue is an Observer Corps report of a fighter crashing near Bradwell on the Blackwater estuary at about the time we were coming home. Not identified, and not found yet.' He sat down and put his feet up on the desk — Jack's old desk and still littered with his papers. Tubby, who did not smoke, lifted in turn the two ashtrays piled high with Jack's cigarette ends and, wrinkling his nose in disgust, emptied them into the waste basket.

'Somewhere amongst that lot,' Tubby continued, pointing at the mass of papers, 'and I'm not even going to try to find it, there's a signal from Fighter Command, no less, instructing Flight-Lieutenant Raymond Cox to take fourteen days' leave. That's better than an engine course.'

'What the hell for?' Raymond asked indignantly. 'Everyone's always trying to get rid of me. I thought there was supposed to be a war on.'

'This is called "Post POW Recovery and Recuperation period" — "PPRRR" in Raf jargon.'

'But I never was a POW,' Raymond protested. 'I was an evader — and it was very restful in the south of France.'

206

'I can't help that, old boy. Group were furious to learn that you flew yesterday, and getting beaten up by the Hun and crash-landing hasn't helped your case. So it's off and away for you.'

As if it was not enough to be attacked by your own CO, missing death by a hair's-breadth, now to have it implied that you had written off your Tiffy because you had lost your touch, and therefore needed a rest — that was, Raymond silently and bitterly concluded, almost too much to bear. For a moment he was tempted to tell the truth of the crash — but, oh my goodness, what a palaver there would be, and what would it do to the Bolands?

Instead, Raymond looked fair and square at Tubby, and said in a clenched-teeth voice, 'If I didn't like you so much I'd smash your face in.'

Tubby Eccles smiled back beautifully. 'That's wizard. Adj's got your pass, and some petrol coupons for Delilah.'

Raymond had been thinking fast, determined to squeeze everything he could out of Tubby's discomfiture. 'I don't want any petrol coupons, thanks. I just want the Moth for a couple of weeks.'

Tubby stared at him in disbelief. Then a benign expression spread slowly over his cheerful face. 'Well, Ray, you've got a cheek.'

'Louise, darling, you know you said the Colonel would do anything for you — anything in the world.'

'What is this leading to?' she asked, laughing down the unscrambled telephone line.

'I thought we might have a few days together. I have been given a fortnight's leave to recover myself. I am, apparently, a menace to the squadron, fit only for the psychiatrist's couch, and in desperate need of a soothing hand on a troubled brow.'

'Gee, is *that* all?'

'It's a start. And talking of starts, I shall whisk you away tomorrow morning at about ten. Unless I hear to the contrary, I'll be there. Just Bonz and me.'

Dick Latchmere told Raymond at breakfast that there was not likely to be much Eighth Air Force serious flying for some time. Sixty-five heavy bombers had been lost in the Schweinfurt raid, with many more than that seriously damaged. One Group, the 305th, had lost thirteen out of sixteen B-17s despatched on the raid.

'There'll be a lot of licking of wounds before they try anything like that again,' Dick had said. 'It's just murder.'

Raymond stacked his basic luggage into the Tiger Moth. Bonz was beside himself with excitement, sitting bolt upright, his lead holding him securely. It was months since the dog had been up in a Moth.

'Where will you be if we need you back?' Tubby Eccles asked. The little wooden prop was turning and Raymond was about to call out 'Chocks away!'

'You mean if you want the Moth back,' Raymond shouted above the sound of the Gipsy Major engine. 'I'll send you a signal.'

He waved goodbye to Tubby, and to Jamie Miller who had come down to the dispersal to see him off. Then he taxied out and took off from the perimeter track in fifty yards.

Fifteen minutes later, with a tightly-secured Bonz leaning out of the front cockpit and his coat streaming in the wind, Raymond was circling Stiplowe at two hundred feet. He could see a group of WACs standing by the guardhouse near the gates, and recognised Louise among them as they looked up, towards him. He raised his goggles to make himself recognisable, waved at her and pointed towards the airfield. She had been expecting the arrival of Delilah, and he could see her burst out laughing with her friends. Quickly she stopped a passing jeep for a lift.

Raymond landed the Moth in a far corner of the airfield, hoping to avoid the ribald comments of American airmen. The ruse worked only partly. Inevitably a jeep, despatched by flying control, arrived to ask if he required assistance. Louise and her friends arrived minutes later in their own vehicle. Keeping the Moth's engine ticking over, Raymond greeted Louise with a formal salute, and announced for all to hear, 'Please hurry, ma'am, we're urgently required at Headquarters.'

Then he passed her a sheepskin-lined leather flying jacket, a helmet and goggles and stowed her small suitcase in the plane's locker.

'But Ray, where are we going?' she asked as he then helped strap her in, with Bonz on her lap.

'Mystery journey,' was all he told her.

As the WAC officer contingent waved her off, Raymond opened the throttle, and a moment later they were flying low over the Thunderbolts parked on their hardstandings, Raymond wagging the wings in acknowledgement of the waving arms below.

The ten-tenths cloud at under one thousand feet added spice to the flight, keeping them interestingly low for the whole journey. When they stopped for fuel at Kidlington near Oxford, Louise asked him again where they were going, but he would say no more than 'A pretty place I know'.

She was obviously exhilarated by the journey, in spite of the cold — pointing out villages and remarkable buildings and waving to people who looked up at them from gardens and fields. After almost two hours' flying, with Raymond navigating by roads he knew so well, the Tiger Moth circled a village with an old church and green, a narrow old bridge and a number of fine old stone mansions flanking a winding river.

He did a single circuit of a grass airfield at five hundred feet, then received a green light from the watch office. Fifteen minutes later, with the Moth secured by a couple of airmen, they walked off down a hill carrying their bags, Bonz bounding ahead, and then through some woods into a valley. Louise stopped by a gate, looking about her in wonder — at the river winding between tree-lined banks, at the rich meadows divided by stone walls, with cattle and sheep grazing, at the centuries-old farmhouses and the ancient bridge spanning the river in the centre of a village. There was a faint smell of autumn and bonfire smoke in the air, and no sound above the steady tearing of grass from some cows on the other side of the lane.

'Ray, this is the most beautiful place I've ever seen in my life. Where have you brought me to?'

'This is the Coln Valley. May used to bring me here when I was a boy. It goes on like this for miles, through villages like Coln St Dennis and Coln Roger and Coln St Aldwyn. This village is called Bibury, and this is where we're going to stay.'

'My God, Ray, you're a magician!'

While they bathed and changed, Louise asked him more about the Bolands. 'I don't really want to hear their names again, but you must tell me what happened when you went round to break the bad news. How did they take it, Ray? It must have been hell for you.'

'I thought it would be. In fact I was dreading it. They're such nice people, and they've been so kind.' He stepped out of the bath and began to dry himself. 'It helped that Rachel wasn't there. She's completing her training. And when I told them he was missing, they reacted almost as if they knew more than I did. "Oh, Jack'll be all right," the father said. "I went missing for a while once, myself. No one's going to kill Jack. He's much too good a pilot."'

'And what did his mother say? Wasn't she in tears, or anything?'

'No, that was the amazing thing. It was as if they had some supernatural line of communication with him and they were convinced he was OK.'

Making up at the dressing table, Louise turned round to face him with an expression of anxiety. 'But he *is* dead, isn't he, Ray?'

'I think almost certainly. We'd have heard by now if he had been picked up.'

'Thank God for that! That man scared me.'

They dined under low sixteenth-century oak beams. There was no menu, and they started with rich pea soup, then mutton and caper sauce with vegetables from the inn's garden, hot apple pie, its pastry wafer thin and flakey, and – what a rarity! — real cream; followed by local Stilton and Double Gloucester cheese.

'How shall we ever go back to service food after this?' Louise asked. She wore a simple long red dress, with a necklace of pearls and the jade earrings which he had bought for her in Burlington Arcade when they stayed at the Ritz Hotel in London. She was sitting back in an old wooden seat with turned arms — 'replete as an over-indulged sultan', she commented.

They had already drunk a bottle of '34 Gevrey-Chambertin, and now Raymond ordered some vintage port to settle everything down nicely.

'Then we'll go for a walk by the river, and afterwards sleep for twelve hours. How's that?'

'Just heaven.' And then Louise sat up straight as if seized with an inspiration. 'Hey, do you remember when *I* had to do everything? You were as green as fresh-mown grass then. And now look at you — organising these marvellous breaks. Well, Ray, I guess you're growing up.'

'I suppose war makes a boy into a man overnight,' was all he could say, self-mockingly.

'And you've been at it long enough. If there was any justice in this world you would be honourably retired — as of this moment.' She looked round the small dining-room, in which was only one other elderly couple who, dinner over, rose from their table, smiling at them and nodding good-night.

Raymond said, 'Let's not talk about the war now. Let's have a few days of fantasy, pretending it's not happening. The nice thing about this place is that we really are miles from the action.'

They, too, made their way out of the dining-room, through the stone-flagged hall and out into the dark night. The river lapped under the bridge; a pair of barn owls exchanged messages.

That night they lay naked under a single sheet in the great four-poster bed. The fire in the grate was little more than a glow, but it remained warm in the room, and they enjoyed the sensuous feel of the linen against their skin.

'In my innocence, as you call it,' Raymond murmured, his hand stroking her breast, 'I used to think that love-making might pall after a while. I certainly never imagined married couples bothering with it much after a year or two — except to produce another child.'

'No, I'm told it gets better and better,' said Louise. 'Of course, we have to rely on what people say, but on present experience, I guess it's true.' She moved against him snugly.

For four unbelievable days and nights, they walked through the Cotswold valleys and over the wolds, tiring themselves out — calling at pubs for beer and cheese in the middle of the day, and succumbing gratefully to the inn food at night. They planned their future together as if the war would be over tomorrow and there was nothing else to consider between them except where they would get married, and how perhaps they might honeymoon in that quaint alpine village Raymond had flown over before *Grable's Legs* had lost her second engine.

They spoke to no one much except intermittently to fellow guests at the inn — who clearly regarded them as a married couple, just as they felt themselves to be.

Then, on Thursday 21 October, Raymond persuaded one of the pilots at Bibury airfield to fly the Moth back to Horning, with Bonz as passenger. Parting was no sweet sorrow for the dog when it meant a Tiger Moth flight, and he went off happily in the front cockpit, to be met at the other end by Raymond's batman.

Then they took an afternoon train from Cirencester, arriving that evening in London, where Raymond had arranged to meet Charlie Dee and Joan for their last night before Louise returned to Stiplowe. Hatchetts in Dover Street was as unlike the inn at Bibury as flying a Typhoon in combat differed from being in a Tiger Moth. The place was packed with officers of all services and their girls, the smoke was as thick as a pea-soup fog, and the noise of music and voices cacophonous.

As soon as they settled at their table, Raymond turned to Charlie. 'If you really want to know what it's like in a B-17 when all guns are firing, then it's about like this.'

But they danced on the tiny floor, drank champagne and laughed a great deal. Joan had an engagingly cheeky manner, a quick tongue and a sharp American wit which they all enjoyed. At one point, as Charlie was ordering a third bottle from a harassed waitress, she leaned across the table and looked intently in turn into the eyes first of Louise and then of Raymond. 'When did you two get married? I don't need to look at that goddamn ring to know you're married. And why weren't we invited to the wedding.'

Louise glanced at her left hand, then put the base of her glass over the ring. She was blushing deeply and giggled like a schoolgirl. 'That's strictly for hotel managers and head waiters,' she said, slipping it off.

Joan turned to Charlie. 'You don't believe that tale, do you?' she said. 'He's just like Brigham Young, Charlie. "He is dreadfully married. He's the most married man I ever saw in my life." Raymond was already feeling rather drunk from the champagne and the noise, but enjoyed being with these Americans. Perhaps he and Louise should live in New York when eventually they did get married. He was about to make this proposal when both girls got up and left.

'Now you boys can talk shop to your hearts' content — for five minutes.'

They did just that. It was Charlie's first opportunity to ask him about Jack Boland. 'How did he get the chop, Ray?'

'No one knows. There was a lot going on at the time.'

'Yeah, I know. We were around, too.'

'He was last seen close to a 190, though no one saw him hit.'

Charlie filled their glasses again and held up his own to clink against Raymond's. 'Here's to your marriage,' he said with a wink, 'even if it is in the future. And here's to your escape on the 14th.'

'So you heard I'd got clobbered.'

Charlie Dee nodded. 'Was that a 190, too?'

Raymond might have hesitated if he had not drunk so much champagne and had not been enjoying himself so much. Anyway, it was worth it for the effect. 'No — it was a Tiffy.'

'Goddamn it, Ray, what in hell do you mean? Not *again?*'

'This time there was a big difference. This time it was not just identification failure. It was the real thing.'

'Do you know why?' Raymond had never seen Charlie Dee look so shocked.

'Yes. It was witnessed by someone who was right there. Someone I believe and trust.'

213

'But, for Christ's sake, what're you going to do about it? You can't have mad murderers in your own squadron.'

Gently Raymond told him to calm down. 'It's all right, Charlie. Obviously I wouldn't be telling you if the fellow was still alive.'

'Was he shot down by your buddy, then?'

'No. This is where the conversation started. We don't know how he was killed. *He* was Jack Boland.'

Charlie Dee's questions dried up, and he sat back in his chair. He stared across the table at Raymond, shaking his head. 'Jesus!' he exclaimed softly. 'Jack Boland — what d'you know!'

Raymond glanced across the night-club to check if the girls were returning. 'You're to say *nothing* to anybody about this, Charlie.'

'Sure, sure.'

'*No one*, and especially not to Louise, though I think she'd be less surprised than you are. She never cared for Jack Boland, and had her suspicions about him. She even warned me he was after my blood — not directly, of course, but sending me on dodgy missions, that sort of thing. Heaven knows why. I thought he was always friendly and generous to me, until this happened.'

Charlie drew on his cigarette and exhaled the smoke vertically. 'You know Rachel used to invite me over to her place. The Bolands were very kind to me — as they were to you. Dorothy sort of mothered me and I used to talk flying with the old man.'

'And the girl?'

'Young and innocent, as you know. I never touched her — I thought of her as a schoolgirl. She once told me how sick Jack was when he got back riddled with malaria from Burma. Went to his head, I guess. I can also remember her saying, "Jack and I are very close. He sometimes says he never wants to marry, he's so jealous."'

'What did you say to that?' Raymond exclaimed.

'I guess I just laughed — maybe a bit nervously. *He* made me nervous, that's for sure. He was a real screwball. We can say that now — now he's dead. As for Rachel . . .'

They had not noticed the return of the women. Joan said over her shoulder in mock weariness, 'Hell, Louise, they're not even talking shop. They're just like all men — girls, girls, girls, that's all they can think about.'

So they danced two more dances, finished their champagne and crossed Piccadilly to the Ritz, uncertainly and noisily in the blackout.

Chapter Thirteen

DICK LATCHMERE WAS standing alone at the bar when Raymond walked in, on his return from leave, and offered him a drink. Raymond decided on a beer then asked him, 'What's the gen? I feel as if I've been away since Dunkirk.'

The IO pushed the pint mug towards him and raised his own. 'Nice to have you back. I suppose you'll have heard that old Tubby has been confirmed as CO. Does that bother you?'

'No, I'm glad of it. I went back on to ops too quickly after my little holiday in Europe. Any sign of Jack yet?'

'Not a thing. But that wreck reported near Bradwell has been identified as a Tiffy — and it's Jack's Tiffy, according to the markings. Engine stuffed with cannon shells. The hood had been ejected and there were no signs of damage to the cockpit, so it looks as if he got out over the sea. Maybe his chute didn't open. Maybe he drowned. It's been known.'

For a moment the vision of Jack Boland flying through the air at 300 mph, tugging fruitlessly at the D-ring of his parachute, and seconds later smashed to pieces by the impact of the sea, filled Raymond's mind. He had seen others killed like this, some with parachute half open, others bunched up in a ball in a pathetic attempt to protect themselves from the blow ... But Jack Boland, so tough and resilient, survivor of the air war from Biggin Hill to Imphal?

And yet, if Jamie Miller had judged right, Jack Boland had actually tried to kill him, a fellow pilot he had previously befriended — and had nearly succeeded in doing so. And then — so it seemed now — nemesis had swiftly followed, and now Jack Boland himself was only one of thousands of airmen's corpses consumed by the voracious North Sea.

Raymond ordered two more pints and asked what the Squadron had been doing in his absence.

'The Americans are lying low after the last Schweinfurt shambles. The bombing wasn't bad, but no one can stand losses like that. Some of the groups were decimated, and morale's got to pick up before they're fit for anything as big as that again. Anyway, the weather's been duff. Colonel Schneider was over here the other day and he told us the big boys wouldn't be doing much until the spring, when some wizard new long-range fighter gets over here.'

The bar suddenly began to fill up. Tubby Eccles greeted Raymond warmly. Wicks Wileski was, as usual, looking very smart in best blue, by contrast with the scruffy battledress and flying boots of the others. Roly and Harry Hobbs had been commissioned in Raymond's absence, and looked rather selfconscious in their old battledresses still showing the stitch marks of the chevrons on their sleeves. Cobber James uttered a few innuendos about Raymond's activities on leave.

So nothing much has changed, Raymond decided, and he felt strangely comforted. The talk was all of dive-bombing now. To their disgust, their Tiffies had been fitted with bomb racks for a 500-pounder under each wing.

'What are the targets?' Raymond inquired.

'No-balls.' Dick Latchmere said obscurely, and before he could explain, Cobber James began to lead a ribald chorus: 'No balls at all, no balls at all . . .'

'It's the codeword for German secret weapon launching sites in the Pas de Calais and the Cherbourg peninsula,' Dick Latchmere continued as soon as he could be heard again. 'Since you took those pictures near Cologne, we've found the Hun's been digging away furiously in France. They look like short railway lines: those in the Pas de Calais all pointing at London, the Cherbourg ones at Bristol. So everyone's been told to bomb them to hell — and that's what we've been doing.

They say you can walk on the flak but no one on 69's been chopped so far.'

It was Dorothy Boland who answered the telephone. It was a bad line and she sounded a long way off. Perhaps she could not clearly hear what Raymond was saying and that would account for her hesitancy. Raymond had dreaded this call but he knew that he had to speak to the stricken family now and again out of courtesy.

'I know there's no news of Jack,' Raymond blurted out, 'but I just wanted to know how you both are?'

There was a pause, as if his words were taking time to reach her. Then he heard, through the interference, 'Oh, we're both very well, Raymond. John's busy of course, and there's plenty for me to do. You know how this dreadful old house is.' Her laugh sounded nervous.

'And how has Rachel taken the news?'

This time Dorothy Boland answered almost before he had finished speaking. 'Just like us, just like us,' she broke in with a trace of irritation — or was that his imagination, or due to the bad line? 'She knows Jack's all right, too. He's always all right.'

Raymond wanted this embarrassing conversation to come to an end. He did not want to find himself invited to the vicarage, even though there had been a time when he looked forward to the warm welcome and hospitality there. But he felt he ought to enquire further about Rachel, so he asked how her training was going.

'Her what? I can't hear you.'

'Her *training* — in the ATA.'

'Oh, John can tell you about that.' Raymond then heard Dorothy calling him to the telephone: 'It's Raymond Cox — you know, dear.'

When Raymond heard the vicar's deep voice he felt almost as if he might need to introduce himself again, so distant from them did he suddenly feel.

'You want to know about Rachel?'

'Yes, I wondered how she was getting on, and —'

'I expected as much,' interrupted the slurred voice which had formerly always seemed so friendly. 'Yes, I expected as

218

much. Well, she's out of harm's way.'

Feeling completely thrown by this response, all Raymond could think of saying was, 'Is she flying?'

'Yes, of course she's flying. That's what she's gone away for. She's out of any risk and she's flying Spitfires.'

The interference on the line grew louder and then an operator's voice cut through, sounding as cold as the voices of Dorothy and John Boland had. 'Have you finished your call? There are others wanting the line.'

Raymond put down the receiver, saying to himself, 'They're welcome to it.' Then, 'What on earth has happened to them? What have I done?'

The dreary dark winter of war closed over the country. For the British it was the fifth winter, but it was the first winter of blackout for most of the American airmen and soldiers who had crossed the Atlantic in hundreds of thousands during 1943. For nearly all of those it was the first time they had left their country, and for many who had previously never even left the state in which they were born it was, especially under military discipline, a hard experience to bear. Except for the endless training, there was little for them to do, and off duty they roamed the countryside and the city streets in search of distractions. With money in their pockets, and the glamorous novelty of being foreign, they attracted the girls more successfully than did the underpaid British troops and airmen. This caused a lot of ill-feeling, and some violence.

On a damp, dark night in the streets of Norwich or London or Liverpool, with the cinemas packed and the pubs out of beer, it was difficult to appreciate that the World War was developing into its final phases. The recapture of the great Russian city of Kiev, the American occupation of the Gilbert Islands on the other side of the world, the implacable Allied advance up Italy, meant little to the millions in uniform still waiting in the United Kingdom — to British, Americans, Canadians, Australians, New Zealanders and those of other Commonwealth countries, to Poles who had not seen their homeland for four years, to Free French troops for whom their homeland was so near and yet so far, and to thousands more in exile from the slave labour camp that Europe had become.

Even the meeting between the three great Allied leaders, Winston Churchill, Franklin D. Roosevelt and Joseph Stalin, in Tehran — where the final plans for the defeat of Germany were agreed — made little impact. The war had been going on for so long that, though everyone yearned for it to end, most people — civilians and servicemen alike — half believed that it would go on for ever.

In the New Year the RAF night bombers continued to drone out on their way to Germany, destroying city after city: to Brunswick on 14 January; 769 to Berlin on 20 January; 648 to Magdeburg the next night; and to Berlin thrice more before the end of the month. But London, in turn, suffered its worst raids since the great blitz. Food rationing became even more severe, and travel within the country became so difficult as to prove impossible for the elderly. It was a very bad winter, and the promise of relief continued to seem distant.

And yet, afterwards, as the days began to lengthen again, and the first green began to appear on hedges and trees, the talk of 'The Second Front' and the landing in Fortress Europe could be heard in the land like a warlike chorus of hope along with the first singing of the spring birds.

15 February 1944 was the first anniversary of Charlie Dee's arrival in England — and the beginning of his war. On the evening before, he had telephoned Raymond at Horning.

'We're having a little party at the Nelson tomorrow,' he said. 'Hope you and some of your buddies can join us. Your sugar'll be there,' he added reassuringly. 'And so will mine.'

'Fine,' said Raymond. 'But what does met say?'

Charlie had obviously done his homework, and replied promptly and decisively. 'Met says 'No go' for tomorrow, or, as you lot say, "Harry clampers".'

For Raymond and Louise the winter had meant periods — sometimes long ones — of separation, scattered with intermittent occasions when they somehow managed to contrive brief meetings. 'This goddamn war was designed, to the last detail, to keep us apart.' Louise had once exclaimed in exasperation on the telephone, when she had to cancel an assignation at the last moment.

At Christmas they again had three magical days in London. The Ritz was full, and all Raymond's persuasion and bribery failed to get them a room, so they had to make do with a bomb-damaged hotel in the Strand, which was already packed with GIs and their girls — 'a heaving great brothel' Louise described it. But nothing could detract from the magic of their being together again, as they walked the Embankment in the moonlight, and joined up with a party of naval officers at the Army and Navy Club to celebrate the sinking of the German battleship *Scharnhorst*. Early on their last morning Raymond stole out while Louise was still asleep, arriving at a jewellers just as it opened and coming out five minutes later with a small packet in his pocket.

Since then they had been unable to arrange a meeting, but to Louise's delight — 'No one, but no one's ever done that to me before!' — Raymond resorted to writing love letters. They had long planned that Raymond would travel to New York the day he was demobilised, and they would marry at St Stephen's Church close to her parents' brownstone house on East 34th Street. *That* was something for them to dream about!

Louise was standing at the far end of the Nelson's bar when Raymond arrived with Bonz under his arm. Their eyes met and she had begun to move towards him until he held up his hand to halt her. He then set Bonz on the bar counter, his customary pub position, placed a packet from his pocket in the little dog's mouth and sent him off. Bonz raced down the counter like a sliding bottle in a Western movie, and halted, tail wagging, in front of Louise. She took the packet from the dog's jaws and glanced up at Raymond, puzzled and intrigued.

Watched intently by those around her, she pulled at the string and unwrapped the brown paper, then a layer of gold paper, to reveal a velvet box. As Raymond watched them, Bonz, the box and Louise's bent head all disappeared behind the crowding of her friends. Then a chorus of 'Ahs' arose, the throng of uniformed figures opened up like the petals of a flower, and there was Louise holding up a ring, its diamonds sparkling in the light of the candles.

The engagement ceremony was brief and chaotic, accompanied by cheering, laughter and barking. Louise was in Raymond's arms as he slipped the ring on the third finger of her left hand; the publican found some champagne he had put away to celebrate the end of the war; and in a brief lull Joan was heard to exclaim — looking hard at Charlie Dee — 'Gee, no one ever proposes to *me!*'

But the war intervened at 9.20 pm. It always did, just when you were near to forgetting it, like pain from an old wound. Someone came running into the bar and shouted that there was a raid on. Remembering only too well how a nearby pub, just as isolated as the Nelson Arms, had been struck two years earlier by a stray bomb with terrible loss of life, the publican ordered everyone outside.

The clear winter sky was criss-crossed with searchlight beams, and there was the sparkle of anti-aircraft fire to the north and the sound of gunfire and the whoomph of bombs. Individual 'intruder' Ju-88s had recently been roving the East Anglian sky at night, bombing and strafing airfields and hovering around night-bomber bases trying to pick out planes as they took off. They were not easy to catch, and this one was evidently proving elusive.

Raymond could just make out the figures of Charlie Dee and Joan watching the display from close to the water's edge, so he and Louise joined them.

'Done any night-fighting in your time, Ray?' Charlie asked.

'No — I find it hard enough to see in daylight, though I believe it's all done by radar nowadays.'

There was renewed firing — this time to the west.

'It looks as if Coltishall is taking a pasting,' Raymond observed.

'Hey, that's where they're keeping our new ships,' Charlie protested.

'What do you mean?'

Louise intervened. 'Listen, you guys, this is a public place and that is confidential conversation. Let's find somewhere quieter if you want to talk shop.'

As it was unlikely that the Nelson would reopen while there was still hostile activity around, the four of them piled into Delilah and drove off into the night. Cruising slowly along the Norfolk lanes, Raymond repeated his question.

Charlie explained 'We're getting our first batch of P-51s tomorrow. We're going over to pick them up from Coltishall.'

'P-51s?' Raymond hated to show his ignorance, but he had never heard of them.

'*You* call them Mustangs.'

'Mustangs? Oh, I've flown them.' Raymond said, sounding unimpressed with the machine. 'They're OK low down but no good above fifteen thousand. And machine-guns! Why not 20 mm cannon, like our Typhoons? They'll be no use for escorting the big boys.'

Louise leant over from the back of the car. 'You just wait and see what's happened to the old Mustang,' she said. 'I've seen all the figures — and, oh boy!'

'I'll stick to Tiffies, thanks.'

Louise laughed and addressed Charlie. 'He doesn't know what you're going to get. Nor what *he's* going to get!'

Raymond jammed on the brakes. They were travelling at no more than 15 mph, so halted at once without loss of dignity. When he turned round in his seat he could just make out Louise's smiling face behind him.

'And just what do you mean by that, Lieutenant Daintree? And kindly remember that you're now my fiancée.'

Charlie laid a hand on his arm. 'In that case, don't strike the dame — not till you're married anyway.' He turned to Louise and Joan. 'Shall I tell him the good news before he drops us all in the ditch?'

'Yes, for Pete's sake do that.'

Charlie then explained how it seemed that Colonel Schneider had told his groups the previous week that they would be re-equipping with P-51s, the Thunderbolts being sent to the Italian campaign; and that several RAF squadrons, including 69, would also be re-equipping for joint operations, escorting American 8th Air Force heavy bombers in a renewed spring offensive.

'I'll tell you something, Ray, these P-51 Mustangs fly higher and faster than the Jug or the Tiffy. They're more manoeuvrable — and guess how long they can stay in the air?'

Knowing that the Tiffy with long-range tanks could stay airborne for around two-and-a-half hours, Raymond made a guess of three-and-a-half hours.

Charlie chuckled. 'Listen, Englishman, thanks to your Rolls-Royce engine and other modifications, and thanks to damn great drop tanks, we'll be able to stay up for *eight* hours! We can go with the big boys all the way — and that means Berlin. Think about that, will you?'

Raymond did. So this was what Dick Latchmere had called the 'wizard new long-range fighter'. As he restarted Delilah he said, 'Right, I've thought about it, and I think it sounds OK.'

'There's someone in the mess asking for you, Ray,' Tubby Eccles informed him. 'You'd better get along, there.'

Raymond noted the slightly mischievous expression on his CO's face but did not comment. He climbed into Delilah and drove away from the dispersal.

The same information was repeated by Jamie Miller before he could even get out of the car. 'There's been someone asking for you, Ray. But I think you may be too late.'

There were few people in the officers' mess: 'Pip' Mandrake and a new pilot officer, and two WAAF officers having an early lunch, and two figures at the bar: Wicks Wileski and a female figure in the dark blue uniform of the ATA. It was notorious on 69 Squadron that if a woman came in to the mess by herself, Wicks would be at her side within two minutes.

As Raymond went straight over to the barman to inquire who had wanted to see him, a woman's voice said, 'Hello, Ray.'

And there was Rachel Boland, looking very neat and winsome, smiling at him and clutching a short gin-looking drink. She had taken off her hat, revealing the same short dark hair and fringe that was his first sight of her a year ago. She was smoking a cigarette and altogether looked very grown-up and poised.

'Good gracious, Rachel. How nice! But what are you doing here?'

'I've just delivered your Squadron its first Mustang P-51B. And very nice she is too. Goodness how she goes!'

Raymond struggled to conceal his surprise, and in doing so sounded banal instead. 'Of course, you girls fly everything nowadays.'

'That's right, everything,' Rachel said decisively. 'And one of these days we might even join you on ops.' Raymond was uncertain how to interpret her sideways smile.

Wicks Wileski meanwhile looked bleakly at Raymond, and failed to sound generous when he offered him a drink. 'So you know my new friend, eh?'

'Yes, Wicks, she's my *old* friend.'

After a while the Pole offered his apologies and slipped away. 'I have flying to do — important flying.'

Raymond seized the opportunity. 'Can you stay to lunch, Rachel?'

'I can, and intend to, Ray. Let's have some together.'

She clearly wanted to talk about flying and ops, and only reluctantly answered Raymond's occasional questions about her family.

'I telephoned them after Jack was shot down, but I haven't visited them, I'm afraid,' Raymond said carefully. 'So what's the news from the vicarage?'

Rachel poured herself a glass of water and sipped it slowly before replying. 'It's good and bad news, a bit of both.'

'Well, tell me. I'm interested. I mean, you were all so kind to me and I really did feel almost one of the family. Is there any more news of Jack?'

'Oh, Jack's a prisoner,' Rachel said casually, as if he must surely know already. And then, her voice went low and sad. 'I'm afraid Papa's not well. I don't think he'll ever get over Arnold.'

'What ever happened to your brother?' Raymond asked, shocked.

'Well, it was ridiculous really — in a ghastly sort of way. He was on Christmas leave ... I wasn't there but Mums told me later. There was some talk about Tiger. It seems Papa was musing about whether it would ever fly again, after being laid up for so long. He asked Arnold if he'd have a look at the engine, to make sure it was properly greased in the right places.'

Raymond offered her a cigarette when she paused, then lit it for her. She inhaled deeply and thankfully, evidently already a confirmed addict, watching him with dark eyes tinged now with tragedy.

'Later that same afternoon, they heard the sound of the engine revving up. That went on for quite a long time, and then seemed to fade away. Papa sent Mums out to see if everything was all right, and she saw Tiger disappearing into the distance. The silly boy had got it off the blocks, opened the doors and taken off — just like that. Half an hour later, Tiger blew up on the beach at Yarmouth.'

'You mean he *crashed* it?'

Rachel looked at him with scorn but her voice trembled. 'Of course not — Bolands don't crash.'

'Then what happened?'

'He must have run out of fuel. Anyway, the anti-aircraft gun crew nearby saw Tiger come in with a dead engine. Arnold did a perfect three-pointer on the sand and then ran onto a minefield. There are mines all along the coast on the sea side of the barbed wire. They couldn't get out what was left of him for hours, because of the mines.'

Rachel stubbed out her cigarette and looked almost accusingly at Raymond. 'I'm surprised you didn't hear about it.'

Raymond did not know how to respond to that. So he simply made do with, 'Poor kid — I *am* sorry.'

The ATA brought in the twenty Mustangs for 69 Squadron over the following three days, and Group informed Tubby Eccles that they had just two days to familiarise themselves with the new plane. It was sad to see the brutish, tough Typhoon go, its place taken by the refined, almost Spitfire-like Mustang P-51, but they had to admit that it was a much superior plane in the rôle of high-level escort fighter.

Raymond was the only pilot in the Squadron who had flown the earlier American-engined version. 'It's a different kite,' he told the pilots of B-Flight — which he had taken over from Wick Wileski, who was due to go on rest. They were standing around the machine Raymond had just been flying, and he patted the warm base of its nose. 'The Merlin engine's done the trick. On that last test-run I was showing a true airspeed of 445 mph at 37,500 feet. Any higher and she gets a bit wallowy, but at that height you can chuck her about like a Tiger Moth.'

Dick Latchmere took over from Raymond, holding a stack of papers in his hand and occasionally referring to them. 'The Mustang, it says here,' he began, 'was a speculative exercise by the North American Corporation. Never heard of them, have you?' No one had. 'Anyway, some Raf brass went over to America in 1940 to see if they had any decent fighters. But there was nothing as good as the Spit. So they left behind some specifications and, believe it or not, in exactly one hundred and seventeen days these North American fellows came up with a prototype, thanks to a German engineer from Messerschmit who quit and went to the States.' He looked up and grinned. 'So it *must* be good. But the American Air Force and the US Navy showed no interest. Only the Raf were impressed. Went like a bat out of hell even with the Allison engine. That was the one you flew, Ray?'

'That's right. Faster than the Spit IX low down.'

The IO referred to his notes and read from them, '"The secret of the Mustang's exceptional speed, range and manoeuvrability lies less in the excellently configured fuselage than in the laminar-flow wing …"' They all looked at the wing, noting that its maximum thickness was well aft. '"This makes for a very smooth airframe, and contributes to the unprecedented range, without drop tanks, of over one thousand miles …"' With drop tanks, that means we can go to Berlin on escort, have fuel for combat with the enemy, and still come home comfortably.'

Dick Latchmere paused a moment for this to sink in, and then added dramatically, 'Which is where you'll all be going in the next few days.'

'You're out of your bloody mind!' Cobber James exclaimed.

For the Luftwaffe, the P-51 Mustang was a new shape and a new menace in the sky. It was not the armament of six .5-inch machine-guns that they feared, for that was less lethal than the Typhoon's four 20 mm cannon and less lethal than that of their own 109 and 190, both of which combined machine-guns with cannon. These two German fighters could also match the manoeuvrability of the Mustang. But no Allied fighter had so far been able to fly five thousand or even ten thousand feet above the bomber formation, ready to swoop down on any attackers, five hundred miles and more from their bases.

No longer could the German fighter pilots tear into the B-17 formations unmolested; no longer could they line up, without a glance behind, and attack the bombers systematically from every point of the compass. Now it was not the machine-guns of the bombers which were the only threat; now these brilliantly fast, well-handled new shapes might come swooping down out of the sub-stratosphere, dropping their tanks and with guns blazing, all over Germany — the Fatherland itself.

In spite of Cobber James's indignation, 69 Squadron was briefed to escort 8th Air Force heavies to Berlin on 4 March 1944. In fact, it was an abortive affair. Weather predictions proved wrong, and the bombers had to withdraw before reaching their target. But two days later it was the real thing.

Seven miles below, the German landscape might have been the surface of another planet. Individual fields merged to give an uneven spread of green, like the first chalk tracings of a young child. Rivers became barely discernible etched squiggles, towns and villages haphazard dark stains. The conception of a living world, of humans and animals, was beyond imagination. The highest flying bird had never penetrated this world that was already beginning to darken towards the blackness of limitless space.

And yet Raymond was not alone. Eleven more of 69 Squadron, men he knew like fellow tribesmen, were poised in this ultimate-altitude world about him, their machines rising and falling like boats in a gentle swell, all farther from home than they had ever been, and seeking a sign of the seven hundred heavy bombers they were due to protect on their run-up to their target, the great city of Berlin.

382 Group was somewhere in the vicinity, too, sharing the same leg as 69 Squadron, a real Anglo-American force

in Anglo-American fighters penetrating deeper into Germany than ever before.

They had been airborne for just two hours when the three squadrons of 382 Group came into sight on the port side, silver-shining machines glinting in the sunlight, by contrast with 69 Squadron's olive-drab camouflage. Raymond knew that Charlie Dee was leading a section of 99 Squadron, four swastikas now on the nose of his Mustang behind the floridly lettered 'Garbo', but they were unlikely to be able to identify one another, unless in the hurly-burly of combat, as 69 Squadron had orders to close-escort the bomber Groups.

The 'big friends' were just visible now, far to the north-east, hundreds of them, dark splashes against an empty sky, several of the lower groups trailing white contrails. Tubby Eccles waggled his wings and turned them fifteen degrees to the left to close the bomber formations, which rapidly took definition and assumed the defensive disciplined stepped Vs which characterised the 8th Air Force heavies. Raymond reckoned they were forty miles from Berlin, but there was still no sign of flak and no warning of the presence of enemy fighters.

The Mustang yawed slightly with the big 108-gallon tanks beneath her wings, though less so now that they were nearly empty, and Raymond longed to release them but waited for the CO's word of command. He glanced round the spacious cockpit, checking instrument readings between more important checks of the sky behind and above.

Now they were directly above the leading groups of B-17s and the flak had begun, radar-directed and instantly on target, spotting the sky black with orange red centres, the later groups flying as if through light cloud, and all of them taking avoiding action and breaking the neat pattern of their formation. Bomb doors were already opening in some of the left groups, breaking the clean line of the fuselage underside.

Cobber James broke radio silence, the Australian twang of his voice a weird anachronism up here in the silence of the sub-stratosphere, 'Where've all the bloody Huns gone?'

'Shut up, Cobber. Here they come!' Raymond, not always first with the sighting, had spotted the distant dots dead ahead and coming in at a devastating speed, straight for the first group, disregarding the flak and their presence.

Raymond momentarily switched to the German wavelength, and his ears were filled with the guttural voices of the German fighter leaders giving urgent orders like an angry crowd of armed protesters. They were clearly outraged to find, for the first time, enemy fighters at this unprecedented distance from England, and these massed bombers over their sacred capital city. As Tubby ordered tanks to be dropped, Raymond led his Flight down to intercept, sensing already, before a shot was fired, the special venom of the German attacks as they developed.

He caught a glimpse of a B-17, victim of a direct hit by flak, exploding with its bomb load in a searing flash — the first to go. Then he was on his back and pulling on the stick, ruddering right, then left, lining up on a twin engine 110 that was despatching rockets which left four grey tails across the sky. Check turn-and-bank, right thumb on the gun button, eyes intently on the reflector sight for deflection. 15 degrees, now 10, pull it through. God, he was going fast, the twin fins of the Messerschmitt half filling the windscreen. He was going to overshoot. No — just time for a short burst.

Christ, he was getting accurate! Well, so he should, after all these years, all these bloody dogfights. But never before with the .5s of a Mustang. The eight guns of the old Hurricane could make a mess at a hundred yards, but these big slugs . . .! The 110 disintegrated as Raymond yanked hard back, blacking out for a fraction of a second. When he could look back he saw debris and smoke streaming away into the distance.

Something else, something big, went by, too — a B-17. He was in the middle of the stream, kicking right, left, to avoid the big friends, coming out below, upside-down again, watching for signs of the enemy below. But this time they were not below. This time, instead of making their single pass and diving away out of sight before climbing to prepare for the next pass . . . this time they were staying to fight it out.

Suddenly the sky over Berlin resembled those fanciful paintings of aerial combat over the Western Front in the First World War — machines everywhere, at every height, in every attitude, some marking their own destruction with smoke trails, others trailing smoke from their firing guns — the ultimate, chaotic, mass dogfight.

On low-level rhubarbs you were often given orders to attack 'targets of opportunity' — trains, vehicles, barges, power stations, railway sidings, and especially military trucks and tankers. Here, now, the targets of opportunity were everywhere, on all sides, above and below. But they did not always give you the opportunity to open fire.

There, right in front, 200 yards range, was a target of opportunity all right. But a silver one, the familiar silhouette of a Mustang with the big air scoop under the belly. Leave that, for God's sake. But a second later he was firing a full deflection burst at — was it a Ju-88? Then, beyond, a straggler B-17, with two engines streaming smoke, was being set upon by a couple of stubby, ugly *hateful* 190s. God, how he hated the 190! Especially *these* 190s. The bomber was already doomed and they were just killing the crew before they could get out.

Raymond threw his machine into a tight turn, straightened up, pulled up, and, by some magic juxtaposition, there was one of the buggers, armoured belly exposed, range fifty yards. He was so angry that his burst was wastefully long. Overkill. Just as *they* were overkilling the B-17. It might have been three seconds long, which is two hundred and forty half-inch slugs — and not many missed. The 190, pilot obviously dead, turned gracefully onto its back, climbed for a few seconds in this unnatural attitude, and then dropped as fast as any of the bombs now raining down on Berlin.

The fight continued at this pitch of ferocity until the surviving bombers had turned through 180 degrees and were on their way home, harried by flak and air rockets and intermittent attacks by 109s and 190s. The price was heavy on both sides, by the bomber groups hellbent on getting their bombs on target, and by the attacking fighters which swooped down again and again like crows on highway carrion, regardless of the stinging Mustangs which were notching up their highest score since they had become operational.

Up here, in the pure air of the sub-stratosphere where the sins of man had never penetrated before, the anger and hate were marked by the smoke and flame of death, of flying debris and missiles. Some of those who fell from the machines at this great height were suddenly, magically held by blossoming parachutes, others continued at terminal velocity to their terminal end; and a wise lucky few free-fell to clear the battle and seek the oxygen of lower altitudes before pulling the ripcord.

More than sixty of the four engine bombers, each with its crew of ten, fell before the fury of the German guns, in spite of the savage defence put up by their gunners and the P-51 Mustangs. But at last, exhausted of ammunition, fuel and the further strength required to fight at this altitude, the Germans withdrew. As for 69 Squadron and the American Mustangs, scattered all over the sky, they too were out of ammunition and would have to nurse their machines home economically after the gluttonous consumption of fuel in those minutes of ultimate combat.

Raymond, who had added two more to his score since he had put down that 110, felt utterly drained and dangerously unalert. Another fresh wing of American Mustangs had taken over the close escort for the bombers' withdrawal across northern Germany. He was relieved to find company in another stray Mustang, and one of his own flight, too. It was J-Johnnie: Jamie Miller. Jamie pulled in close, rocking his wings and giving the thumbs-up sign, then two fingers to represent his own score. Raymond unsnapped his mask for a second to grin and clap his gauntleted hands before settling back for the long run home, full coarse pitch, full weak mix, +2 boost.

No one was interested in them, not even the flak boys outside the big cities, and they might have been on a training recce over England — until they skirted Emden. Here the heavy 88s threw up a couple of dozen rounds — uneasily accurate, too — just to show bad feeling. Then they were over the sea and they felt able to chatter freely to keep up their spirits.

'Quite a do, Ray!'

'What were yours?'

'Both 109s. I think they were both Gs. One of them took me up to thirty-nine thousand feet and the stick was like a spoon in thin milk.'

Pause. Then Raymond: 'How're your legs, Jamie?'

'They'll never move again.'

They had been sitting still for over five hours and Raymond's own legs felt like ballast. He pulled away from Jamie's Mustang and said, 'Why don't we try this?'

He inverted his Mustang with a gentle half slow roll and eased forward the stick in order to maintain position on Jamie's machine. The effect was magical. Flying upside-down like this, all the pressures on his body were reversed, the blood flowed out of his legs, relieving the strain on the veins, and the whole world took on a rosier, if upside-down, aspect. Jamie followed his Flight Commander's example and, for fifteen minutes and for almost half the distance across the North Sea, the two fighters cruised serenely through a clear blue March sky, in loose inverted formation.

They were quite alone. No one saw them until Raymond heard a voice on the radio channel exclaiming, 'I'm going nuts, Willie! Look at that, over at 3 o'clock.'

'Christ, they're Mustangs! What's got into their heads?'

Raymond could see a pair of twin engine Mosquitoes, probably returning from a shipping recce, off to their left. He flipped over the transmitter lever and called out, 'Balls! It's you Mossies who're upside-down.'

Without a word, and a few seconds later, the two Mosquitoes flipped over onto *their* backs. At once Raymond and Jamie, as if linked by wire, reinverted themselves and Jamie transmitted, 'Look at those Mossies over there. I wonder why they're upside-down.'

That made them feel much better. After a day like today, it was not only their legs that needed relief.

Chapter Fourteen

'YOU'RE WANTED ON the blower, Ray,' Tubby Eccles called out from his office. 'A woman, of course,' he added in a world-weary voice. 'And on the scrambler. Misuse of official communications.'

Raymond darted in from the ops room. By contrast with the CO's desk in Jack Boland's time, Tubby Eccles kept it clear of all papers except a few in the out-tray. Now he handed the instrument over to Raymond, who heard Louise's voice, sounding metallic as always on the scrambler, saying anxiously, 'Darling, Charlie's just been shot up. They're operating on him now.'

'How bad is he? Will he pull through?' Cheerful Charlie Dee, a survivor if there ever was one. It did not seem possible — or right. Funny how, after all this time, you never became reconciled to this sort of thing.

Louise continued reassuringly, 'Oh, sure. He's not on the danger list. But they're trying to save his right leg. He got a shell in his thigh. And why only there I don't understand. You should see his ship, Ray. It's incredible he got it back.'

Raymond promised he would be over the next day if ops permitted. 'I'll let you know when I arrive.'

Charlie was sitting up in bed, looking fresh and perky but pale. His leg, in plaster from the top of his thigh to his ankle, was under a protective cage. Joan and Louise were sitting on either side of his bed when Raymond arrived with a box of

234

chocolates he had winkled out of the village stores.

'It was a goddamn milk-run compared with some of those Berlin trips,' Charlie said. 'Just across the Channel to those secret weapon sites we're hammering. The flak was filthy — it always is there — but there wasn't a kraut in the sky. I was just wondering why we were needed, when I was jumped out of the sun.'

'Same old story,' Raymond said sympathetically. 'Don't worry, it happens to the best of us.'

'But what bugs me is maybe I'm not going to fly for a while.'

'Don't you worry. Duggy Bader flew through the Battle of Britain without *any* legs. You'll manage with *one*.'

'Oh, sure!' a voice behind them confirmed. 'We'll strap him in somehow.' It was the American orthopaedic surgeon who had operated on Charlie, a young fresh-faced major who had come to check on his patient.

'And you'll be getting your new "Garbo" tomorrow,' said Louise. 'The British ATA are bringing in three P-51s, so I read in the intelligence bulletin this morning. And one of them'll be G for Greta Garbo, and the name'll already be painted on.'

The major struck a more serious note by asking Charlie how he'd slept, and if he was feeling any pain.

'Oh, I'm swell, sir. Can I get up tomorrow? I'd like to see my new ship.'

'Maybe not quite yet, Lieutenant. But you're doing just fine.' And the surgeon walked off down the ward to visit his other patients.

Louise and Raymond took their leave soon after, so Charlie could be alone with Joan. Walking away from the Stiplowe base hospital Louise said sadly. 'I'm afraid Charlie's flying days are over, Ray. Last night the major told me he'll be shipped home as soon as he's fit to travel. And isn't it just great, the Colonel's recommended him for the DFC.'

'That's grand — but I'll miss him,' said Raymond. 'I've become very fond of Charlie since he tried to kill me.'

'I'll tell you something else: he proposed to Joan just before he got shot up. And what she doesn't know and what he doesn't know is that she'll be allowed to go back to the States with him.'

Raymond smiled. 'I'd put up with a cannon shell in my own leg if it meant we could spend the rest of the war together.'

They were now standing in the spring sunshine outside the big HQ building where Louise worked.

'Oh, darling, don't joke like that. It's bad enough already, seeing so little of you.' She began to reach out a hand towards him, then withdrew it, aware that there were curious eyes all round them. 'Ray, my love, how much longer will this war go on for?'

'A while yet. But I've booked another weekend at the Ritz for the beginning of June. You can fix it with the Colonel?'

'Oh, I'll try.' Her grey eyes traced over his face as if painting him in her imagination. 'Oh Jesus, how I'll try! Good-bye, my sweet beloved.'

In this very public place, all Raymond could do was salute her with a cheerful smile and turn away.

Raymond had been right. The war in Europe was still weeks away from its climax. In that month of April 1944, the RAF and the USAAF dropped over eighty thousand tons of bombs on Germany and on German-occupied Europe. 'When is D-Day coming?' everyone was asking. In Italy, the Allies had at last broken the back of the German forces, and were marching on Rome.

When King George VI spoke to his people, saying, 'I hope that throughout the present crisis of the liberation of Europe there may be offered up earnest, continuous and widespread prayer,' everyone knew that an invasion must be imminent. On Monday, 15 May 1944, the King himself, Churchill and Eisenhower and the commanders and principal staff officers of the cross-Channel expedition were briefed in London, with the assistance of a huge map of the beaches of Normandy where (unknown to the Germans until the Allies landed) the invasion — 'Operation Overlord' — would take place.

Meanwhile, up in East Anglia, the great air war continued unceasingly, and not even Colonel Schneider, nor his Chief Intelligence Officer, nor his deputy, Lieutenant Louise Daintree, knew the precise date of D-Day or where the Allies were going to strike. For 69 Squadron and the other RAF fighter squadrons of 12 Group and of 382 Fighter Group of the 8th Air Force, flying continued as intensely and as dangerously as ever.

On the day after Raymond visited Charlie Dee in hospital, the American heavy bombers were again diverted from their regular targets in Germany — oil supplies, chemical works, aircraft manufacturing plants, etc. — to the 'No-ball' sites in northern France, the secret weapon — the *Wunderwaffen* — launching trenches which were daily growing in number and in their potential danger to Britain and to the outcome of the war.

'Now this,' said Jamie Miller, 'is what I call a civilised hour for ops.' It was, in fact, just after 10 o'clock in the morning, five hours later than they had been called over the past days. So the B-Flight officer pilots were in a relaxed frame of mind, and Jamie, having consumed two helpings of bacon and eggs, now spent several minutes filling his pipe.

'What's met say?' asked Harry Hobbs.

'Ten-tenths at five thou., clearing at the coast,' said his brother. 'I called in on the way.'

'Hoping it might be scrubbed, I suppose,' said Raymond. 'But it's not. So let's get cracking.'

Raymond was again filling in for Tubby Eccles, who was currently on leave. Now he would be leading a full quota of twelve Mustangs to escort 8th Air Force bombers to the Pas de Calais. Standing behind his chair, he continued more seriously to those pilots present. 'And don't, for Christ's sake, take it for granted this is going to be a piece of cake. That's what the Yanks at Stiplowe thought yesterday, only they call it a "milk-run". And a chap I know there got a cannon shell in his leg. There may be fewer Huns about but they can still bite.'

Met was right. Over Norfolk, it was ten-tenths, and Raymond had to lead his Squadron through two thousand feet of cloud in tight formation before they broke through into the sun. They caught up with the leading groups of heavies ten miles east of North Foreland, their contrails so heavy that they formed a man-made cloud layer. It was seven months since Raymond had flown in *Grable's Legs*, but the memory of that flight was so fresh that it might have been yesterday.

237

At least this was a safer run for them, though the flak, when it opened up, was heavier than anything Raymond had seen over any German target, spotting the sky so densely that it added new depth to the contrails.

He stationed 69 Squadron five thousand feet above the Americans, scanning every point of the compass continuously. Below, the landscape south of Calais had been pockmarked, by heavy, medium and fighter bombers, with thousands upon thousands of bomb craters. These made white circles of varying sizes in the chalk soil, with overlapping concentrations where the ski sites of the secret weapons were closest together. It seemed as if nothing could have survived down there but Raymond knew from long experience, at the receiving as well as the giving end, how rapidly bomb damage could be repaired, and he had heard from the Spy that many of the launching sites had been buried deep underground with concrete roofs like the U-boat shelters, which had proved indestructible.

The B-17s went into the wall of flak like foot soldiers going over the top at the Somme, falling by the same arbitrary whims of fate, one here, one there, two side-by-side as if in a deliberately shared ordeal. Spread across the open sky of northern France, it was a scene so familiar to him by now that Raymond could not conceive of a time when this aerial slaughter might cease: on and on, hundreds of thousands of workers in America building these great chariots of destruction, thousands of young Americans training to crew them, and hundreds of thousands more Germans exclusively preoccupied with their demolition, generation after generation of them . . .

Raymond's mind had momentarily wandered but his eyes remained as sharp as that time (was it before the Battle of Waterloo?) when he had first spotted a Ju-88. One thing that had never changed was the reaction as you identified a 'bandit' for sure, that little *frisson* followed at once by the sharpening of the senses. Raymond felt it now, even though the enemy was ten or fifteen thousand feet below and as harmless as an Imperial Airways 'Hannibal'. It was, in fact, a tri-motor Junkers 52, perhaps fat with staff officers speeding to an urgent meeting.

Raymond deliberately chose Red Section to go down. One of the pilots was as green as the landscape, and it would do him a power of good to warm up his guns against the enemy.

'Red one and two, there's a bogey nine o'clock below heading due east. Go get it. Out.'

The two Mustangs broke away with the eagerness of greyhounds out of the traps, diving flat out. Feeling suddenly patriarchal in his senior rôle, Raymond watched the leading bomber groups dropping their loads, black confetti for a marriage of death with death. Then, before the bombs had found their targets, the planes turned away from this cauldron of flak and broke into individual evasive action.

'Buttercup Red One to Buttercup Leader,' Raymond heard faintly from his detached pair. 'Have dealt with bandit. OK to go home?'

'Buttercup Leader — OK. Out.'

Behind, the American P-51 groups, including 382 Group from Stiplowe, were dealing with an intervention by Messerschmitts, and judging by the overlapping exclamations and violent claims, it was a scrap all right. But it was 69's task to remain with their own groups, which they did without incident. Raymond detached another section to close in on a straggler B-17 with three working engines and, as far as he could see, less than half its tailplane left. Then they came round south of Boulogne — renewed flak — and over the blessed Channel, heading for the white cliffs to the north. 'There'll be bluebirds over,' Raymond hummed silently, 'the white cliffs of Dover ... light and laughter and peace ever after ...' Like hell — not tomorrow, not the next day, not the next year. Only B-17s over the white cliffs of Dover — those lucky enough to get this far.

At Horning, Bonz was sitting on the lip of the blast bay in his customary stance, forbidden to move until engine switch-off. He seemed more content now that Raymond was flying Merlin-engined machines again, and came dashing down the bank to greet him and take his helmet between his jaws.

'Chiefy would like a word with you, sir,' Raymond's fitter greeted him. 'As soon as you can, he said.'

Raymond watched the last of his Squadron touch down — no one missing — and then walked towards the Flight-Sergeant's office. Normally Chiefy would be out on the perimeter track, supervising the parking of the aircraft, but instead Raymond could see him seated at his desk, talking to someone.

'What's up, Chiefy?' he broke in.

Flight-Sergeant Mullard had more service in than the total of half the Squadron's erks: dating back to the RFC. He sported faded Palestine, North-West Frontier and First World War ribbons. His skull might have been covered with old tightly-stretched dark leather, his face was dominated by a waxed moustache, and his voice was like a cement-mixer. He now stood to attention and saluted Raymond, as did the young corporal standing on the other side of the desk.

'Well, sir, I doesn't know how to put it.'

'Let's sit down, shall we,' Raymond suggested, and did so himself. The op. had taken less than three hours but he felt tired and in need of a cigarette, which he lit up, and a drink, which would have to wait.

'Well, sir, it seems that our old CO's back. So Corporal Baines says.'

Raymond turned to the corporal, whom he knew and trusted: a wizard with a Merlin. 'What do you mean? What old CO?'

Corporal Baines sat very upright in the upright chair, oil-stained hands on his knees. 'I really couldn't believe my eyes, sir. I though he went for a burton months ago. But I had just finished checking M-Mother — been a bit of trouble with the boost control, just got the cowling on — when a Commer stopped beside me. I was right up at the end, out of sight from here, so no one else saw what happened. You had all been gone about ten minutes, I suppose.'

'Who do you *mean*?' Raymond asked brusquely, and then the thought struck him like a blow to the head. 'You don't mean Squadron-Leader Boland?'

The corporal nodded. 'Yes, sir. He was like a ghost ... I mean, he was so pale. I've never been so scared in my life.'

Raymond asked, 'What did he do, for God's sake?'

'He was dressed in his best blue uniform, sir, decorations and all. Quite smart. No flying gear or anything. He greeted me by my name and then he asked, 'Is this kite serviceable?' So I said, 'Yes, sir. Just finished work.' And he climbed into the cockpit. He was very impatient.'

Chiefy broke in at this point. 'I told him 'e shouldn't have done, sir. Squadron Leader Boland wasn't fit to fly — 'e must've escaped from 'ospital, sir.'

Raymond considered the crazy scene this must have presented. Then he said to the corporal. 'I suppose it wasn't easy to disobey a squadron-leader. Especially your old CO. Force of habit, force of training.'

The corporal looked down at his hands. No gunk would ever quite clear his pores of the years of oil and grease. 'I suppose I should have refused, sir. But he was so *definite*.'

Raymond stubbed out the cigarette in Chiefy's ashtray. 'You mean he took off?'

'Yes, sir. He didn't run up the engine or check the mags or nothing, sir. He just taxied out and took off — not wasting no time, neither.'

'I confirmed that with flying control, sir,' said Chiefy, 'I was too busy at the time. But the duty officer saw it take off. 'e thought it was just one of the Squadron who'd been a bit delayed. 'e thought the kite might join up with the Yanks from Stiplowe which had just flown over on the same op.'

Knowing the answer, Raymond asked, 'And I suppose he hasn't come back?'

'Not 'ere, sir. Not 'ere.'

Raymond looked at the two faces in turn, at the two pairs of eyes watching him curiously. 'Well,' he said slowly, 'that's a bit of a turn-up. Does anyone else know?'

Firmly, almost indignantly, Flight-Sergeant Mullard said, 'Oh no, sir.'

'I'd better do some checking. Keep it under your hat for now. And thanks for letting me know.'

In the security of Tubby Eccles's office, Raymond got on the scrambler to Group.

'Chris, is there any news of a missing RAF Mustang?'

'Not a thing. Ray. Yours was the only British squadron on the "No-ball" op, and your Spy reported all home, and one

241

bloody great Junkers to your credit.'

'Yes, but there was a gatecrasher, too. It's all very rum but our "Missing presumed killed" Squadron-Leader Jack Boland turned up here just after we took off . . .'

Raymond told him then about Corporal Baines's experience, and when the AOC's number two made doubting noises, Raymond reassured him. 'Baines is as straight as a die — and anyway, who'd make up a story like that? I mean, where's Jack *been* all this time?'

'If it wasn't his ghost, then it looks as if he'll be one now,' said Squadron-Leader Chris Berry. 'Nothing in from Air Sea Rescue either. Where and when will the mystery intrepid birdman strike again?'

Raymond laughed bitterly. 'It's all very well for you, making jokes from behind your cosy desk at Group. But I've got to account for one lost Mustang and keep this story quiet as well — at least for a day or two.'

Later Louise exclaimed, 'Gee, Ray, if I have to use my charm on Colonel Schneider once more, I'll *have* to go to bed with him.' She added grimly, 'That's something he's been trying to bring about for the past twelve months.'

Raymond laughed. 'Oh, come on, you're not *that* wanton. Anyway, think of that moustache and the smell of cheap cigars and bourbon.'

'Well, its not been easy to get away this time,' Louise said emphatically. She cupped his face with her hands and kissed him half a dozen times very quickly, and then once very slowly. 'But worth it,' she added, when she had finished.

The evenings had grown long and warm again, and they sauntered slowly along the bank of the broad towards the Nelson Arms. 'Why was it so urgent?' she asked teasingly. 'Just lust?'

'That's a good enough reason, isn't it? And let's be lustful if we can. But for now I want to ask your advice.' He told her briefly about the Jack Boland business: his surprise reappearance and immediate disappearance again. Louise perched on the top rung of a fence to consider the matter.

'Those Bolands!' she exclaimed at length, accepting from Raymond the proffered lit cigarette. 'They're what you might call ubiquitous. Do you suppose he'd been in hiding all these months? But why hiding, unless he thought you were going to charge him with attempted murder? And that wouldn't be like him. Or do you think he was in hospital with loss of memory? But then he'd be identifiable. Wherever he was, he couldn't be kept away from a good fight any longer. But how did he know about that big op. to the Pas de Calais?'

'He could've telephoned intelligence at Horning, or Stiplowe, flung his rank around. Then after he took off, he could've kept at a distance until the scrap started, then no one would've noticed he wasn't wearing flying gear.'

'And he was real sick and wouldn't have stood a chance in a dogfight,' added Louise. She held up her cigarette and studied it, a habit of hers when brooding on a problem. 'Ray, I think you ought to call up his mother. I've got a hunch she knows more than she let on to you. Anyway, I guess she ought to know.'

'No answer to the telephone.'

'Then go see her, Ray.' Then quickly correcting herself, 'No, on second thoughts don't. I'm sorry about her troubles, but I don't trust anyone in that family by now. Who knows if that mad Jack hasn't baled out somewhere and is lying low again. Remember, he damn nearly killed you once.'

Raymond took her arm to help her down. 'Bonz needs a walk,' he said. 'He's been cooped up all day.'

Louise clasped his hand tight as they started away from the pub along the path they knew so well. 'What rubbish!' she exclaimed. 'He doesn't need a walk at all. He hates walks. He likes flying. But if *you* want a little walk, and a rest at the end of it, then I'm your girl.'

17th May 1944 was a dirty day, 'Harry clampers' at first, which gave Raymond the chance to slip away. Cloud four hundred feet. Light drizzle. Delilah's wipers going click-clack through their short arc on the seven-inch-deep windscreen. Out of the front gates, right, second left and over the next crossroads. Like every town and village in the country, for fear of guiding invaders, West Aitcham was not signposted, but Raymond could have driven to the vicarage blindfold.

The short gravel drive was as overgrown as ever, and the brown front door had not only lost still more of its paint; it looked as if it had not been opened for weeks.

There was no response to either the bell or the knocker. Leaving Bonz tied up in the car, Raymond walked round to the back, where he could hear an intermittent banging sound. The hens were loose and wandering about the yard with its two-foot-high nettles and the couch grass growing between the cobbles. There was that banging again: *crash, crash.* He walked a few yards, and the hens came clucking up beside him as if he ought to have had corn to scatter. Another bang, and this time Raymond saw the reason. The big double doors of the makeshift hangar which had housed 'Tiger' were swinging free in the wind, perhaps as they had done since that first and last fatal flight. He secured them to make himself feel less uneasy, glancing briefly inside at the emptiness.

Then he walked back to the house. He knocked on one of the cracked panes of the back door. When there was still no response, he entered. But, oh God, the smell! At first it was no worse than cooking cabbage, then recognisable as putrefying flesh. At the entrance to the scullery the two black labradors lay sprawled out dead, side by side. Not all that long dead, but long enough to have begun smelling in the unventilated rear quarters of the house.

With two dead dogs at your feet, it seemed a faintly ridiculous thing to do, but he called out, 'Is anyone at home?'

The kitchen looked as if someone had got up in the middle of a meal and forgotten to return. The Aga was cold, there was congealing food on the plates, and one glass half full of water, the other turned on its side. Raymond opened a window to let out the stench, then moved towards the hall, feeling like an interloper, and on into the vicar's study.

He remembered it as he had last seen it: heaped coal and wood fire, John Boland rising cheerfully and limping over on his stick to greet him. 'A little life-saver?' Then perhaps a little quote from the Good Book. And Rachel stroking the velvet ears of the two dogs. Or Dorothy Boland bustling in full of talk of lunch. Or Jack in his dressing- gown and slippers, looking ill but full of seeming friendliness and hospitality, like the rest of them. But the smell of pipe smoke had dispersed,

244

to be replaced by the smell of dead dog filtering in from the scullery.

It had always been a dark room — mainly because of the laurels outside obstructing the light — but a cheerful room. And *noisy*. Not noisy now, however. The only sound, from outside, was the distant hum of a Merlin engine. Probably a Spit going out on a met flight. Then a cat mewed in the dim corner, and before he could move towards the sound, Dorothy Boland greeted him.

'Hello, Ray. How nice of you to come! And how brave!'

He could see her, in the same corner, huddled up in a rocking-chair with the two cats on her lap.

'Dorothy, for God's sake, what's happened?'

'Come and give me a kiss, you nice motherless boy.'

He went towards her and bent down, the cats springing protestingly away. She put her arms round his neck and kissed him on the cheek.

'I'm sorry no one else is here. I've only one left now, Ray, and she's flying somewhere far away.'

'What do you mean, Dorothy?' Raymond pulled up a chair and sat in front of her. 'What on earth's happened?'

Dorothy Boland rocked gently to and fro, hands clasped in her lap, fingers twisting against fingers, staring up at him with her bright blue eyes. 'Don't think I'm mad, Ray, just sitting here like this. It's just that the grief has paralysed me and I don't know what to do.'

'Go on, tell me,' Raymond said gently.

'Jack was the last to go, and he, my dear Ray — he was not himself, I'm afraid. I think it was some pernicious strain of malaria he had on top of all that terrible time and terrible responsibility in Burma, and then straight back into leading a squadron here. You remember how he never really got over that malaria in spite of all the drugs, and when he was shot down something seemed to crack in his brain.'

Calmly and articulately Dorothy Boland told Raymond how Jack said he had crash-landed his Typhoon on marshland by the sea and had walked home through the night. 'He arrived at five in the morning. He was in a very bad way, not physically at first, just his mind, poor darling. He kept claiming that no German could ever shoot him down. He said it had to be you

245

and that American boy who came here once or twice — you know, Charlie. "They were always after me," he said "because they knew I was protecting Rachel from them. The two devils shot me down, working together. *They* did it for revenge, and so they could get at Rachel — my Rachel!"'

Dorothy Boland was sobbing silently, her head rocking from side to side in her grief. 'My poor Jack, my poor boy. He didn't know what he was saying or what he was doing. It was no good trying to reason with him. He just got terribly angry and broke out into awful sweats and shaking, saying over and over, "I'll have to deal with them, I'll have to deal with them." Oh, Ray, it was awful. I think he was going mad.'

With his hand on hers, Raymond was thinking of how this mother must have tended her sick son over all those weeks, knowing that if she called the doctor he would certainly be taken away. She never locked his door so that he knew he could leave at any time, but he also sensed the truth that he was totally dependent on his mother for his freedom, not from the medical authorities but from the provost-marshall for attempted murder.

'But what about John? How did it affect him?'

At the mention of her husband's name, Dorothy eased herself out of her chair and walked over to the sideboard. She took out a bottle of whisky and two glasses.

'It affected him very badly. One boy killed, the other what he took to be incurably insane.' She held up the bottle, smiling wistfully. 'I have always been afraid his "little life-savers" would kill him eventually. But all that speeded things up — the consumption, I mean, and the destruction of his liver. He had been terribly ill for months.'

Raymond got up and stared in horror at this tough, grey-haired woman for whom the tragedies had piled up in such swift and agonising succession. 'My poor, poor Dorothy. You haven't deserved all this.'

She filled the glasses with a steady hand, and held hers up. 'John's last words to me were from St Matthew, of course — 'To what purpose is this waste?' And then he closed his eyes. It was quite peaceful — not like poor little Arnold's end, or Jack's, "In all the full fury of violence."'

'But Dorothy, Jack may still be all right. He's gone missing before.'

'Oh, I know he is dead, dear Ray. A woman knows these things when it comes to her own blood. He dressed himself in his best blue, with all his decorations, just as if for some formal occasion. I asked him if he was going somewhere, and he said, "Yes, I have a duty to perform. There's something big on and I must hurry. Good-bye, Mums." And he kissed me. Then he strapped on his revolver, just like you all do on operations. I called out, "Don't go, don't go, Jack." Then those lazy old dogs who never seem to be aroused by anything suddenly sprang to life when they heard my voice and saw Jack going downstairs. They jumped up, barking and trying to stop him. So — oh dear God forgive him for he did not know . . .'

She put down her drink and began sobbing uncontrollably. Raymond put an arm round her shoulder. After a while, when she could speak again, she said, 'Isn't it awful? But somehow the death of a harmless animal is almost worse than that of a person — a person you love, even.'

'Yes, yes, I can understand. But I don't understand why no one in the village, none of John's parishioners, came to see how you were.'

'Oh yes, they wanted to, bless them. But I didn't want to see anyone — not even the new vicar — and the word got round. I don't mind now, though.'

They finished their drinks and then Raymond said, 'I know what happened to Jack immediately after he left you.'

He began to tell her, but she shook her head and said, 'Yes, I know, Ray. I knew he was going to fly and I knew he would never come back, although I don't think we'll ever know what happened. He wasn't fit for flying. But he kept saying, "I have a duty to perform."'

Later, Raymond went to put the two dogs in a sack and bury them in the garden. There were other practical things to see to: food and care and someone to come in and clean up. 'Oh, I'll be all right now,' she assured him. 'What a blessing you have been! Wouldn't your aunt have been proud of you.'

'Poor Dorothy, what a ghastly business! Now what about Rachel? Does she know? Do you know where she is?'

Dorothy spread her hands wide and smiled. 'You never can tell with that girl — here, there and everywhere. Last time I heard she was somewhere up in Scotland. It might be Timbuctoo today.'

'She knew you were caring for Jack, I suppose?' Raymond asked, recalling the confidence with which Rachel had said he was a prisoner, which was as near to the truth as she could have come.

'Oh, yes. She was very good with him, whenever she could get here. How they loved one another, those two!' And she smiled at the memory.

'I'll get onto ATA when I get back. One other practical thing, Dorothy,' he went on gently. 'It'll have to come out now — I mean about Jack. The word's bound to get round, and we've got to account for the plane. But I'm sure it'll be all right as far as you're concerned.'

'That doesn't matter. None of that matters. But I would like to see my little girl.'

Raymond almost laughed. 'Not so little now, Dorothy. You should just see her climbing out of a Typhoon!'

He kissed her cheek and told her he would come back the next day if he could, and urged her to answer the telephone if it rang and to ask the new vicar to call by. She was back in her rocking-chair as he left and the cats were back on her lap. But she looked a changed woman now, and had promised him she would fix herself something to eat.

'Holy Jesus!' Charlie Dee exclaimed. 'What d'you think he was going to do? Was it some suicide mission?'

'I think he was after us — one or both.'

'You're kidding, Ray?'

'Oh no, not kidding at all. As you know, he'd certainly had one go at me. And his poor crazed mind worked the same way about you. Allies in the seduction of his beloved sister.'

Charlie sat up indignantly. 'But I never *touched* her! I never thought of touching her.'

'Of course you didn't. And *my* kisses were only social — a peck on the cheek.'

'But all that hospitality! Heck, he *kept* inviting me over to his place — and you, too. Almost as if he wanted her seduced, and then wanted to take it out on us.' Charlie flipped a Camel at Raymond and shrugged his shoulders. 'Still, I guess if you're screwy, everything's screwy.' He glanced down the ward and turned with a grin. 'Well, here come the dolls. No one's going to kill us for seducing these two. And, oh boy, do you get randy just lying here!'

Every pair of eyes from every bed followed the progress of the two elegant WAC officers as they moved down the ward, waving and smiling at patients they recognised. 'Lucky they're officers, or we'd be deafened by the whistles,' Charlie remarked. 'Good evening, girls. No one'll mind if you kiss us.'

It was almost a farewell session, for Charlie had now been told he was to be shipped home to the States in two days, and the sentiment flowed freely ... 'What're we going to do without you?' And, 'Honey, I'm going to miss you so I'll die.'

Charlie said, 'We'll have reunions, just like college grads. Every year we'll get together and talk about our heroic past — here in little ol' England.'

Joan turned to Raymond. 'We're giving Charlie a farewell party tomorrow evening. Six o'clock — you *must* be there.'

'And before that,' Charlie added, 'there's going to be a ritual farewell down at the dispersal. The doc says I can be wheeled down to kiss the tail of my new ship — the P-51 I'll never fly. Just sitting there waiting for me — my Garbo. Whoever flies her will have to be shit hot, I'll tell you. No goddamn flak holes.'

Five minutes later, outside the sick bay, Louise was looking more serious as she confided in Raymond, 'No one's had the heart to tell him yet.'

'Tell him what?'

'His replacement "Greta Garbo" never came — and it was painted all ready for him too. The other two were delivered OK, and landed just a few minutes after the Group took off on a mission. The two ATA 1st officer girls who brought them in said they flew down together from the USAAF depot but they lost contact with the third ship at the end of the flight. We've no report of any crash. Just disappeared, sort of clairvoyant, as if the pilot knew there was no one to fly it.'

Raymond did not comment at once. Then he said thoughtfully, 'Poor old Charlie. He'll be disappointed. I suppose it's too late to trace where it went. Those girls are usually so hot on navigation, too.'

Several times during the morning Raymond tried to get through ATA at White Waltham, but the telephone lines seemed to be inextricably entangled, crossed and double-crossed. 'It's the same everywhere — GPO lines, service lines, even the scrambler lines are scrambled,' George Lubbock complained. 'I couldn't even get through to Group earlier. It's all because of this bloody invasion.'

'This bloody invasion's going to be a bloody cock-up if no one's going to be able to talk to anyone else,' Raymond remarked bitterly.

'It can't be long now,' said Jamie Miller. 'I had to fly down to Shoreham yesterday and the roads were *crammed*. There must've been a thousand tanks on one stretch of the Brighton road, and the fields were like the biggest Scout jamboree of all time — millions of tents.'

It was 31 May 1944 and the tension everyone felt was reflected in short tempers, too much drink and not enough sleep. Even the equable Tubby Eccles, back from leave, was liable to give sharp answers.

With an hour to spare before a late afternoon op., Raymond settled himself in his Flight Commander's office with the telephone, determined to get through to Rachel Boland or at least find out where she was.

After fifty minutes of frustration and failure, he thought of getting the private home number of Rachel's Pool Commander who — she had once told him — lived in Leicester. Directory Enquiries got him the number — after he had thrown his rank around, and promoted it to Air Commodore and threatened a report to the area supervisor. That number got him through to the Pool Commander's mother who promised to do her best to relay a message asking her son to telephone Raymond urgently that evening.

It was not until dinner that a steward called Raymond to the telephone. It was the Group Commander, sounding concerned. 'Are you a relation of Rachel Boland?' he asked.

'No, but I'm speaking for her mother, and it's pretty damn urgent. Can you either get hold of her or let me know where she is?'

'I wish I could. I certainly wish I could. She took off from the depot early two days ago with two other 1st officers. She was delivering a P-51 Mustang to 382 Group. She was due back that evening after delivering it but never made it.'

The line was being interfered with, a second and then a third voice becoming audible, while the Pool Commander's voice was fading.

Raymond half-shouted, 'Did the plane land somewhere else?'

'I can't hear you.'

'DID — IT — LAND . . .?'

Raymond could not be sure whether the answer he heard was 'No it didn't' or 'No, I can't hear you'.

'This is it, chaps. The real thing.' Tubby Eccles walked into the ops room from his office, tying up his Mae West. 'They're going ashore now, God help them.'

'You mean the bloody invasion?' Cobber James asked innocently, not looking up from his game of poker.

'No, my Aunt Clara's birthday.'

Jamie Miller said, 'The sixth hour of the sixth day of the sixth month. How about that?'

'Very quick calculation,' said one of the Hobbs brothers, gathering up his winnings. 'Now work out how much I've won.'

Two hours later, Raymond led B-Flight over the Channel at seven thousand feet, heading for the Normandy countryside which lay behind the invasion beaches. Between breaks in the cloud he looked down on a sight he would remember all his life, a breathtaking expression of military power on a scale the world had never seen before. Thousands of ships, from giant battleships to barely visible auxiliary vessels, crowded the ocean for as far as the eye could see, carving white wakes on the water behind them; hundreds upon hundreds of landing craft delivering men and vehicles to the scarred, burning shore, with many more following in second, third and fourth waves, some of them burning or abandoned.

The shelling from the sea, which had begun before dawn, still continued, the guns of the men-o'-war sparkling with muzzle flashes like a million struck matches, and relays of multiple rockets adding to the hell of destruction. Smoke spread from burning buildings and tanks; and up and down this French shore, from west to east, the figures of the assaulting troops were like plague flies setting about their devastation.

The sky was as full and as busy as the sea and the land below, and Raymond's memory went back to the time in September 1940 when Winston Churchill had referred to RAF Fighter Command as 'the few'. In those days, if the odds of Germans against you were only five to one you were thankful. Now, today, D-Day, there was not an enemy aircraft to be seen, and the sky was full of thousands of fighters and bombers — of the good old Spitfire, updated from that earlier battle; of Typhoons and Thunderbolts, Lightnings and Mustangs; of medium bombers like the Mosquito, Boston and Mitchell (the Americans at the same height as they were, in groups of eighteen, maybe two or three hundred of them), the familiar silhouette of the American B-17s and B-24s; the British heavies, the Lancasters and Halifaxes, with their massive bomb-carrying capacity: all hell-bent on destruction out of the raging sky.

'Going down — *now!*' Raymond ordered. And he pushed forward the stick, at once picking up speed, his flight conforming, through a gap in the clouds the city of Caen visible on the right, already a cauldron of smoke and rubble dust from bombing. At one thousand feet, when Raymond raised his hand, his flight broke up, following the orders — being repeated that day by hundreds of fighters and fighter-bombers — to search for targets of opportunity. Especially trains and everything moving on the roads, and above all signs of reinforcing German Panzer divisions.

Intermittently over the next forty minutes, Raymond followed the pattern of low-level strafing he had first practised — how many years ago? The weaving over fields and trees, the scattering livestock, the white, upturned faces of startled people in village street and field, and the little domestic detail that imprinted itself on your mind — like a woman in black taking down the checked family tablecloth from her washing line — and the hazards of church steeples and electricity pylons, and, above all, the flak towers that could fire level at you.

This time he was lucky early: a long freight train, each truck with bulging tarpaulin load, moving in stately style over a level crossing. Raymond swung round, lined up, dipped down, and released his half-empty drop tanks on the leading truck, did a quick 180 degree turn and opened fire on the same spot. The incendiary .5s in his ammunition belts did the rest, the explosion of flame consuming the big black locomotive and the first dozen trucks.

Never hang around, and never attack twice — that was the rule. But from ten miles away, when he glanced back, the smoke was rising in black gouts into the sky. A single lorry he found entering a village went up in flames, too, and later, a platoon of infantry, given no time to scatter, went down like skittles.

Kill, destroy, kill, destroy. *Am I just a hardened old killer? Will compassion ever creep back? Will I ever 'know what 'tis to pity' again?* Louise always pooh-poohed such considerations as this — 'You've never lost your pity, Ray. It's just a job, a temporary, not-very-nice job.' But, oh how he hated it — while yet, as always, relishing his skill.

But 'those that dance must pay the piper', even now, after such a heavy price had been paid in suffering and injury. Raymond saw that nemesis was upon him long before it descended — or so it seemed in the sudden acceleration of time violence brings about. At one moment, he was racing low above the Normandy *bocage* of tight little hedged fields, and the next, like 'a gathering of evil intent', he was two hundred feet above a group of Tiger tanks, their 88 mm guns elevated on to some unseen target.

But these giant killers were also equipped to deal with the threat from the air, and keen gunners with their own survival at stake had spotted Raymond's lone Mustang speeding north towards the Allied bridgehead. The Tigers' 7.9 mm guns coned Raymond as if someone had tipped the gunners off about his direction and time, the mg bullets spattering him from nose to tail.

Perhaps fifty, perhaps one hundred of these lethal little bullets struck Raymond's plane. By the grace of good luck, or the grace of God (and who is to make the distinction?), not one of them struck Raymond fatally or even seriously. A chance fragment of his own Mustang's alloy nicked his right ankle, scarcely drawing blood.

Raymond winced at the pain, expecting worse, thrust his Mustang's stick forward as if he was Joe Louis throwing a right punch, kicked left-right-left rudder, and flew clear of the danger, ruddering right and left at twenty-five feet at the same time thinking *September 1940 to June 1944, with hardly a break. And still alive. Do I deserve it?*

And at this precise moment, 10.27 am, 6 June 1944, the Mustang's Merlin engine decided enough was enough. And who could blame it, with no fewer than seven 7.9 mm bullets embedded in its crank-case? Raymond felt the familiar emptiness in his stomach at the onset of serious crisis, pulled back the stick, considered briefly the idea of baling out, decided against at seven hundred feet, and prepared to put down — somewhere, anywhere.

In fact there was little choice. Anything behind was still enemy-occupied territory, where on this of all days his reception would be hostile, while ahead he could just discern through the smoke of battle a stretch of shell-torn beach. Raymond was aware that in almost four years of flying in a number of degrees of hazard, never had he flown through such metal-filled air — air thick with heavy, medium and light shellfire, from naval rockets and 8-inch through 88 mm down to 20 mm and .303 and 7.9 mm gunfire.

It made the flak over Dover, or Berlin, over Dutch coast convoys and 'No-ball' targets, seem like the shuttlecocks in a game of badminton. Raymond had long since given up praying. He just guided his dead-engine Mustang through the lot, looking for once neither to right nor left, nor behind, steadying his concentration on a stretch of beach dead ahead. But this was not the Normandy holiday beach of the 1930s *avec les petits enfants* digging sandcastles and paddling in the sea, mother and father stretched out under a parasol sipping *vin du pays*.

This was a very special and very busy beach, littered with artillery and the trucks and tracked personnel carriers towing them, with intact tanks slow-moving inland and mined tanks stationery and askew, with the litter and detritus of war from smashed-open ammunition boxes to smashed-open infantrymen, blankets and markers, abandoned guns and firing guns, and the wire and obstructions which had been overcome — at a price — three hours earlier.

It was suicide to crash-land here, and the sea was little clearer with its LCTs and other landing craft, some moving, some knocked out and half sunk, many more disgorging their tanks and trucks and half-tracks and infantrymen.

Was this finally it? Raymond chose the sea as the better of two evils. With canopy ejected and his engine dead, the wailing chorus and ear-stunning sounds of battle penetrated his helmet and distracted his brain — when it was no time to be distracted. Through the smoke and dust he eased his Mustang to a relatively clear stretch of water, stalled her some ten feet above the sea and smacked in.

It was said you had thirty seconds to get out of a Mustang after ditching. If this was so, it was the shortest half minute Raymond had ever recorded. He had already snatched off his helmet, and he scarcely had time to unclip his straps and bang his 'chute release before the water rose round him and he was in the icy, choppy water. With his Mae West inflated, there was no risk of drowning but he had already taken in a choking amount of water when he caught sight of a destroyer's grey hull no more than fifty yards distant. It disappeared from sight as he sank into the trough of a wave and reappeared as he rose on a crest. All the guns were firing — c-r-a-c-k, c-r-a-c-k, c-r-a-c-k — and the pain in his ears was abominable; and, anyway, who was going to pay any attention to a single airman in the sea at this critical stage of the invasion . . . ?

Raymond prepared himself for a long wait, but in the event an inflatable dinghy with an outboard motor came alongside him in less than five minutes. Feeling distinctly the worse for wear, and very sorry for himself, Raymond was dragged aboard by a couple of burly ABs. He might have been no more than a bit of obstructing flotsam, but they did strip off his sodden clothes and flying boots, and they did wrap two blankets round him with surprising tenderness, and in proper Royal Navy style held a bottle of Royal Navy rum to his lips

— burning to his throat it was, but — oh God be praised! — blood-warming from head to ice-cold toes.

George Lubbock handed Raymond the signal from Bentley Priory without a word. *'Flight-Lieutenant Raymond Cox DFC to US 8th AFHQ wef 7 June as Chief Liaison Officer. Promoted Squadron-Leader.'*

Raymond handed the piece of paper back to the veteran Adjutant with a bleak expression on his face. 'No chance of getting it negatived, I suppose, George?'

Flight-Lieutenant Lubbock shook his head slowly. 'None whatever. Some penguin statistician leafing through the records with nothing better to do has found out how long you've been on ops. And there are at least a thousand fully trained single engine pilots hanging about waiting for a job. So . . .'

Lubbock hauled Raymond off forcibly for a drink. 'And I think it may have got around that you get on rather well with the Yanks.'

'What are you suggesting, George?'

'Oh, nothing, nothing. Then, of course,' he added, steering the glass towards him, 'It's rather wizard having two-and-a-half rings. Better money, too.'

'I suppose it was bound to come. But, my God, George, I'm going to miss it — and miss all of you!'

'You don't want me to pretend that I'm not thankful, darling, do you?'

'No, of course not. No more tears in bed.'

'Tears of relief maybe. You know, Ray, I hadn't cried since I was a baby until we met.' Louise turned Raymond's head round on the pillow, kissing him lingeringly. 'There were nights when I cried myself to sleep with worry in my little bed where we first made love.'

'I *told* you I'd be all right.'

And those were his last words before he was lulled into a deep sleep by the scent of roses and a sense of fulfilment and total satisfaction.

They did not hear about Rachel Boland for another week, and then it was only negative news, elicited from the ATA by Colonel Schneider, who had to account to HQ for the missing P-51 Mustang from 382 Group's strength. The ready-painted replacement G for Greta Garbo, number 44-06069, had taken off from the depot where American Air Force planes were uncrated, assembled and prepared before delivery, at ten in the morning, a minute after the other two which had subsequently arrived safely. These pilots had been too preoccupied with landing procedures to notice her disappearance. The weather was clear and there was no reported enemy activity over the country. The pilot, 1st Officer Rachel Boland, was experienced and had a clean record. Next of kin had been informed that she was 'missing'.

These mid-June days, when the Allied armies in France were fighting to retain and expand their toehold inland from the beaches where they had landed, were also intensely busy for everyone at the High Wycombe headquarters of 8th Air Force where Raymond was now working. But he had managed to find time to put at least half a dozen calls through to the vicarage at West Aitcham. On each occasion there had been no reply.

It was not until the belated capture of Caen, where the German defence had been particularly ferocious, on 9 July, and the start of General George Patton's spectacular sweep across France, that Raymond had managed to get away for twenty-four hours.

He drove to Norfolk, picked up Louise and headed for West Aitcham. It was the first time she had visited the house which had figured strongly in her suspicions and fears for so long. Her first comment was typically blunt as Raymond stopped the car in the overgrown drive.

'What a goddamn dump, Ray! No one can really *live* here.'

'Oh yes, they do — or at least they did. You should have seen it a year ago. The place was jumping with life then.' Raymond's memory switched briefly to the hard-drinking, hearty, Bible-quoting father, the eager young boy full of promise, his strange, sick elder brother, the warm-hearted but down-to-earth daughter, and the hospitable, plump mother whose domestic arrangements were forever almost out of control.

And now? The young boy dead, the father dead of grief and whisky, the two other children somewhere in that world of the 'missing', that poignant, haunting, sky-embracing word coined for the lost aviator.

And Dorothy Boland? Louise was the first out of the car, knocking on the almost paint-less front door and peering through windows obscured by dust and cobwebs. Then they went round to the back, Bonz sniffing about familiar corners and showing signs of the unease they both felt. The back door was unlocked, but this time no stench of putrefying dogs, and the place had been cleaned up even if the air was stale. Louise glanced curiously at the aircraft pictures on the walls and counted the pipes in the rack.

'I didn't like the idea of this place when you used to come here and I don't much like it now, but I'm sorry about your friend, Ray. She was a sort of mother-figure to you — that right?'

'She certainly wanted to be. I think she wanted to be a surrogate mother to Charlie, too — and anyone else she thought in need. But now . . .'

'How d'you mean?'

'Well now, wherever she is, she'll be the one who'll need looking after — the lonely one. Oh Christ!' he suddenly exclaimed as he stood in the middle of the room looking miserably about him. 'This bloody, bloody war!'

They learned from the village shop that a distant relative — or so it was said — had come to pick her up. Dorothy had left without a word to anyone. She had allowed no one from the village to talk to her after the telegram (no doubt read avidly in the post office) which announced that Rachel was missing.

Outside, in the village street, they heard the growing rumble of the bombers going out, and B-17s could be glimpsed through gaps in the clouds, several hundred of them labouring for altitude and forming up for the North Sea crossing.

'They're off to the oil plants again,' said Louise. 'Like to be going with them, Ray?'

'I'd rather be here with you,' he replied, even though the pull of the sky and the heart-pumping memory of combat qualified his preference. Not by much, though, and it would surely diminish with the passing years. But the germ would always be there: through future peace and marriage, amid family life and civilian work so tame and humdrum after the raging sky that it was hard now to envisage how it would be.

'There go our boys,' murmured Louise, watching the P-51s rising from Stiplowe, climbing like larks to join their 'big friends' over enemy soil.

Epilogue

THE GIRL WITH short hair, who held a clipboard as if it was a handgun, exclaimed, 'God, what a stink!'

No one responded because they could not hear. All they could hear was the engine grind from the JCB earth remover.

'Take it easy,' she ordered the driver, a long-haired bloke with a fanatical gleam in his eye as he operated the twin levers and stared into the ten-feet-deep hole he had gouged in the clay soil. He *was* taking it easy. As an old hand in the Weald Aircraft Recovery Group he knew he was near to the heart of the matter. And the stench confirmed it — a sharp smell like the back of an old garage: of oil mixed with the equally clinging odour, almost hospital-like, of ancient glycol. Yet, as he reminded himself in the solitariness of his cab, new glycol, old glycol, it all smelt the same — not like maturing wine. But glycol, once smelt never forgotten. The cooling agent for an engine that had not required cooling for nearly half a century.

With extra care, Jos and Harry picked over the next scoop deposited beside them. Brian was down in the pit in thigh boots, probing the water and clay like a surgeon. He signalled lowering of the scoop, then just before its shovel bit, he swung round and shouted, 'Hold it!'

Gerda echoed the cry, 'Hold it!' The long-haired driver jammed on the brake and raised his eyes to heaven in mock despair. But no one saw. Everyone was poised round the lip of the crater, watching Brian scraping away sodden clay with his hands.

'Plug!' he suddenly shouted.

'Bloody hell!' said Gerda.

Brian's hands and wrists were submerged in the clay and water, but you could see they were moving.

'Another plug!'

'Bang on!' said Gerda, whose father had told her that was RAF language. 'Gumboots on, all.'

They usually took a break for lunch — bread, cheese, beer — but not today. By half past two they had exposed all the twin V banks. It was, indisputably, a Merlin, and only two of the twelve plugs were damaged.

Every time Mick Horsley eased a shovel-load of clay from the side of the engine block, brown water poured in to take its place. 'A pump, a pump, my kingdom for a pump!' he cried out.

Brian in his thigh boots was the only one safe from the liquid mud, and he operated in the deepest part of the crater. He had his back to the others when his shovel brought up a small object with glass in it. When he washed it off, it was revealed unmistakably as a pair of goggles, one lens cracked, the other missing, and only fragments of the leather and fabric remaining. 'Oh God!' he said quietly and slipped the sodden object into the pocket of his bomber jacket. 'What next?' What next indeed! Pilots did sometimes become separated from their goggles in a hurried exit, but it was an ominous sign.

They worked on in silence, clearing the clay from around the engine. With luck, Gerda calculated, they would be able to get the chains round before dark, and if all went well, the Merlin would be out on dry ground and they could spend Sunday searching for pieces of cockpit. They had found a blind-flying panel complete with instruments last year.

But this time their luck ran out. 'Look, you guys, we'll have to stop.' Jos was holding up a femur, as clean and white as in a path lab, and Harry found, at the same time, half a flying boot. He held it up, dripping, like a fisherman with no joy in his work.

Gerda looked like thunder. 'Bloody hell — bury it again, quickly Jos. That may be all.'

'It isn't.' Brian had found the other boot, and the remains of a foot in it, tattered material spilling out.

'That's it, then.'

'Home for tea.'

Mick, 'who had education', as Gerda once claimed, quoted more Shakespeare:

> 'Duncan is in his grave;
> After life's fitful fever he sleeps
> well . . .'

Gerda said sharply, 'He bloody doesn't, not all in bits like that.'

So now it would be the police, and reporters, and questioning by the MOD. A full exhumation. But how were they to know? When they applied to the authorities for the licence they were told the records were not complete. How could they be? Just a rather dodgy map reference. The farmer had not minded. Said he would come along later . . . And now all that waste, and the cost of hiring the JCB.

It was raining when they got back into the Land Rover, with all their wet gear and tools piled into the back. It was 4.45, 19 April, and that poor bugger had been lying there in bits like that since God knows when.

It wasn't until 20 May that the police telephoned Gerda. 'I have the commissioner's authority to say you may carry on with that dig, Miss Whitehead.'

'Thanks,' she said. She had not been called 'Miss' for bloody years, she realised. 'All cleared up, is it then?'

'I don't know about "cleared up", madam. But the inquest will be next week and the coroner says he'd like to hear if you recover anything that might help with the identification of the aeroplane. And, of course, the deceased.'

'OK. That's a deal. 'Bye.'

Gerda dialled Brian's number. 'OK, for Saturday? The police said we must look for what they call the deceased and what we call the poor bloody pilot.' She giggled.

Brian said, 'Christ, what've they been doing, then, the last four weeks?'

'I'll fix the JCB.'

The fancy white tape was still round the site, though the prohibition-of-entry notice had been removed. The Merlin was still lying there at the bottom like an outsize coffin in its grave. Mick Horsley said, 'Looks the same as we left it. I'll bet they didn't dig up any more of our poor sod.'

It took them six hours to get the engine out. When it was resting on the lip of the crater, Jos and Harry got busy cleaning it up, while Mick began serious work with the JCB. It had not rained since they had quit the site on 19 April, and although the going was heavy, at least the clay was dry. They went on until dusk, the JCB groaning away. By then there was a great mound of soil on one side of the crater, and on the other side the Merlin looked quite spruce. Harry was being very professional, making notes though it was almost too dark to read.

'OK — port side. Prop shaft — and, shit, it's bent. Camshaft cover OK. Identity plate, thank God, OK. Come back to that. Plugs on this side all OK. Generator drive bracket dented. After cooler pump looks OK. Hydraulic pump adaptor looks OK, but hard to see. Ditto coolant pump . . .'

Harry suddenly stopped, went back to the plate, rubbed it, pulled a torch from his pocket, and shouted. Harry did not often shout, so everyone knew it was important. 'Hey, Gerda, come here and look. It's not a Rolls Merlin, it's a bloody Packard-built job. Look at that.'

'Christ!' exclaimed Gerda a minute later. 'It's a bloody Mustang. It's not a Spit or a Hurry at all. It's a bloody Mustang. Must he, if its the American engine.'

The next day was Sunday, 21 May, and the whole Weald Aircraft Recovery Group was on site by 8 am, the word having spread very rapidly. 'The whole bloody lot of you!' Gerda exclaimed in her own delicate fashion as she surveyed all thirty-five of the team with their metal-detectors and shovels and heaven knows what. No one, but no one, had ever found a Packard-Merlin powered P-51 Mustang, and, boy, were they going to dig!

Gerda was in her seventh heaven of power-display organising, and very good she was, too, in spite of her expletives and shouting. The JCB ground away, depositing great wads of Weald clay for the termites to pick over. 'Bloody hell' this, and 'Bloody hell' that all morning, as fragment after fragment was eased out of the cloying, clinging clay, one of them showing the all-important numerals 44-06069.

They drove themselves to an exhausted halt at 1.30, when it was out with the sandwiches and beer and Thermos flasks. The stack of 24ST alloy fragments, some of them lethally sharp, and some after a quick rub as shiny as when they had left the Inglewood plant forty-five years ago, were lying beside the engine like corpses after a bombing. Les from Petworth (no one knew his second name) was sitting on the engine's supercharger wheelcase, sandwich in one hand, a small bit of alloy and a bullet in the other.

No one was watching as he got out a rag and then a calliper and bent over a hole in the metal. And no one heard him the first time when he said, 'That's a fifty-calibre.' The second time he said it, Micky Horsley, who was also picking over their finds, asked, 'What d'you mean, Les?'

'That's a .5 machine-gun hole. Not a German 7.9 mm, not a .303, certainly not a 20 mil. cannon. That's a fifty-calibre. Yank. No one else used them.'

'But this is a Yank plane, so don't be daft. Maybe a Raf Mustang, but the chances are it's a Yank. There were ten times as many.'

'I don't care a bugger,' said Les from Horsham with uncustomary heat. 'That's a .5 machine-gun hole.'

Gerda came over as the news spread. 'Bloody hell,' she said. 'You're right, Les.'

Mickey Horsley said, with a cunning expression on his face, 'Can you tell the difference between a German heavy machine-gun and an American heavy machine-gun, Les?'

'You mean between the Colt .5-inch and the German MG1517?'

'That's right. The size of the cavity — one half an inch, the other 13 mm.'

Les from Horsham did not reply at once, allowing the silence to give the impression that he was cornered. Then he spoke slowly and not very loudly so that some of them could scarcely hear him. But they could all watch as he pulled the big bullet out of his pocket, as shiny as the day it was fed into its belt back in 1944. 'It *might* be tricky without this confirming evidence. That,' he said, holding it up, 'is a Colt slug — a 50-calibre, or .5-inch, made in the US of A.'

'Bloody hell — where did you find it, Les?'

'Just nestling in the clay. I expect there're more about. He pointed at the flattening in the nose. 'This one hit something tougher than 24ST alloy, that's why it stayed with the wreck.' And that settled that.

Soon after the break, they found nine more bits of alloy, two of them — they thought — from a wing, and one which Les (a previously underestimated member) said was a piece of engine cowling. At one end there were two letters, 'B' and 'O', in florid, slanting lettering; and beside them, very faded but indisputably, a fragment of a painted face, just the cheek and one eye and the beginning of a nose, and some hair.

Before they packed up for the day, Gerda counted thirty-seven fragments of fuselage, varying in size from a few inches long to over three feet. This last had five holes through it, each with a circle of bent-back metal like a small, lethal crown. They were all exactly a half inch in diameter.

Then there were two fragments of what Brian was sure was rudder, and — prize of prizes — most of the blind flying panel, with three holes through it, one of which had smashed the turn-and-bank.

'No wonder the pilot didn't get out, poor bugger,' Joss remarked.

'Bloody good shooting,' Harry said callously.

It was not until they were cleaning off their tools, and Gerda was supervising the stacking of their day's treasure in the back of the truck, that Brian was heard to exclaim, 'Look at this, for God's sake! I thought the police said they'd been through this lot with a toothcomb.'

A large chunk of dried Wealden clay had been lying some yards from the site where it had rolled soon after they had begun operations. For some reason no one — police or them — had bothered to split it open.

'I saw something white sticking out so I stuck my shovel in and it came open like a chunk of slate.'

What it revealed might have been the world's oldest fossil. But it was not a fossil — it was a human bone, not yet half a century old. Brian held it up, and even Gerda did not say,

'Bloody hell!' For once they stood in reverent silence, until Sandy Shore from Steyning stepped forward and took the large white bone from Brian. Sandy was a fourth-year medical student, already so confident and serious in his work that Brian had once been heard to say, 'There's my future doc!'

Sandy studied the bone like a jeweller valuing a diamond — though this was twenty times the size of the Koh-i-Noor.

'This,' he said at length in his Sussex-country voice, 'is a pelvis.' He paused, his timing like an actor's. 'And it is a female pelvis.'

From his thirty-first-floor apartment overlooking Central Park, New York, Raymond Cox glanced at the spectacular, castellated skyline formed by the Park West skyscrapers. He read again the item in the newspaper, dropped it onto the table and glanced at his watch. It was 11.05 am here, so would be 8.05 in LA. Charlie would be up, for sure — would have had a long swim in his pool. Might be eating breakfast.

'Honey, come and listen to this. I'm phoning Charlie.'

Louise came in from their bedroom, her hair wrapped in a turban. Raymond indicated the item on page two of the news section of the fat *New York Times*. 'Take a look at that and then listen to what Charlie and Joan have to say.'

Raymond dialled the Los Angeles code and Charlie's number. 'Hi — have you got your LA *Times*?'

Charlie Dee said he did not get a newspaper on Sunday. Too heavy to carry, he said. 'Anyway, it's all muck about schmucks.'

'Well, listen to this, Charlie boy.' Raymond reached for the newspaper and Louise gave it up reluctantly. 'The item's headed "Mystery of World War II wreck", and it goes on: "Aviation historians in England are puzzled by the discovery in West Sussex of an American fighter plane dug up not far from the market town of Horsham. The aviation archaeologists exploring the suspected site of the downed machine reported that it was a P-51, rarely found on English soil as they operated mainly over the Continent of Europe, chiefly over Germany during the 8th Air Force bombing offensive of 1944-45. It is also unusual to find body fragments, which in turn lead to legal and ethical complications." Are you listening to this, Charlie?'

Charlie Dee said he sure was, every word, and so was Joan on the other line.

In the New York apartment, Louise sat close to Raymond, to scan over his shoulder what he was reading to their old friends on the other side of the continent.

'Hey now, what about this? "It has been established by medical authorities that these body fragments are those of a woman, probably less than twenty-five years, who evidently died in combat, as the fragments of the P-51 reveal signs of battle damage."

'What do you make of that?' Raymond asked rhetorically.

'Is that it?' Charlie Dee asked from three thousand miles away.

'The best is yet to come,' said Raymond. 'Now hear this: "Aviation historians in London confirm that the only female flying combatants in World War II were Russian, and they never served in the English theatre of operations, but from the reference identification found in the wreck, it has been established that this fighter airplane was due for delivery by a woman pilot belonging to the British delivery service, the Air Transport Auxiliary. The name of this pilot has not yet been established, but these same aviation historians believe that she was inadvertantly involved in a combat mission, which led to her being shot down and killed in the remains of her aircraft."'

There was a brief silence on the line from Los Angeles. Then Charlie Dee took a deep breath, and asked again, 'Is that all?'

'Almost,' replied Raymond. 'But here's the punchline. "The aviation archaeologists conducting the 'dig' have put forward the theory that this P-51 was in fact shot down by a machine of the same type. While this is not yet credited by the historians, the archaeologists insist that they have incontrovertible evidence."

'End of story. What do you make of all that, Charlie?'

Raymond and Louise had their eyes fixed on one another as Charlie's voice filled their living-room on this fine May Sunday morning.

'Well, I guess it figures. You told me, Ray, that she once said she might get into combat flying, so I suppose poor little Rachel seized her chance when she saw 382 Group scrambling, and joined in. Unfortunately, she chose the one mission that mad Jack Boland had also grabbed in order to shoot me down. And how in God's name was he to know that I was laid up, and that his sister — his beloved sister — was flying *Greta Garbo*.'

After a pause Raymond said sadly. 'I think I'll fly over for the funeral, even if its just for the sake of that tragic family. Do you remember, Charlie, we once said, "Every year we'll get together and talk about our heroic past." Well, we've not done that, even if we're still buddies. But we could look up old places, Stiplowe, Horning and the Nelson Arms — and maybe put some flowers on Rachel Boland's grave.'

THE POPPY FACTORY

William Fairchild

'Gripping and poignant' *Guardian*

. . . I've lived with it on my conscience all my life and now I've got to rid myself of it before I die. It will all seem ancient history to you – and yet, if it hadn't happened . . .

Upon the death of his estranged grandfather, the General, Adrian Garrard received a large and heavily sealed parcel. Inside was a Colt revolver and a manuscript. The revolver had belonged to his grandfather. The manuscript concerned the General's war – the Great War, the war that was to end all others. It was about secrets that had been guarded for decades – secrets so dark and fantastic they could not have been guessed at or imagined; secrets next to which the horrors of battle seemed almost comforting. And it told of the General's guilt. Guilt for the consequences of his loyal and soldierly behaviour. Guilt for the part he had played in allowing evil to win that war.

But it was not a story, the General's manuscript. It was the truth.

THE POPPY FACTORY
Its suspense will hold you.
Its horror will haunt you.

'This is the best novel I've read so far this year . . . and one of the best war novels I've ever read' *The Australian*

'It is the pity of war, its futility and its effect on men that Fairchild sensitively captures' *Sunday Mirror*

'Brilliant' *Daily Telegraph*

FUTURA PUBLICATIONS
FICTION
0 7088 4222 4

SLAUGHTER AT SALERNO
Wotan 20

Leo Kessler

The Vulture gave the assembled officers one of his crooked, perverted smiles. 'The Tommies' prime objective must be the seizure of Montecorvino. I propose to take that town first.'

For Colonel Geier, the Vulture, the arrival of British troops at Salerno is another chance – maybe his last – to win the coveted general's stars. And he determines to make it his own personal Dunkirk

But it is now September 1943. British morale is high, whereas three-quarters of his own troops are untried greenbeaks fresh from German cadet school. And following Mussolini's disappearance who knows which way the Italians will swing . . .

FUTURA PUBLICATIONS
FICTION/WAR
0 7088 2660 1

REBEL 2: THE DIE-HARDS

Leo Kessler

THE DIE HARDS – VICTORY OR DEATH!

Dunkirk burned. The horizon blazed as German dive-bombers gunned the port. The British Army looked defeat in the eye. And Hitler's three reluctant Brown-Shirts were ready to go home . . .

'Ami' – son of an unknown American father

Karl – whose father was in Neuengamme concentration camp

'Polack' – whose family had disappeared in Poland

– they had no place in Hitler's Reich, three misfits allied against the grinding brutality of the Fourth Grenadier Regiment!

Then Montgomery's army mustered in a last all-out offensive. The survivors of the First Battalion, the Die-hards, made a furious attack for victory or death. And for the rebels, it's back to the hated German lines . . .

FUTUTRA PUBLICATIONS
FICTION/WAR
0 7088 3994 0